Dollars for National Goals:

Looking Ahead to 1980

DOLLARS FOR NATIONAL GOALS:

LOOKING AHEAD TO 1980

LEONARD A. LECHT

National Planning Association

A WILEY-INTERSCIENCE PUBLICATION

JOHN WILEY & SONS, New York · London · Sydney · Toronto

Library of Congress Cataloging in Publication Data:

Lecht, Leonard Abe, 1920—
    Dollars for national goals.

    "A Wiley-Interscience publication."
    Includes bibliographical references.
    1. United States—Economic policy—1971—
2. United States—Social policy. 3. United States—
Appropriations and expenditures. I. Title.

HC106.6.L392   309.1′73′0924   74-8353
ISBN 0-471-52095-0

Printed in The United States of America

10 9 8 7 6 5 4 3 2 1

FOREWORD

A Statement by the NPA National Committee on America's Goals and Resources

This is the second report of the National Planning Association dealing with the dollar costs of achieving an illustrative series of national goals. The theme of the report focuses on the problem of priorities, of choosing "what comes first." Even the world's wealthiest society, as the study indicates, is unable simultaneously to maintain high and rising standards of consumption, add to the economy's productive capacity, and supply resources to protect the nation's security while also providing for an expanding array of pressing economic, social, and environmental goals. An attempt to achieve the standards for all 14 goals included in the report, for example, would involve an estimated deficit in the GNP in 1980 of $236 billion (in 1969 dollars) or 17 percent of the anticipated $1.4 trillion GNP in that year.

Protection of environmental quality has emerged as a major new goal in the past decade. Concern with environmental quality has transformed the nation's earlier approach to natural resource policy. Problems of energy supply and utilization, for instance, have been redefined by the emphasis on "clean" energy, (i.e., nonpolluting energy), and by the greater requirements for gasoline partially brought about by the pollution abatement equipment added to motor vehicles. These problems have been accentuated by the greater demands and supply bottlenecks for many different types of energy. Changes in the stringency and comprehensiveness of pollution control standards are the basis for most of the projected increase to attain the environmental quality goal, an increase from $16 billion in 1969 to $56 billion in 1980.

Developments in the past decade include an expansion of objectives in the human welfare service goal areas with many implications for expenditures in the coming decade. Spending for the education, health, manpower training, and social welfare goals increased by $71 billion between 1962 and 1969 (in dollars of 1969 purchasing power). Attaining goals in the human welfare service areas, as they are currently conceived, would entail spending $265 billion more in 1980 than in 1969.

The report assesses the costs of achieving goals in terms of dollar spending. The dollar indicators, after allowing for price changes, are measures of our willingness to commit resources to the objectives included in the pursuit of individual goals. By themselves, the dollar figures often obscure the changes that must occur if the goals considered are to be pursued more effectively in the next decade than in the past one. In health, for example, in the absence of institutional changes, shortages of manpower and facilities will continue to frustrate efforts to make medical care more available to Americans by spending more dollars. Accordingly, while more·dollars are frequently a necessary condition for making greater progress toward attaining goals, planning and institutional changes are equally (and sometimes more) important elements in increasing society's capability for realizing widely shared aspirations.

The present study raises, although it does not answer, the question of how the nation can realize more of its goals in the decade ahead. There are three apparent routes for increasing the country's capability for pursuing goals. One is economic growth, thereby increasing the resources available for all goals. A second route takes account of recent shifts in standards and priorities and involves transferring a larger percentage of the national income from the private to the public sector. A third is the route of institutional change to increase the efficiency with which resources are used to pursue agreed-upon objectives.

There has been much discussion in the recent past of the costs and benefits of economic growth as measured by increases in the GNP. Much of the questioning of the desirability of GNP growth represents a questioning of our priorities, of the uses made of the growth in output. GNP includes many trivial items such as the large-scale expenditures for frequent automobile style changes. Part of the GNP growth reflects the costs of offsetting the undesirable effects of other economic growth—for example, the investment in equipment by industry to reduce the pollution created in the course of production.

More resources and more production will be required in the decade ahead to remedy poverty, to rebuild the cities, and to supply resources for many other goals. More growth is likely to be required, particularly, for that part of GNP that is made up of services to enhance human welfare, such as health and education services. With a growing labor force, a static economy in the decade ahead also implies a society with persistent and rising mass unemployment. While we recognize that the desirability and even the wisdom of continued economic growth are being questioned by intelligent and concerned members of the public, we cannot see a nongrowth policy as feasible in the near future if we are to meet the social goals usually held most strongly by the very people who question the need for an emphasis on continued economic growth. It is clear, however, that the economic growth that is desirable would include a greater reliance than in the past on measures for reducing waste, for eliminating the undesirable side effects of growth, and for more effectively utilizing nonrecoverable resources.

Economic growth minimizes social and political conflicts by making it possible to assign a higher priority to some goals without diminishing the resources available for others. The tax system provides a mechanism for pursuing selected goals (e.g., those financed by government) by redistributing resources from the private to the public sector. Americans are demanding many more services from government in education, health, law enforcement, pollution control, recreation, social welfare, and other areas. Attempting to achieve the goals considered in the present study by 1980, for example, would involve over \$100 billion more in government purchases of goods and services in 1980 than are otherwise anticipated in NPA's projections on the basis of current government programs after allowing for "built-in" increases and for a larger population. Despite anticipated growth in income levels, it is likely that increases in public expenditures of this magnitude could not be financed without higher-than-present tax rates.

Economic growth, or higher tax rates, would leave unchanged the institutions involved in the activities required for achieving goals—institutions that are often ineffective or unresponsive to changing needs. Education, health, transportation, or urban development, among others, can supply instances. In urban development, to cite one illustration, the total private and public outlays in 1969 amounted to \$95 billion, or one-fifth more than the spending for national defense in that year. However, the present bifurcation of the metropolitan areas into central cities and suburbs with many overlapping and sometimes conflicting jurisdictions, jurisdictions frequently divided along lines of race and income, make it difficult to plan rational programs for meeting the needs of the urban areas. The net effect of the massive outlays for urban development has frequently been to make the cities less hospitable to human habitation. In other instances, as in education or housing, obsolete organizational patterns and institutional resistances have come to constitute formidable barriers to utilizing the technological advances and the scientific knowledge that is available. We therefore repeat that allocating more dollars within the existing institutional framework is not always the best course for attaining goals; in some cases it may not even be a good idea. In many instances, institutional reforms should be given as high or even a higher priority than greater dollar allocations.[a]

[a] "Among America's goals the utmost priority should be given to the reestablishment of our moral stature at home and abroad. The failure to do this will inevitably render it infinitely more difficult to attain some of the other goals listed antd in particular those covered by Chapter 4."   FRANK ALTSCHUL

The significance of the present study lies in its overview of the implications of pursuing a system of goals reflecting current conceptions of standards that involve competing claims on resources. The dollar estimates in the study represent a first step in devising better systems of social indicators for assessing our progress in utilizing limited resources to achieve a variety of objectives. The Committee accepts the broad conclusions of the study without subscribing to all aspects of the report. We recommend publication of the report as a contribution to the national discussion of changes in priorities and to stimulate further research in this important field.

NATIONAL COMMITTEE ON
AMERICA'S GOALS AND RESOURCES

Advisory Committee Members
Who Signed the Statement

PREFACE

This study was undertaken by the National Planning Association as part of an on-going research effort to provide more and better information concerning national goals and resources to decision makers in the private and public sectors of our society. It represents a logical "next step" in proceeding from earlier research dealing with the dollar costs of achieving goals as they were conceived in the early 1960's and with the manpower requirements generated by the purchases of goods and services in pursuit of national goals.

A study of so broad a scope is inevitably the product of the efforts of many people. Many individuals in different organizations and agencies, private and public, have contributed ideas and source materials. Research memoranda have been prepared in each goal area by a consultant or a member of the NPA staff. I have written the individual chapters drawing on the research memoranda and on other materials. Needless to say, I am responsible for the errors of omission and commission in the report.

The following individuals participated in preparing the research memoranda.

Goal Area	Authors of Research Memoranda	Affiliation
Agricultural support	Alvin Egbert	World Bank
	J. Dawson Ahalt	U.S. Department of Agriculture
Education	Tom Lieser	NPA Staff
Environmental quality	Robert U. Ayres	International Research and Technology Corporation
	Neal Potter	Resources for the Future
Health	Gerald Rosenthal	Brandeis University
	Richard J. Rosen	NPA Staff

Household consumption	Chong K. Park	NPA Staff
	Ahmad Al-Samarrie	NPA Staff
Housing	Peter Wagner	Federal Reserve Board
International aid	Chong K. Park	NPA Staff
Manpower training	Chong K. Park	NPA Staff
	Richard J. Rosen	NPA Staff
National defense	Tom Lieser	NPA Staff
Private plant and equipment	Ahmad Al-Samarrie	NPA Staff
	Paul J. Cicurel	NPA Staff
Research and development	Mary H. Holman	George Washington University
	Theodore Suranyi-Ungar	George Washington University
Social welfare	Raymond Munts	University of Wisconsin
Transportation	Chong K. Park	NPA Staff
Urban development	Peter Wagner	Federal Reserve Board

    This study owes much to the inspiration of the late Gerhard Colm, formerly Chief Economist of the National Planning Association, and to the support of John Miller, President of the National Planning Association. I am indebted to the Ford Foundation for the financial support that made this study possible. The study also owes much to the members of the National Committee on America's Goals and Resources, persons drawn from business, labor, government, and academic life who have served as a continuing advisory board from the inception of NPA's research in priority analysis. Members of the NPA research staff have contributed to this book in many ways. Paul Cicurel, Tom Lieser, and Richard Rosen have supplied invaluable research competence and specialized knowledge. Ahmad Al-Samarrie and Chong K. Park have provided a high level of economic expertise in a number of fields. The work of typing and editing the many drafts and memoranda has been ably performed by Nancy Monroe and Michele Moncarz. Ms. Moncarz prepared the index.

LEONARD A. LECHT
Washington, D.C.

May 1974

CONTENTS

TABLES

Dollars for National Goals:

Looking Ahead to 1980

Chapter One

GOALS ANALYSIS:

INTRODUCTION AND SUMMARY

I

Changes in the nation's choice of goals, and in priorities among them, can have far-reaching consequences for human well-being, for private and public expenditures, for employment opportunities and markets, for industry, and for America's international posture. Changes in popular concerns manifested in legislation and national programs and in spending patterns in the past decade show that a significant, if sometimes inconsistent, shift in goals and priorities has been taking place in the 1960's with many implications for the 1970's and 1980's.

Concern with the nation's goals is, of course, nothing new. In the past this interest focused on the economy's overall performance and on obtaining the maximum levels of production and employment. The new element is the far greater interest in the uses made of the economy's growth in output. In the public economy, interest in goals and priorities frequently centers on the size of the defense budget, on the uses made of the Highway Trust Fund, on reform in public welfare assistance, or on the priorities implied in devoting four-fifths of the Federal Government's expenditures for the conduct of research and development to problems relating to national defense, space exploration, or atomic energy.[1] In the private sector, part of the growth appears to be devoted to trivial purposes or to represent the use of resources to counter the undesirable by-products of GNP growth. For example, private industry, according to the Council on Environmental Quality, is expected to spend $27.5 billion between 1971 and 1980 to meet legislative requirements in effect early in 1972 to reduce the two major types of pollution: the air and water pollution stemming from factories, feedlots, incinerators, power plants, and similar sources.[2]

Where and how priorities are assigned in a democracy is determined by the decisions of consumers, firms, trade unions, and voluntary associations and by legislation and budgetary appropriations at all levels of government.

[1] U.S. Office of Management and Budget, *Special Analyses: The Budget of the United States Government, Fiscal Year 1973*, p. 281.

[2] Council on Environmental Quality, *Environmental Quality*, 1972, pp. 276–277. The amendments to the Water Quality Act adopted later in 1972 would substantially increase the required private capital outlays during the 1970's.

These decisions are made, as they must be, in the light of the information available at the time. Research and analysis can expand the information base available for making choices by indicating where economic and social developments are leading to redefinitions of goals or by changing the standards that are likely to generate new claims on resources. It can also assess the anticipated consequences for the uses of resources 5 or 10 years from now of pursuing objectives similar to those currently receiving widespread consideration. In the absence of information about the costs, benefits, and side effects of pursuing many different goals that compete for resources, the choices implemented often create unexpected problems that cancel out the intended benefits, or they may reflect the options of narrowly based pressure groups and special interests.

This study was undertaken with the aid of a grant from the Ford Foundation to appraise how the developments in the past decade have induced changes in goals and standards that can influence national policy and national expenditures in the next 5 or 10 years. To illustrate these consequences, the report focuses on the estimated dollar costs in 1980 of achieving an illustrative series of national goals as they have been conceived in the early 1970's. The present report is the third in a series of reports based on studies undertaken by the National Planning Association dealing with the dollar costs or manpower requirements for attaining national objectives.[3]

The overall conclusion that emerges from the study is that an underlying shift in national priorities, as indicated by expenditures, occurred during the 1960's with many consequences for 1980. Goals concerned with providing services that promote human welfare—education, health, manpower training, and social welfare—received a higher priority. Goals linked with the nation's international posture—national defense, research and development, and aid to the developing nations—received a lesser priority. Government expenditures were responsible for a majority of the shifts in priorities; however, private outlays have been the critical element in the rapid growth in spending for such goals as transportation. Looking ahead to 1980, large increases in expenditure would be required to attain most of the goals considered. The largest percentage increase (more than a tripling of outlays) is listed for the environmental quality goal, the major new goal to have emerged in the past decade. The costs projected for attaining the entire system of goals is estimated to exceed the $1.4 trillion GNP anticipated in 1980 by $236 billion, or by 17 percent of the GNP.

The "gap" in resources projected for 1980 underscores that the problem of priorities, of choosing "what comes first," will remain an important issue

[3] See L. Lecht, *Goals, Priorities, and Dollars—The Next Decade,* The Free Press, 1966 and L. Lecht, *Manpower Needs for National Goals in the 1970's,* Praeger, 1969.

in the 1980's as it has been in the 1960's and 1970's and earlier. The pace of economic growth in the next decade will be the most important single factor in determining the extent to which more resources will be available to pursue goals. The need to expand employment opportunities for a growing labor force, to remedy poverty, and to supply resources for an entire system of goals makes it likely that the national concern with the quality of life will be less involved with slowing down economic growth than in seeking to influence how the growth in output is used.

II

The 1960's mark a watershed in American history in which the concerns arising from the Great Depression of the 1930's and the Cold War of the late 1940's and early 1950's became superseded by other issues. The effects of these changes show up in the shifts in priorities and in the new formulations of goals and standards that emerged during the decade.

It appeared to many in the 1960's and early 1970's that the nation was in the midst of a fundamental institutional crisis, a crisis symbolized in such terms as "future shock," "the greening of America," "black power," "crime in the streets," "the generation gap," "the drug culture," "Women's Lib" and, more recently, "Watergate." More generally, all of these slogans reflect the diminished power of old values and responses to command loyalty.

The changes in institutions and aspirations taking place during the 1960's were accelerated by a "one-time" demographic shift that occurred then. The population in the 14- to 24-year age group grew by nearly 14 million during the decade, an increase greater than the growth in numbers in this age group in the preceding 70 years.[4] Accordingly, the civil disturbances in the cities and on the campuses, the divisions over the war in Vietnam, and the involvement with ecology and the environment were becoming everyday aspects of American life at a time when the age group most likely to constitute a force for change was increasing more rapidly than in any other period in the country's history.

The economic progress characterizing the decade existed side-by-side

---

[4] For an analysis of the significance of this demographic shift see D. Moynihan, "Youth and a Troubled World," *The Washington Post,* July 29, 1973, Section C, pp. 1, 5.

with an accumulating backlog of unresolved problems, problems sometimes intensified by the rapid growth. As the size of the poverty population declined during the 1960's, it appeared plausible to many persons in and out of government that, with continued economic growth (to quote the Council of Economic Advisers in their 1969 *Report),* "poverty would be eliminated entirely in about ten years."[5] In contrast with this optimistic expectation, however, the number of families on the welfare rolls receiving benefits under the Aid to Families with Dependent Children (AFDC) program rose by more than 1.7 million between 1960 and 1970, a growth of over 200 percent.[6] Although the income gap between black and white families narrowed until the last part of the decade, the median income of black families in 1969 was only 61 percent of that of white families, and the ratio dropped to 59 percent in 1972.[7] The social and physical disorganization in many of the inner cities had their counterparts in the more prosperous suburbs in a way of life described by one authority on urban problems, Wilfred Owen, as "cars without community."[8] In fields contributing to human welfare, such as health, spending rose rapidly during the 1960's, increasing, in constant dollars, by 125 percent. However, the death rate from cancer also increased during this period, rising from 149 per 100,000 population to a rate of 160.[9]

The changes in the perceptions of problems and goals separating the generation of the 1960's and 1970's from the Depression generation is highlighted by the recent questioning of the values represented by the emphasis on a high GNP growth rate or on continually increasing levels of private consumption. So, *The Wall Street Journal,* in discussing the doubts expressed about the relevance of the standard measures of economic growth, points out that many persons, especially younger persons, have been asking if the United States was "recording its progress on a faulty report card."[10] The shift in outlook between the generations is underscored by comparing the policy statement in the Employment Act of 1946 with the comparable statement in the National Environmental Policy Act of 1970.

The Employment Act states that "it is . . . [the] continuing policy and responsibility of the Federal Government . . . to promote maximum employment, production, and purchasing power." The Environmental Policy

[5] Council of Economic Advisers, *Annual Report,* 1969, p. 159.

[6] *Statistical Abstract, 1972,* p. 299.

[7] U.S. Dept. of Commerce, *The Social and Economic Status of the Black Population in the United States, 1972,* 1973, p. 17.

[8] W. Owen, *The Accessible City,* 1972, p. 111.

[9] U.S. Public Health Service, *Vital Statistics of the United States,* 1970.

[10] *The Wall Street Journal,* December 16, 1971, p. 1.

Act declares that it is the Federal Government's continuing policy "to create and maintain conditions under which man and nature can exist in productive harmony, and fulfill the social, economic, and other requirements of present and future generations of Americans." The operational difference between the two policy statements is summarized by the observation in the White House National Goals Research Staff's report that, a generation ago, "smoke billowing from a factory chimney was a reassuring sight," indicating that there was economic activity and people at work earning income.[11] By the late 1960's, the same smoke would figure in popular and legislative concerns as contributing to pollution.

The changes in perceptions of problems that influenced attitudes toward economic growth are also evident in the positions taken toward population growth and technological advance. The desirability of rapid population growth was taken for granted earlier as creating larger markets for industry, adding more new entrants to the labor force, and promoting the country's security by enlarging the population base on which the armed forces could draw in the event of an emergency. By the beginning of the 1970's, rapid population growth had come to be widely associated with depletion of natural resources, with congestion and pollution at home, and as a primary cause of the inability of the less-developed nations such as India to increase their low average per-capita incomes. Within the United States, the Commission on Population Growth and the American Future stressed that "there is hardly any social problem confronting this Nation whose solution would be easier if our population were larger."[12] In science and technology, the theme that "knowledge is useful power," as in health research, had become transformed into the theme of knowledge as "dangerous power," with the prime dangers illustrated by the research in developing more powerful nuclear weapons. The "technological renunciation" involved in the defeat of the proposed Federal appropriation of an additional $300 million in the early 1970's for development of a commercial supersonic air transport is one important indicator of the changes in attitudes toward technological advance. The defeat of the SST appropriation was largely attributable to apprehension that its potential contributions to technological and economic advance were insufficient to outweigh such anticipated environmental side effects as greater noise and atmospheric pollution.

The effects of these developments are evident in the fears expressed that we are "backing into the future," that is, seeking to solve long-term changes

[11] National Goals Research Staff, *Toward Balanced Growth: Quantity With Quality,* 1970, p. 163.

[12] Commission on Population Growth and the American Future, *Population and the American Future,* 1972.

with measures that are frequently unrelated to the strategic variables that must respond to devise effective solutions. The enactment of Medicare and Medicaid is an example. The social conscience and political pressures that prompted the nation to adopt these measures were unaccompanied by a comparable effort to encourage the large-scale introduction of more efficient systems for providing medical services or to increase the supply of health manpower. Accordingly, close to half of the increase in spending for health services in the past decade was accounted for by higher prices for medical care and not by increased services.[13] Similarly, the optimism attending the introduction of the "Great Society" programs in the mid-1960's frequently gave way to skepticism and disillusionment as new measures initially enjoying general support (i.e., compensatory education or the New Careers movement) appeared to yield limited benefits according to the available yardsticks of performance. These growing doubts about the efficacy, if not the benevolence, of government existed alongside of greater demands for services and benefits in many areas from Federal, state, and local units of government.

The changes in American society in the past decade suggest several tendencies with implications for the pursuit of national goals in the next decade. For one, inflation and the slowing down of productivity growth raised many questions concerning the extent to which the United States was becoming chronically prone to inflation and less competitive in world trade. While inflation, like the youth culture, has been characteristic of most industrially advanced non-Communist nations, and the rate of price increases in the United States was less than in these other countries, the persistence of the increases in prices suggested the likelihood that the pressures for controlling inflation will influence the pursuit of domestic goals to a greater extent in the next 10 years than in the past 10. For another consideration, the social and demographic changes that stood out so sharply in the 1960's have as yet to affect the commitment of most Americans to high and rising levels of household consumption. The personal consumption expenditures that accounted for fractionally more than 62 percent of the Gross National Product in 1969 made up 63 percent in 1962 and slightly less than 63 percent in 1972.[14] A third tendency is the greater demand for services from government in education, health, protection of environmental quality, social welfare, and other areas. Accordingly, the government expenditures that repre-

[13] Medical care costs rose at a more rapid rate in the past decade than any other item in the Consumer Price Index. See Council of Economic Advisers, *op. cit.,* 1972, p. 248.

[14] Percentages refer to current dollar ratios. See Council of Economic Advisers, *op. cit.,* 1973, p. 193.

sented the equivalent of 28 percent of the GNP in 1955 had increased to 34 percent by 1970.[15]

III

The massive needs for physical facilities of many kinds in the large cities, the prevalence of pollution, the failures of the public welfare system, and the inadequacies of our educational and health systems have been the subjects for general public discussions in the recent past. Concern with these and similar problems has led to a mushrooming of interest in a reordering of the nation's priorities.

This interest notwithstanding, terms such as "goals" or "priorities" frequently refer to abstract purposes divorced from everyday experience. To quote the late Dr. Gerhard Colm, formerly the National Planning Association's Chief Economist, "a salesclerk who sells cereal to a housewife, a teacher who instructs a class, a doctor who treats a patient, a businessman who decides to build a factory—all would be astonished to be told that they were engaged in the pursuit of national goals, namely, increasing the standard of living, promoting education and health, and increasing the economic strength of the country. They would be as astonished as the man who was told that he had been talking prose all his life."[16]

Goals, in this context, refer to "areas of concern" such as education, health, housing, household consumption, research and development, urban development, and so on. They are objects of concern because of a prevailing interest in change and in improvement, that is, in eliminating slums or narrowing the gap between the potentials of modern medical technology and the health services available to Americans. Research in national goals received its current impetus as far back as the late 1950's when dissatisfaction with the progress made in education, in research, and in technological achievements was intensified by the evidence of accomplishments in other nations, especially the orbiting of the Sputnik spacecraft by the Soviet Union

[15] E. R. Fried, et al., *Setting National Priorities: The 1974 Budget*, 1973, p. 8. Estimates refer to fiscal years 1955 and 1970.
[16] G. Colm, "Goals Research in Dollar and Manpower Terms" in L. Lecht, *Manpower Needs for National Goals in the 1970's*, 1969, p. vii.

in 1957. The Commission on National Goals was established by President Eisenhower as a response to these developments. The Commission in its report, *Goals for Americans,* identified and discussed goals in 15 areas affecting most aspects of American life.[17] President Kennedy identified space exploration as an additional goal in 1961 when he proposed that it become a national objective "to put men on the moon and bring them back."

The areas identified by the Goals Commission, together with space exploration, provided the framework for the National Planning Association's initial study of the dollar costs of achieving a quantitative standard for each goal in the mid-1970's reflecting the informed opinion, national programs and policy, and legislation in the early 1960's. The areas for which the cost estimates were presented included household consumption, urban development, social welfare, health, education, housing, research and development, and aid to the developing nations. The overall finding in the study stressed the existence of an important problem of priorities in the United States since the costs listed for full realization of the standards for all of the goals considered were estimated to exceed the GNP anticipated in 1975 by approximately $150 billion (in 1962 dollars) or by 15 percent of the GNP.[18]

It appeared more reasonable in many ways to think of national goals in the climate of opinion and policy prevailing in the early and mid-1960's than in the late 1960's or early 1970's. There was a closer approximation to a national consensus in these earlier periods as the Administration's Great Society, civil rights, and tax reduction programs came to command support from a variety of publics including business groups, Congress, the academic community, the labor movement, and members of minority groups. As the war in Vietnam and the turmoil in the central cities and on the campuses accelerated in the second half of the 1960's, divisiveness rather than consensus often appeared to have become characteristic of much of American life. It was difficult to believe that the demonstrators and protestors shared the same goals as the establishments they were demonstrating against or that the life styles symbolized by the "youth culture" maintained a common set of aspirations with the over-30 generation, the "hard hats" and other blue-collar workers, or the black militants in the large urban ghettos. While the war in Vietnam has ended, and the disturbances in the central cities and campuses have subsided, the existence of a common framework of consensus goals based on a broadly shared definition of the national or individual interest is far from self-evident in many aspects of American life.

In a decentralized pluralistic society such as our own, the mechanisms by

---

[17] *Goals for Americans, The Report of the President's Commission on National Goals,* 1960.

[18] *Goals, Priorities, and Dollars, op. cit.,* p. 42.

which goals are identified and standards determined are frequently obscure. In contrast, the process of goal setting in a totalitarian society is less ambiguous since goals are defined by a national authority, and their definition has the force of law. The targets in the Soviet Five Year Plans, for example, have possessed an imperative character. Many groups in America, private as well as public, participate officially and unofficially in determining objectives and in implementing them. Voluntary associations publicize and lobby for better schools, for mental health, to preserve wilderness areas, and for a variety of other purposes. In many areas, the role of public authority is minimal. For example, consumers determine the manner in which they spend their incomes. In others, as in national defense, public authority alone determines the standard and makes the decisions controlling expenditures. In a number of goal areas, education or social welfare are instances, the Federal Government makes use of its own expenditures to encourage state and local governments to develop more adequate education and public assistance programs. Some goal areas (e.g., health) include a variety of private and public activities such as research, construction, and the provision of services to indigent, aged and other individuals. Other goal areas, as in manpower training, are closely identified with ongoing government programs intended for more or less specific target groups.

General agreement on the areas of concern—on goals—and on broad directions for change frequently coexists with extensive disagreement as to priorities and specific programs for achieving objectives. For example, Americans are generally agreed on the need to expand and upgrade urban mass transit. There is considerably less agreement on how far funds in the Highway Trust Fund should be made available for this purpose. Or, persons who are equally committed to the goal of assuring an adequate national defense are less agreed on the desirability of maintaining the present level of armed forces in Europe, or on the need for maintaining a triple land, sea and air nuclear deterrent. Similarly, a strong national commitment to greater equality of opportunity has been accompanied by substantial disagreement as to the wisdom of continuing the traditional reliance on expanding educational opportunity as the primary means for achieving this result. As Charles Schultze, formerly Director of the Bureau of the Budget, comments, "there is a widespread consensus, transcending party lines, that increasing equality of opportunity, improving the quality of public services, and rescuing the environment are, and should be, important concerns of the Federal Government. There is far less consensus, however, on how these objectives ought to be attained."[19] While the Administration's proposed budget for the 1974 fiscal year was aimed at achieving a number of changes in existing priorities, it

[19] C. L. Schultze, et al., *Setting National Priorities: The 1973 Budget*, 1972, p. 12.

is at least equally significant that expenditures for the major Great Society programs rose from $21 billion in fiscal 1970 to $36 billion in fiscal 1973. The rate of increase in spending for these programs was more than double the growth in all Federal outlays in this period, 68 percent as compared with 29 percent.[20]

The relevance of the national goals concept is often more obvious in the areas that involve public expenditures, areas characterized by collective decision making, than in the goal areas in which private spending predominates. One of the underlying themes in American history is the commitment to high and rising living standards, a goal largely pursued in the private sector. Moreover, few sharp lines can be drawn on the basis of the source of expenditures since both the private and public sectors contribute to the pursuit of goals. Implementing the objectives expressed or implied in national legislation or new government programs typically requires expenditures that extend well beyond the Federal Government's budget. So, as the Council of Economic Advisers points out in its 1971 *Report,* the Federal Government's objectives in housing (i.e., the targets for the construction of dwelling units in the 1968 Housing and Urban Development Act) concern "the share of GNP devoted to housing, not the share of the Federal budget related to housing."[21] Attaining the objectives of the Clean Air Act and the Water Quality Act plus their amendments primarily entails expenditures by private industry for pollution abatement equipment and by individuals who purchase automobiles equipped with the pollution controls. Appraising how the economy's resources should be allocated to national defense, highways, health care, or urban development requires consideration of the resources available in the private as well as the public economy.

IV

The changes in private and public expenditures in the individual goal areas can provide an overview of the shifts in priorities that took place during the 1960's. The dollar indicators show that the goals concerned with

[20] *Ibid.,* p. 11.

[21] The original Act stipulated a target of 26-million housing units for the 1968–1978 period. Council of Economic Advisers, *op. cit.,* 1971, p. 93.

providing services that enhance human welfare received a high priority during the decade while the goals involved with making the cities more viable
places to live in were accorded a lesser priority. The most consistent underlying tendency was the lesser priority given to the goals closely linked with
the nation's international posture.

Dollar expenditures, even after adjusting for price changes, constitute an
incomplete and, in some instances, misleading yardstick for measuring
changes in national priorities or in the means required for implementing
them. Population growth alone would lead to larger outlays for hospitals,
schools, household consumption, and old-age benefits even in the absence of
improvements in standards. Furthermore, a greater input of dollars need not
be associated with a corresponding increase in the attainment of the objectives for which the larger dollar outlays are intended. More dollars may be
spent for health care without reducing the number of days lost because of
illness, and greater spending for education in the inner-city schools or elsewhere need not lead to improvements in reading ability or in problem-solv-
ing capabilities. In some goal areas, health again is an instance, shortages of
specialized manpower or facilities can frustrate attempts to change priorities by spending more dollars. In addition, the dollar figures are often incomplete because they do not include the costs of the side effects induced
by the activities entered into in pursuing goals. The outlays for the transportation goal, to cite an illustration, are understated because they do not take
into account the costs to society of the pollution, the congestion, and the
highway accidents attributable to motor vehicles. Similarly, the spending for
the agricultural support goal refers only to government outlays for attaining
income goals in agriculture. The costs to consumers in higher prices and the
lesser availability of farm products from reinstating the price support and
land diversion programs of the 1960's included as an alternative policy option in this goal are estimated to be $13 billion a year by 1980.

Yet, after voicing these caveats, it is apparent that choices in assigning
priorities to competing goals are considered in terms of allocating more dollars or fewer dollars for one purpose as compared with another. Therefore,
debates in Congress and among the public on national priorities have focused on the desirability of spending more dollars for national defense, highway construction, or space exploration, to cite examples, as compared with
social welfare, mass transit, or health programs. Dollars, in this context,
supply a measure of the claims on economy's resources expected to arise
from the pursuit of a system of goals. The dollar expenditures indicate a
"willingness" on the part of the relevant publics to commit a greater or lesser proportion of their limited resources to particular goals. While the ex-

penditure of more dollars alone is insufficient to assure that greater progress will be made toward attaining goals, it is difficult to conceive of programs for the more effective pursuit of goals in areas such as health, housing, or urban development that would not involve a substantially greater input of public and private dollars in the decade ahead.

The areas for which the cost of attaining goals in 1980 have been "priced out" in this report provide a point of departure for assessing the changes in priorities that have taken place during the past 10 years. They are listed in order of expenditures in 1969, the base year for the present study:

Household consumption
Private plant and equipment
Urban development
National defense
Social welfare
Education
Health
Transportation
Housing
Research and development
Environmental quality
Agricultural support
International aid
Manpower training

Outlays for the individual goal areas in 1962 (the base year in NPA's initial goals study) and in 1969 are summarized in Table 1-1.[22] To facilitate comparability, expenditures in both years are expressed in dollars of 1969 purchasing power.

The data in Table 1-1 point to the wide range of differences in the emphasis given to individual goal areas during the 1960's. Spending for the goals supplying services contributing to human welfare—social welfare, health, education, and manpower training—increased by nearly $71 billion (in 1969 dollars) between 1962 and 1969. The large increase listed for the private plant and equipment goal reflects the expectations of continued inflation in the late 1960's and the need to add to the economy's capacity for

---

[22] The list of goal areas in this report differs from the list in *Goals, Priorities, and Dollars—The Next Decade* in several respects. For a comparison of the differences between the two goals classifications, see Appendix Table C-10.

Table 1-1   Estimated Expenditures for National Goals, 1962 and 1969 (in billions of 1969 dollars)

Goal Area	Expenditures 1962[a]	Expenditures 1969	Percent Change, 1962 to 1969
Household consumption	$420.0	$579.6	38.0%
Private plant and equipment	58.7	99.3	69.0
Urban development	85.2	89.9	5.5
National defense	65.5	81.0[c]	23.5
Social welfare	45.0	73.0	62.0
Education	43.6	64.4	48.0
Health	43.9	63.8	45.5
Transportation	39.3	61.4	56.0
Housing	38.0	35.4	− 7.0
Research and development	21.1	27.3	29.0
Environmental quality	10.9[b]	15.8	45.0
Agricultural support	8.2	7.8	− 5.5
International aid	6.1	5.4	−12.0
Manpower training	0.1	2.0	[d]
GNP	679.1	930.3	37.0

[a] Derived from L. A. Lecht, *Goals, Priorities, and Dollars—The Next Decade,* 1966, Table 1-2, p. 36. The estimates in Table 1-2 have been converted from 1962 to 1969 dollars.

[b] The spending for the environmental quality goal in 1962 includes $7.1 billion in outlays for the natural resources goal listed in the earlier study together with an estimated $3.8 billion added as the cost of solid waste collection and disposal.

[c] The estimate for the national defense goal includes $78.4 billion of government purchases and $2.6 billion largely made up of transfer payments and grants-in-aid.

[d] 1962 outlays are a poor basis for estimating the percentage change in spending since the present program was started in 1962.

producing goods and services. At the other extreme, the agricultural support and international aid goals received a sufficiently low priority so that spending, after adjusting for price increases, declined during the decade.

    The priorities given to different goals can be described as "high" or "low" by relating the changes in spending in each of the areas to a common standard. The relevant standard for this purpose is the percentage increase in GNP, in 1969 dollars, over the 1962–1969 period. The goals for which spending grew at a more rapid rate than the GNP were the beneficiaries of a larger share of the economy's resources devoted to their pursuit.[23] The goals for which spending grew at a less rapid pace, or decreased, were receiving a diminished claim on the GNP. The GNP grew by 37 percent, in constant dollars, between 1962 and 1969. High-priority goals are defined as those for which the increase in spending was at least one-fifth greater than the GNP, or an increase of 44.5 percent or more. Low-priority goals are those for which spending decreased, or increased at a rate of one-fifth less than the GNP, or by under 29.5 percent. Average-priority goals are those whose growth rates fall between these two limits. The classifications or priorities for the different goals arrived at on this basis are described in Table 1–2.

Table 1-2   Classification of Goals According to Their Priority Status During the 1960's

Priority Status	Percent Change in Expenditures, 1962 to 1969
High-priority goals	
Private plant and equipment	69.0%
Social welfare	62.0
Transportation	56.0
Education	48.0
Health	45.5
Environmental quality	45.0
Manpower training	—
Average-priority goals	
Household consumption	38.0
Low-priority goals	
Research and development	29.0
National defense	23.5
Urban development	5.5
Agricultural support	− 5.5
Housing	− 7.0
International aid	−12.0

The large percentage increases are shown for the areas dealing with human welfare services and for the transportation and plant and equipment goals. The high priority for the transportation goal stems from consumers' preference for their individual automobiles, a preference encouraged by the all-too-frequent absence of attractive alternatives in public transportation,

---

[23] Minor aspects of several goals (e.g., the purchase of land for recreational facilities in the environmental quality goal) do not involve any claims on GNP.

and from the spectacular increase in air travel. The relatively modest increase for the environmental quality goal grows out of the fact that concern for pollution in the late 1960's was just beginning to become translated into programs and legislative standards requiring substantial expenditures. The average priority for the household consumption goal shows household consumption as a close-to-constant proportion of the GNP.

While the human welfare service goals received a high priority during the 1960's, outlays for the closely related objective of making the cities more viable places in which to live, work, shop, move about, and play were accorded a low priority. Although there has been much discussion of far-reaching measures to rebuild the cities (i.e., an urban land bank or a "Marshall Plan for the cities"), spending for urban physical facilities declined from 12.5 percent of the GNP in 1962 to under 10 percent by the end of the decade. The low priority for the one goal intended solely for the rural areas, the agricultural support goal, shows the effects of a decline in farm population and of the extensive questioning of measures that primarily benefit the larger and the commercially organized farm units.

The goals closely identified with the nation's international posture, national defense and international aid, received a low priority during the decade. Spending for national defense increased by less than one-fourth, while public and private aid and capital supply to the developing nations underwent the most sizable percentage decrease of any single goal. The research and development goal is also closely linked with the nation's international posture since the largest element in public research and development outlays is made up of expenditures for national defense and for maintaining the country's lead in space research and technology. The low priority for this goal was the result of cutbacks in spending for research and development related to the space program and to national defense.

The changes in the expenditure patterns and priorities in the different goal areas during the 1960's have continued, with individual exceptions, through the early 1970's. The low-priority designations for national defense, research and development, international aid, and agricultural support have shown few signs, up through 1973, of reversal. Government expenditures for national defense, for example, have continued to decline as a proportion of the GNP, falling from 8.7 percent of the Gross National Product in 1969 to an estimated 6.7 percent in 1972.[24] The high priority for the human welfare service goals has also continued. The outlays for health that amounted to 6.8 percent of the GNP in 1969 rose to 7.4 percent in 1971, while spending for education went up from 6.9 percent in 1969 to 8.2 percent of the GNP in 1972. In other areas such as housing, changes in the availability and cost of mortgage credit often make for sharp year-to-year fluctuations in

[24] Council of Economic Advisers, *op. cit.*, 1973, p. 193.

residential construction so that the expenditures for housing in any single year are an inadequate representation of the underlying changes. The number of new private housing starts, accordingly, rose from nearly 1.9 million in 1969 to over 2.5 million in 1971.[25]

A majority of the shifts in priorities during the 1960's involved areas in which government spending, largely the Federal Government's expenditures, was the predominant element in the total outlays or in the changes in spending that took place at that time (see Appendix Tables C-8 and C-9). National defense, research and development, international aid, and agricultural support received a low priority in the past decade either because the Federal Government's spending grew slowly in these areas or it declined. The high priority for the human welfare service goals was the consequence of a substantial growth in Federal, state, and local government outlays in these areas. In health, more than five-eighths of the total outlays in 1969 were made up of private expenditures. However, focusing on the increases in spending for health between 1962 and 1969, about the same proportion—five-eighths—represented increases stemming from government sources.

The experience of the 1960's and its continuation in the early 1970's highlights the importance of government budgetary appropriations and legislation as sources of change in national priorities. New departures in government expenditures and in regulatory programs, as in pollution control currently or the space program a decade ago, have an important bearing on economic activity in the private sector. The effects of the unrest in the cities, the apprehension over the quality of life, the disenchantment with the war in Vietnam, and the other pressures for change show up in a shift in priorities within the public sector. These developments have prompted, although with many inconsistencies, a greater concern with domestic welfare and a lesser concern with the nation's international stance.

V

The cost projections for attaining the individual goals refer to the economic and social framework anticipated in 1980. As in the 1960's, changes in the age composition of the population and in family size will make up an under-

[25] *Statistical Abstract, 1972*, pp. 65, 105, 682. Estimate of housing starts includes mobile homes.

lying theme influencing many other changes in American society. The most important single factor affecting the pace at which goals can be pursued is a projected increase in the GNP of about half between 1969 and 1980, an increase of nearly $470 billion.

The basic elements entering into the economic and social environment anticipated for 1980 are summarized in Table 1-3.

Table 1-3.   Selected Economic and Social Indicators, 1969 and Projected 1980[a]
(dollar totals are in 1969 dollars)

	1969	Projected 1980	Percent Change, 1969 to 1980
GNP (in billions)	$ 930	$ 1,399	50.5%
Population (in millions)	203	228	12.5
Civilian labor force (in millions)	81	100	23.5
GNP per worker	$11,940	$14,700	23.0
Average household personal income[b]	$11,440	$14,625	28.0

[a] National Planning Association, *U.S. Economic and Demographic Projections, 1972–81, Report No. 72-N-2*, 1973, pp. 51, 58, 65, 78. See also Appendix Tables C-1, C-2, C-4 and C-5.
[b] Refers to "consumer units," that is, to families and unrelated individuals.

The increase in the GNP from over $900 billion in 1969 to nearly $1.4 trillion by 1980 implies a growth rate of 3.8 percent a year (in constant dollars) during this period. This rate of growth would be about equivalent to the overall change for the 1948 to 1970 period, but it would be somewhat less than the 4 percent growth characterizing the 1960 to 1970 period or the 4.6 percent actual rate between 1962 and 1969.[26] This slowing down in GNP growth is expected to reflect, in part, a greater emphasis on "balanced growth," that is, on taking into account the undesirable side effects of economic growth for the quality of life and for the environment. Protecting the environment will require large investments by industry and government in facilities to abate pollution, that is, to bring about an improvement in the

[26] These estimates refer to the growth rates from the actual levels of the GNP in 1962 and 1969. Translating the 1962, 1969, and 1980 GNP estimates into "full-employment" Gross National Products (i.e., assuming a level of output consistent with a 4 percent unemployment rate in each of these years) would yield growth rates of 4.3 percent a year in the 1962 to 1969 period and 3.9 percent for the 1969 to 1980 period.

quality of life that is not taken into account in the GNP. The projected 3.8 percent annual growth rate in GNP is based on an anticipated 2.8 percent increase in productivity, conventionally measured in output per man-hour, in the private economy, a 1.9 percent annual growth in the civilian labor force, and close to one-half of 1 percent average annual decrease in hours of work per employee. The decrease in hours worked would represent the equivalent of an additional vacation of a week and a half a year. These changes in the economic framework are consistent with a 4.4 percent unemployment rate in 1980. This is substantially less than the greater than 5 percent rates in 1971 or 1972 but more than the 4 percent unemployment rate widely regarded as a noninflationary full employment target a decade ago.

The social and economic environment in the 1960's was affected at many points by a "one-time" rapid increase in the size of the population in the 14- to 24-year age group. Partly because this group will grow older, the 1970's will be influenced by rapid growth in the population in the 25- to 34-year age group, an estimated growth of nearly 12 million between 1970 and 1980.[27] This is roughly five times as large as the increase in the same age group in the preceding decade. The "generation gap," therefore, should become less evident in the next decade because the population of young persons under 25 will loom less large. These demographic developments help explain why the labor force is expected to grow at a considerably more rapid rate than total population, 23.5 percent for the labor force as compared with 12.5 percent for population during the overall 1969 to 1980 period. In addition, the large population increase in the age group most likely to be engaged in rearing families, a group whose incomes are typically increasing because of experience and upgrading, will provide a basis for a renewed burst of urban growth, residential construction, and community formation in the next 10 years.

While there will be many more persons in the child-rearing age groups in the 1970's, the families they rear will typically be smaller than in the past generation. The transition from an approximately three- to a two-child family as the norm desired by most women in the child-rearing age group was clearly evident by the end of the 1960's.[28] As two-child families become more prevalent, more married women will seek careers, while employment opportunities for teachers and others who serve or produce goods intended for young persons will diminish. Growth in the number of two-child, two-career families will increase the demand for smaller homes located reasonably

[27] *Manpower Report of the President,* 1973, p. 219.

[28] In 1972 70 percent of young wives in the 18- to 24-year age group expected to have two or fewer children. Only 9 percent expected to have four or more. *Ibid.,* p. 61.

close to places of work, and this development is expected to increase the preference for urban as compared with suburban life-styles and for facilities for recreation and leisure. This slowly growing population, largely made up of small families, will be concentrated in a dozen large metropolitan centers. Although the large urban centers occupy only a tenth of the land area, they are expected to contain over 70 percent of the population by the end of the century.[29] Economic resources, technological advance, and the "knowledge industries" will be concentrated in these areas with many fewer opportunities and resources in small towns and rural areas. The problem of population distribution, therefore, is likely to figure as an added dimension to the more familiar problems of economic growth and full employment in the next 10 or 20 years.

The civilian labor force is projected to reach 100 million by 1980, 19 million more than 1969. About half of this increase is expected to be made up of women, and about a sixth will consist of nonwhites. Planning for second careers, for less-than-full-time jobs, for more effective vocational education, and for the elimination of discriminatory barriers in employment will assume a more important role in the next decade than in the past one. The potentials for increasing and upgrading job opportunities for women and nonwhites (the economy's major reserves of underutilized human resources) will constitute a major consideration in determining how far the nation will be able to pursue its goals without encountering manpower bottlenecks.

The occupational makeup of the larger labor force in 1980 will show many signs of the much-discussed shift to a "postindustrial" society. Employment opportunities will continue to be dominated by activities in providing services, with especially rapid growth in the occupations requiring specialized knowledge and skills acquired through post-high school education in technical institutes, community colleges, and four-year colleges and graduate or professional schools. By 1980, according to the U.S. Department of Labor, nearly seven out of 10 nonagricultural wage and salary workers will be employed in the service industries—in health, in teaching, in finance and insurance, in providing transportation services, in research and development, or in government. Although employment opportunities for teachers are expected to grow slowly during the 1970's, and in some instances to diminish, employment for professional and technical workers, again to quote the Department of Labor, is projected to undergo the most rapid growth rate for any occupational group. Employment is expected to decrease in the occupational groups characterized least by skills acquired through schooling, laborers and smaller farmers.[30]

[29] *Toward Balanced Growth, op. cit.,* p. 44.

[30] *Manpower Report, op. cit.,* 1973, p. 225.

The greater skills and productivity of most persons in the labor force, and the greater prevalence of two-career families, show up in the projected increase in average income per household to over $14,600 in 1980, an increase of nearly three-tenths beyond the 1969 level. As in the past, higher family incomes, it is anticipated, will lead to marked increases in spending for services and for consumer durables, especially in spending for automobiles, for travel, and for recreation. Not all Americans will participate in this greater affluence. Nearly 18 million Americans are still estimated to be included in the households receiving poverty incomes in 1980, a decrease from 24 million in 1969 (see Appendix Table C-3). This would represent a drop from 12 to 8 percent of the population.

The typically more prosperous families in the coming decade, because of their greater incomes, would be paying higher taxes even if present tax rates were to remain unchanged. The projections show an average personal tax burden per household in 1980 of $2700 with present tax rates, about $900 more than in 1969. This would represent an increase in the ratio of personal taxes to personal income from 15.5 percent in 1969 to 18.5 percent in 1980 (see Appendix Table C-5). If, as many observers anticipate, the more educated, larger, and better-off population in the 1970's demands significantly more and better services from government in health care, education, environmental protection, or income maintenance, to cite instances, the level of tax rates is expected to rise. According to Andrew Brimmer, a member of the Federal Reserve's Board of Governors, merely to avoid "a serious deterioration in the scope and quality of our public services" will involve higher tax rates in the next five or ten years."[31] A major priority decision in the next 10 years, therefore, will concern the extent to which public services are to be expanded at the points that the expansion would require higher tax levels to shift resources from the private to the public economy.

VI

The costs of pursuing or attaining the goals considered in 1980 pertain to a future in which the available resources or the expenditures in many of the different goal areas are expected to diverge markedly from the present. The

[31] *The Wall Street Journal*, December 3, 1971, p. 1.

implications for the utilization of the economy's resources from pursuing national goals in the decade ahead can be illustrated in terms of "surprise free" projections that appear reasonable in the light of standards stemming from recent experience.

It is unlikely, in most instances, that the pace of change in spending in the different goal areas in the 1960's, and the priorities the spending levels imply, would continue unabated through the 1970's. Continuing past spending patterns into the future overlooks the cumulative effects of a high or a low priority in generating pressures for change. An extended erosion of support for research and development, for example, could lead to a deepening imbalance in international economic relations as other nations such as Japan forged ahead in the high technology industries. Continuation of a low priority for urban development would lead to massive deterioration of the physical facilities of the central cities. The worsening of facilities could encourage a further exodus of the middle class and of many business firms to the suburbs together with an explosive buildup of tensions in the urban ghettos.

An alternative to projecting past trends in spending to assess the implications of pursuing national goals is to project the cost of attaining standards reflecting current policy and informed opinion. The expenditure estimates for the goals prepared on this basis, therefore, show the anticipated significance for the use of resources in 1980 of what were widely regarded as desirable improvements in American life in the early 1970's. The standards are derived from legislation, from national programs and policy, from the recommendations of expert studies such as those of the National Academy of Sciences study groups, and from the behavior of decision-making units in American society. The standards seek to reflect issues as they have been conceived by the public and in the political process rather than attempting to present "optimum solutions" to problems of resource use or judgments concerning the desirability or undesirability of a high priority for attaining particular goals. Where it is apparent that important differences in standards provide the dominant note, as in the national defense or agricultural support goals, alternative standards are listed and "costed" out. The projections based on the standards are "surprise free" in that they reflect current developments and current opinion in these areas, and, separately, they represent levels of achievement regarded as reasonable and within reach on the basis of present knowledge and in a free enterprise system.

To cite instances, the standards adopted by the Federal Government to implement the Clean Air and Water Quality Acts, together with their amendments, supply the basis for the pollution abatement standard in the environmental quality goal. Similarly, the targets in the Housing and Urban Development Act, targets initially calling for the construction or subsidized rehabilitation of 26 million dwelling units in the 1969 to 1978 period, provide the point of departure for the standard in the housing goal. In research and development, the standard illustrates a scenario in which defense-related R & D increases at about the same rate as the GNP with the bulk of the increases in the country's R & D effort taking place in private and public outlays devoted to civilian-society needs or for more basic research. In household consumption the standard mirrors the spending patterns of private consumers who have consistently chosen to spend more than nine-tenths of their disposable incomes for consumer goods and services. The alternative standards for the national defense goal stem from different scenarios about the state of international relations in the next decade, primarily relations between the United States, the USSR, and mainland China. The less optimistic version of the future assuming a return to the Cold War projects a level of defense spending in 1980 of $102 billion (in 1969 dollars). This is $47 billion more than the alternative anticipating that the recent relaxation in United States-USSR-China tensions, developments symbolized by the President's visits to mainland China and the USSR, lead to partial disarmament by 1980. The standards for each goal are discussed in greater detail in the individual chapters, and they are summarized in Appendix B.

The expenditure estimates for attaining the goals refer to social rather than to market demand. But, in a society in which priorities and expenditures often undergo marked change in response to new problems and shifts in public concerns, many of the unmet social demands of the present are likely to become translated into market demands for goods and services and, therefore, into claims on resources in the next five, 10, or 20 years. Projections that attempt to take these aspirations into account often provide a perspective for anticipating future changes in private and public expenditures, or in job opportunities and markets for business, as well as future issues in national policy that would be lacking in forecasts based on extrapolations of past trends. For example, projections of expenditures and employment requirements in the health area made in the early 1960's, and based on the experience of the 1950's, would have overlooked the forces making for the changes resulting in Medicaid and Medicare and, consequently, in a formidable increase in spending for medical services and in the manpower required to provide them.

While the projections for attaining the goals are concerned with dollar costs, little attempt has been made to provide corresponding measures of dollar benefits. In part, this omission grows out of the aim of the study, to assess the claims on resources likely to arise in the next decade from the pursuit of a system of goals that seeks to reflect widely shared current aspirations. The omission partly arises from technical reasons. While meaningful indicators of benefits are available in a number of individual areas (e.g., days lost because of illness in health or reductions in the inventory of pollutants in environmental quality programs), a common denominator is lacking for aggregating measures of benefits that are sometimes expressed in different physical units and sometimes in dollar terms into a total comparable to the Gross National Product or labor force concepts. Research in developing more adequate social and economic indicators is substantially enlarging our ability to measure the benefits, as well as the dollar costs, of public programs and private activities that contribute to the pursuit of goals. However, the present "state of the art" does not permit consistent and integrated cost-benefit formulations for the individual goals comparable to the dollar estimates.

VII

Two cost estimates and two growth rates in expenditures are presented in each goal area. These include the actual expenditures in 1962 and the projected outlays for attaining the individual goals in 1980. A comparison of the annual average growth rates in spending in the different goal areas in the 1962 to 1969 period with the projected rates in the 1969 to 1980 period can provide an indication of the dimensions of the shifts in expenditures involved in attaining specific goals.

The expenditure estimates for 1969 and 1980 are listed in Table 1–4. The projections for 1980 range from $8 billion for the manpower training goal to over $900 billion for the household consumption goal, an area that includes aspects of many other goals. Where alternative standards have been prepared for specific goals, the estimate in the table refers to the standard that more closely reflects the experience in the early 1970's.

The estimates suggest prospective changes in the claims on the economy's resources that would arise if a high priority were assigned to particular goals in the decade ahead. Health, for instance, would move up from seventh place in the order of expenditures in 1969 to fifth in 1980. National defense would shift from fourth place in 1969 to ninth. Attaining the goals concerned with human welfare services—education, health, manpower training, and social welfare—would entail spending $265 billion more in these areas in 1980 than in 1969, a growth of 130 percent. The largest dollar increase

Table 1-4   Estimated Gross Expenditures in Individual Goal Areas,
1969 and Projected 1980
(in billions of 1969 dollars)

Goal Area	Expenditures in 1969[a]	Projected Expenditures in 1980	Percent Change, 1969 to 1980
Household consumption	$ 579.6	$ 931.3	60.5%
Private plant and equipment	99.3	207.8	109.5
Urban development	89.9	196.0	118.0
National defense	81.0	80.9	0.0
Social welfare	73.0	188.8	158.5
Education	64.4	123.8	92.5
Health	63.8	148.4	132.5
Transportation	61.4	104.3	70.0
Housing	35.4	85.4	141.0
Research and development	27.3	48.8	78.5
Environmental quality	15.8	55.9	254.0
Agricultural support	7.8	11.0	42.0
International aid	5.4	15.5	187.5
Manpower training	2.0	8.0	299.5
Gross total	1206.0	2205.7	—
GNP	$ 930.3	$1398.9	50.5%

[a] See Table 1-1.

in this group would be the one for the social welfare goal, a growth of $116 billion. The bulk of the larger social welfare expenditures would represent the cost of providing retirement incomes to aged couples in 1980 approximating the Department of Labor's "modest" budgets for these households in the early 1970's. The largest increase in dollar spending is the one for the household consumption goal, a growth of over $351 billion. All of the goals list increases in spending for 1980 other than the national defense goal standard assuming limited arms stabilization and continuation of the present state of international relations through the 1970's. The outlays for this standard assume a smaller but considerably more highly paid volunteer army in 1980 and a continued expansion of defense capabilities through research and development to devise new weapons systems and to update the conventional forces. If this version of the future were to materialize, defense spending, including both purchases of goods and services and other outlays, would decline from the 8.7 percent of the GNP that it was equivalent to in 1969 to 5.8 percent of the far larger Gross National Product in 1980.

The increases in spending to attain the standards in the different goal areas are summarized in Table 1–5. The table classifies the goals on the basis of the estimated percentage increase in expenditures between 1969 and 1980, and it also shows the projected growth in dollar outlays for each goal.

Table 1-5   Projected Increases in Spending in Individual Goal Areas, 1969 to 1980

By 1980 Spending Projected to	Percent Increase in Spending, 1969 to 1980	Increase in Dollar Spending, 1969 to 1980 (in billions of 1969 dollars)
Triple 1969 levels or more		
Manpower training	299.5%	$ 6.0
Environmental quality	254.0	40.1
Double 1969 levels		
International aid	187.5	10.1
Social welfare	158.5	115.8
Housing	141.0	50.0
Health	132.5	84.6
Urban development	118.0	106.1
Private plant and equipment	109.5	108.5
Less than double 1969 levels		
Education	92.5	59.4
Research and development	78.5	21.5
Transportation	70.0	42.9
Household consumption	60.5	351.7
Agricultural support	42.0	3.2
National defense	0.0	−0.2

The large percentage increases for the manpower training goal represents growth in outlays for a relatively new program that figures as an important element in many of the suggested reforms of the present public welfare system such as the Administration's proposed Family Assistance Plan in the early 1970's. The close-to-comparable percentage growth for the environmental protection goal stems from far-reaching changes in public conceptions of needs in dealing with the deterioration of the natural environment and the translation of these conceptions into legislation and national programs. The percentage growth listed for the education goal is considerably less than for the other human welfare service goals because of the anticipated slow increase in enrollment in elementary and secondary education. While the rate of increase in expenditures for the urban development goal is among the more moderate growth rates, the growth in dollar expenditures would amount to $106 billion, or to $25 billion more than the total spending for the national defense goal. Expenditures of this magnitude could make cities less hospitable to human habitation if they were unaccompanied by adequate land use planning by metropolitan-wide units of government to eliminate the congestion, pollution, and sprawl that now diminish the attractiveness of so many urban areas.

The achievement of some goals, again urban development is an instance, would involve a major change from the spending patterns in the 1960's. Others would entail only moderate changes from the growth in spending of the previous decade while still others (e.g., transportation) could be attained with a decrease in the rate of growth in expenditures. The degree that the projections for 1980 imply a continuity or a break with the trends in spending in the recent past is described in Table 1–6 by a comparison of the projected growth rates in expenditures in each goal area between 1969 and 1980 with the actual growth rates between 1962 and 1969.

Table 1-6 Average Annual Growth Rates in Expenditures in Individual Goal Areas, 1962 to 1969 and Projected 1969 to 1980[a]

Goal Area	Growth Rate in Expenditures, 1962 to 1969	Projected Growth Rate, 1969 to 1980
Household consumption	4.7%	4.4%
Private plant and equipment	7.8	6.9
Urban development	0.8	7.3
National defense	3.1	0.0
Social welfare	7.1	9.0
Education	5.7	6.1
Health	5.5	8.0
Transportation	6.6	4.9
Housing	−1.0	8.3
Research and development	3.7	5.4
Environmental quality	5.4	12.2
Agricultural support	−0.8	3.2
International aid	−1.8	10.1
Manpower training	—	13.4

[a] See Tables 1-1 and 1-5.

The projections for the human welfare service goals continue the higher-than-average growth rates in expenditures that characterized these goal areas in the 1960's so that a high priority to attain these goals in the 1970's represents an acceleration rather than a break in trend. The decrease in the projected growth rate for the transportation goal comes about because of the expectation that achieving this goal would involve especially rapid increases in spending for commercial carriers and for public transport facilities, modes of travel requiring lesser outlays for facilities for each million or billion passenger miles than private automobiles. The major breaks from the experience of the 1960's show up for the environmental quality goal and for a number of goals that received a low priority in that decade. The effects of the recent growth in interest in environmental quality is reflected in a projected growth rate in the 1970's more than double the comparable rate in the 1960's. The modest increase in growth rates in spending for the research and development goal arises out of the anticipation that the rapid growth in R & D will take place in the areas related to civilian society needs, types of research that seldom require the elaborate and costly development projects found in R & D to devise new weapons systems or spacecraft.

Not surprisingly, the large reversals in growth rates are concentrated among the goals receiving a low priority during the 1960's such as housing, urban development, agricultural support, and international aid. In many of these areas, standards are in flux, and the underlying consensus on which they are based has as yet to emerge. Reversing the low growth rate for urban development, for example, would involve public decisions as to whether to concentrate resources on rebuilding the central cities or to assign the primary emphasis to providing utilities, housing, expressways, and other facilities to encourage the continued movement of people and jobs to the suburbs. In the international aid goal area, the nominal standard, the United Nation's target that the advanced nations make available 1 percent of their domestic GNP in public and private capital supply and other economic assistance to the less-developed countries has become less relevant to experience with the aid programs in the United States. Conflicting aid objectives that join long-term development aims with short-term goals in military assistance, humanitarian aid, and political aims have prompted a continuing low priority for aid to the developing nations for over a decade.

The classification of goals employed in this analysis omits a number of areas of concern that have received extensive consideration in the recent past. For instance, maintenance of law and order in the large cities and elsewhere does not figure as a separate goal. Official statistics based on offenses known to the police estimate that crimes of violence rose from a rate of 160 per 100,000 population in 1960 to 325 in 1969 and 393 in 1971.[32] The

[32] *Statistical Abstract, 1972,* p. 143.

prevalence of crime is related to the drug culture, the unrest in the ghettos, the persistence of poverty, and the opportunities for earning income that organized crime frequently offers to persons who are otherwise on the margins of the labor market. It is also linked with an insufficiency of policemen, lengthy delays in the administration of justice, and to the inability of most penal institutions to rehabilitate their charges. Programs for lessening the incidence of crime cut across many goals including education, health, manpower training, social welfare, and urban development, and they would also involve improvements in police, judicial, and penal establishments. A high priority for law and order in the next decade would entail more effective pursuit of objectives in all of these areas.

VIII

The gross total obtained by adding up the projected expenditures for attaining all the individual goals in 1980 amounts to over $2.2 trillion. This total overstates the costs for achieving the entire system of goals because it contains substantial elements of double counting. After eliminating the double counting, the net cost of all the goals considered would exceed the $1.4 trillion Gross National Product anticipated for 1980 by $236 billion, or by 17 percent of the GNP.

Maintaining the everyday concepts of goal areas as they are discussed by the public or in Congress involves defining goals in ways that frequently include elements of overlapping with other goals. For example, the $49 billion expenditures listed for the research and development goal in 1980 includes $11 billion for the conduct of defense-related R & D. The defense-related R & D figures both in the R & D goal and in the national defense goal. For another instance, over half of the expenditures listed for the health goal represent personal consumption expenditures for medical care services that are also included in the household consumption goal. In effect, eliminating the double counting reduces the costs of all of the goals to expenditures included in one of the sectors of the national income accounts, that is, to personal consumption outlays, private domestic investment, net exports, or government purchases of goods and services. Eliminating the double counting reduces the total cost of the 14 goals from $2206 billion to $1635 billion.

The GNP is expected to increase from $930 billion in 1969 to nearly $1.4 trillion in 1980. Not all of this $470 billion growth in resources would be available to pursue improvements in standards. A substantial part of the anticipated increase would be absorbed in maintaining present levels of performance for a larger population. For example, providing the 1969 average level of household consumption, $8837, to the additional 13.5 million households expected by 1980 would absorb $120 billion of the projected $351 billion growth in expenditures listed for the household consumption goal between 1969 and 1980. As with the Federal Government's budget, the discretionary resources available for improvements in standards or for new initiatives would be substantially less than the total increase in resources because of "growing workloads, rising numbers of beneficiaries, and in some cases legislated improvement in benefit levels under existing programs."[33] In addition, sustaining the $1.4 trillion volume of output in 1980 would preempt an additional $64 billion more in that year than in 1969 in private capital outlays to add to the economy's productive capacity.

The additional resources available in 1980 because of economic growth in the preceding decade are estimated to be almost as large as the entire GNP in the early 1950's. Growth of these dimensions should allow for the greater absorption of resources from such sources as population growth and also allow for many improvements in performance. However, this massive growth in resources would be insufficient to provide the output necessary to achieve the standards for all of the 14 goals. The derivation of the estimate of the deficit in resources for achieving the system of goals is summarized in Table 1-7.

Table 1-7   Estimated Deficit in GNP for Attaining Goals in 1980
(in billions of 1969 dollars)

Item	Projected Value in 1980
Gross outlays for goals	$2205.7
Double counting	571.1
Net outlays for goals	1634.6
GNP in 1980	1398.9
Deficit in GNP for goals	235.7
Deficit as percent of GNP	17.0%

[33] *Setting National Priorities: The 1973 Budget, op. cit.,* p. 415.

Our society could choose to eliminate slums in the 1970's, to provide the $6500 nationwide minimum family income proposed several years ago by the national organization of public assistance beneficiaries, or to triple the present outlays for R & D related to social, economic, and environmental needs. The nation can achieve many of its goals in the decade ahead and more fully pursue others. However, it is also evident that even with reasonably optimistic economic growth, a growth rate estimated at slightly less than 4 percent a year during the 1970's, the resources available would be inadequate to attain all of the goals considered at the same time. Hence the need for priorities, for determining "what comes first" as a claim on resources and by how much.

Achieving all of the goals would involve a distribution of the GNP in 1980 different from what would otherwise be anticipated on the basis of recent experience. Private plant and equipment outlays and government purchases of goods and services would account for a larger share of the Gross National Product and personal consumption expenditures for a smaller share (see Appendix A). Attaining the entire system of goals would also require a higher GNP growth rate, 5.3 percent a year during the 1969 to 1980 period as compared with the projected 3.8 percent rate in the same period or with the annual average of 3.7 percent for the overall 1948 to 1970 period. Sustaining a 5.3 percent rate would require discontinuous growth in productivity in an increasingly service-oriented economy, longer hours of work, or a more rapid labor force growth than is expected in the next decade. Institutional changes that enabled the economy to maintain price increases at an acceptable level, for example, about 3 percent a year, while maintaining unemployment rates in a 2.5 to 3.5 percent range by 1980, as compared with the 5.6 percent rate in 1972, could also make a significant contribution toward more fully realizing goals. A reduction in the unemployment rate of one percentage point from the 4.4 percent rate projected for 1980 would increase the economy's output by an estimated $14 to $15 billion.

More currently, the inflation that accelerated in the United States as an aftermath of the war in Vietnam highlights the problem of priorities. This experience shows that even the world's most affluent society lacks the resources to maintain high and rising standards of private consumption while simultaneously adding to its stock of plant and equipment, supplying greater resources for national defense objectives, and also adding expenditures for an expanding array of pressing economic, environmental, and social goals.

IX

The estimates of the costs of the goals or of the deficit in resources for fully achieving the entire system of goals represent points on a scale reflecting the anticipated resources and the claims on resources expected to arise from the attainment of a series of goals. Similarly, the projected GNP for 1980 is derived from the current estimates of labor force growth in the 1970's, productivity increases, and reductions in hours of work. Changes in these variables, like a reduction in the unemployment rate, add to the resources available for pursuing goals. An increase of 0.1 percent in the rate of productivity growth in 1971, for example, would have added about $1 billion to the GNP that year.

To an observer from the less developed nations, or from most of the rest of the world, the American economy would be set apart by its abundance. Yet, the leapfrogging of resources and aspirations makes it unlikely that the problem of scarcity of resources, the basic condition that creates the need for priorities, would disappear in the United States in the foreseeable future because of economic growth and scientific advance.[34] A greater-than-expected growth in the GNP would carry with it larger-than-anticipated increases in household consumption by most Americans, greater needs for public services (e.g., environmental protection activities), and greater requirements for private capital outlays to provide the additional productive capacity needed to sustain the larger volume of output. With the passage of another 5 or 10 years, continued growth in resources in an environment in which problems and opportunities were changing would lead to reformulations of presently held standards and to the emergence of new goals. For instance, expanding the availability of medical care by financing it through a Government Trust Fund supported by payroll taxes and general revenues, as proposed in the Kennedy-Griffiths National Health Insurance legislation, could well cause national health expenditures to substantially exceed the $148 billion projected as the cost of achieving health goals in 1980. By

---

[34] While the problem of scarcity has not been eliminated by scientific advance, the critical scarce resources have shifted in this century to include a far heavier stress on human resources (i.e., on theoretically based "expertise" and the abilities to innovate and to manage large-scale organizations) and on energy resources.

1980 present commitments to expenditures for leisure-time activities, including lifelong schooling, may accelerate as the four-day week becomes generalized in American industry. With the passage of time and with more resources, the relatively limited standard of retirement benefits for the aged included in the social welfare goal would probably be revised upwards. This standard would provide by 1980 the approximate equivalent of the Department of Labor's suggested income requirement of $4200 a year in the early 1970's to maintain a "modest" level of living for elderly couples in urban areas. The Labor Department suggests, for example, an income requirement of $6620 for a "high" budget for a retired couple. Growth in the volume of resources may be consistent with sharply rising costs for some products such as petroleum products. This development could affect objectives in urban development by reducing the attractiveness of the suburbs as places to live in and commute to work in the city.

Emphasis on the gap in resources for attaining goals points to the necessity for making choices rather than to the desirability of diminishing aspirations. Concentration on requirements in individual goal areas obscures the need for choice because it overlooks the fact that the specific goals considered are part of a larger system of competing claims on resources. From the perspective of the system, the task of policy and, essentially, of politics is to reconcile the claims arising from different goals and to keep a multitude of competing claims within the constraints set by the economy's resources. Looking ahead to 1980, the outlines of some of the current issues likely to involve continuing choices for the next 10 years appear evident. For instance, to what extent does the diminution of human well-being from pollution, congestion, and sprawl warrant an emphasis on control measures that pose a likelihood of a reduction in economic growth and, therefore, in the resources available for other goals? Can more resources devoted to research and planning make a large difference in needs for this type of choice in the next 5 or 10 years? Should public and private resources be devoted to rebuilding the core of the central cities, or should the bulk of the resources be applied to develop new towns and satellite cities on the periphery of the metropolitan areas at the probable cost of a large-scale disinvestment in the physical facilities, including housing, already in place in the central cities? Will relaxation of international tensions in the 1970's facilitate continuation of the recent lesser priority for the goals concerned with the nation's international posture and a greater priority for the domestic human welfare service goals? Does the national commitment to equality of opportunity carry along with it a commitment to a considerably closer approximation to equality of results for Americans? Each of the choices made in these areas will have its particular pattern of consequences for the uses of the economy's resources in the decade ahead.

Chapter Two

PRIVATE SECTOR GOALS: HOUSEHOLD CONSUMPTION AND PRIVATE PLANT AND EQUIPMENT

I

Personal consumption expenditures and outlays for private plant and equipment are categories in the national income accounts. They are treated as goals because an analysis of the expenditures in the two areas serves to underscore the role of the private sector in the pursuit of national goals and also to highlight the relationships between the private and the public sectors in seeking to achieve goals. In an economy in which over three-fourths of the output is absorbed in the private sector, and in which government programs in pursuit of goals can substantially influence private spending, consumer expenditures and private outlays for plant and equipment can provide much of the impetus for economic growth and the means for pursuing a variety of goals.

The massive aggregates that make up personal consumption expenditures are treated as a single goal area—household consumption—because of the deep-seated conviction held by most Americans that high and rising levels of private consumption figure in their individual goals. While the youth culture, the consumer movement, and the greater concern with the environment have raised many questions about the values represented by this emphasis on private consumption and about the quality of much of what is consumed, the persistence of this attachment is apparent in the near constancy in the proportion of the GNP that is utilized for private consumption. For instance, the personal consumption expenditures that accounted for fractionally more than 62 percent of the GNP in 1969 made up 63 percent of the GNP in 1962 and slightly less than 63 percent in 1972.[1] In addition, treating personal consumption expenditures as constituting a separate goal area related to family living standards provides a perspective for integrating a number of different activities that contribute to the achievement of goals. Most of the spending for goals in health or transportation, to cite instances, represents spending by private consumers.

Creating productive capacity for industry and agriculture, and facilities for nonprofit organizations, is a means of supporting the pursuit of all goals

[1] Percentages refer to current dollar ratios. See *Annual Report, Council of Economic Advisers*, 1973, p. 193.

rather than a separate independent goal. Private outlays for plant and equipment are treated as a separate goal because the construction of plant and the production of equipment, while adding to productive capacity, is also one of the major claimants on the economy's resources. To estimate the amount of resources required for all goals, the expenditures for the productive capacity needed to pursue them must be included. Aside from these considerations, account should also be taken of the impact of the society's choice of priorities for private capital outlays in the next decade. A high priority for urban development in the 1970's, to cite a leading instance, could add close to $20 billion to the capital outlays projected for 1980 as otherwise arising in a growing economy. These additional outlays would be largely spent for public utilities, for industrial and commercial buildings, for urban mass transit, and for religious, cultural, and recreational facilities for nonprofit organizations.

The relationship between the private and the public sectors is often expressed in terms of the share of the GNP made up of government purchases, personal consumption expenditures, or gross private domestic investment. Yet, as Murray Weidenbaum, formerly Assistant Secretary of the Treasury, notes, consideration of the role of government "needs to be updated to reflect a far more complex . . . array of relationships . . . between the public and private sectors."[2] To cite one important instance, the $79 billion in estimated Federal outlays for money income transfers to individuals in the 1973 fiscal year very largely becomes translated into personal consumption outlays by the aged, the unemployed, the disabled, and by low-income families receiving the income transfers. Similarly, implementing the environmental quality standards in the Clean Air Act and the Water Quality Act primarily increases expenditures in the private sector by firms required to purchase equipment to abate pollution and by consumers in the form of the higher prices paid for automobiles because of engine modifications and add-on devices to reduce the emission of pollutants.

The social changes and shifts in national aspirations that have characterized the 1960's can be expected to influence personal consumption expenditures and private capital outlays in the 1970's. Changes in consumers' aspirations are illustrated by the resurgence of the consumer movement, a movement more concerned with receiving good value for money spent than with a downgrading of material well-being. Apprehension over the ecological consequences of constructing an oil pipeline in the Alaskan tundra has been the motivating force in the opposition to plans to build a pipeline from the Alaskan North Slope to the West Coast states. While there is little evi-

[2] M. L. Weidenbaum, *The Modern Public Sector,* 1969, p. 4.

dence in these shifts of a diminishing role for private consumption or private capital outlays, they do suggest a lesser emphasis on quantitative increases in consumption or in capital outlays as synonymous with economic or social progress.

II

Americans expressed their preference for rising levels of personal consumption during the 1960's by spending nine-tenths or more of their personal income after taxes for consumer goods and services. Personal savings during this period typically fluctuated between 5 and 7.5 percent of disposable personal income.[3] Consumer spending in the past decade showed many signs of an underlying shift toward a more service-oriented and a more leisure-oriented society.

The changes characterizing American society in the recent past show up in the growth in average consumption outlays per household and in the distribution of these expenditures between consumer durables, nondurables, and services. These developments are summarized in Table 2–1.

Between 1950 and 1972, average consumption expenditures per household increased, in 1969 prices, by three-fifths. This increase stemmed from higher levels of personal income arising out of productivity growth, a growth summarized in a 3.2 percent average annual increase in output per manhour in the private economy during the overall post-World War II period.[4] Occupational shifts within the labor force also help to account for the higher personal income and household consumption expenditures. Total employment, for instance, grew by 16 million between 1960 and 1972. Over 12.5 million of this increase took place in the generally better-paid and less unemployment-prone, white-collar, and skilled-craft occupations.[5]

The increases in consumption levels since 1950 obscure differences in trend in the distribution of consumer expenditures, trends often closely

[3] *Council of Economic Advisers,* 1973, *op. cit.,* p. 212. While the savings rate rose to 8 percent and slightly more in 1970 and 1971, it fell to 6.9 percent in 1972; *ibid.*

[4] National Planning Association, *Revised National Economic Projections to 1980, Report No. 71-N-2,* 1971, p. S8.

[5] *Manpower Report of the President,* 1973, p. 141.

Table 2-1 Selected Indicators, Personal Consumption Expenditures,
1950, 1960, 1969, and 1972[a]
(in 1969 dollars)

Item	Year			
	1950	1960	1969	1972
Total personal consumption expenditures (in billion dollars)	$285.0	$390.2	$579.6	$648.1
Average consumption expenditures per household[b]	5771	6902	8823	9273
Distribution of consumer expenditures by type of product				
Durables	12.9%	12.1%	15.5%	16.3%
Nondurables	48.8	46.6	42.7	41.8
Services	38.3	41.3	41.8	41.9
Total	100.0	100.0	100.0	100.0

[a] National Planning Association, *U.S. Economic and Demographic Projections: 1972–81, Report No. 72-N-2*, 1973, pp. 51,52,65,99; *National Income and Product Accounts of the United States, 1929-1965, Supplement to Survey of Current Business,* 1966. See also Appendix Table C-6.
[b] These estimates refer to "consumer units," that is, to families and unrelated individuals.

linked to changes in consumers' aspirations as well as to larger household incomes. These shifts amount to a decrease in the share of consumer spending allocated to nondurables such as food together with an increase in the proportion represented by durables and services. Consumer spending over the entire period increased most rapidly for durables, for example, for color television sets, automobiles, automatic dishwashers, and stereo sets. The values implied by this growing accumulation of durables are convenience, mobility, opportunities for the passive enjoyment of leisure, and the abridgment of time and effort spent in household drudgery. The values receiving less emphasis are those summed up in the traditional concept of ownership. Consumers, to a large extent, in effect rent their durables by borrowing the funds with which to pay for them. Between 1960 and 1972, for example, consumer installment debt nearly tripled, increasing from $43 billion to $127 billion.[6]

By the early 1970's spending for consumer services had become the largest component in personal consumption expenditures exceeding spending for

[6] *Council of Economic Advisers,* 1973, *op. cit.,* p. 262.

nondurables for the first time. While the increase (in current dollars) partially reflects the more rapid price rises for consumer services,[7] the growth in service outlays also stems from rising income and educational levels, greater leisure, and from growth in the possession of durable products often requiring costly maintenance and repair service. Consumers' outlays for automobile repair and related services in 1972, to cite an illustration, amounted to $10.6 billion. Similarly, spending for foreign travel by residents of the United States rose from $2.3 billion in 1960 to $6.2 billion in 1972.[8] In keeping with the growth in spending for consumer services, by the early 1970's about three-fifths of the employed workers in the United States were engaged in providing services to others—such as giving legal advice, teaching children, cleaning clothes, driving buses and airplanes, administering government programs, cutting hair, presenting entertainment, and treating patients.

Emphasis on the growth in household consumption levels overlooks the fact that Americans are "something else than a 'buying machine'—a robot created to consume the good, bad, and indifferent products and services of our economic system."[9] The forces tending to define Americans as "buying machines" are illustrated by the $20 billion spent annually on advertising. Some 560 messages of one kind or another impinge on the average American consumer each day, according to *Business Week*.[10] Consumers, to quote the President, require protection in the face of the seeming "impenetrable complexity in many of our consumer goods, in the advertising claims that surround them, the merchandising methods that purvey them, and the means available to conceal their quality."[11] The search for more effective consumer protection made itself evident in the reawakening of the consumer movement in the 1960's, a reawakening manifested in the mushrooming of consumer-oriented organizations and publications, in the emergence of persons such as Ralph Nader as national figures, and in the debates within and without industry over the social responsibilities of the large corporations.

[7] For instance, between 1967 and 1972 the consumer price index for services rose by 36 percent; the comparable increases for durables and nondurables were 19 and 20 percent respectively. The weight given to the increase in service outlays in constant dollar comparisons over time, therefore, is substantially affected by the recency of the base year selected for this purpose. See *Council of Economic Advisers, 1973, op. cit.,* p. 246.

[8] National Planning Association, *U.S. Economic and Demographic Projections: 1972–81, Report No. 72-N-2,* 1973, p. 62.

[9] A. W. Troelstrup, *The Consumer in American Society,* 1970, p. 14.

[10] *Business Week,* October 17, 1970, p. 132.

[11] *Message to Congress,* February 24, 1971.

The same considerations show up in legislation enacted during the 1960's to strengthen the legal position of consumers—truth in lending, truth in packaging, and similar legislation. Allowing for the resurgence of interest in consumerism, it is also significant that the total outlays for the Federal Food and Drug Administration, the agency most directly concerned with product safety and consumer protection, amounted to an estimated $156 million in the 1973 fiscal year, or to approximately 75 cents per person.[12]

The discussion of total and average household consumption, of the distribution of consumer expenditures by type of product, or of the need for consumer protection, refers to developments affecting most consumers to one degree or another. The aggregates and the averages derived from them obscure the extent to which living standards for large groups of people are concentrated at levels far below the averages. The problem the aggregates conceal is the problem of poverty.

There is little evidence that the degree of inequality in the income distribution has changed significantly since World War II. The lowest fifth of the households received 4.4 percent of total money income in 1947 and 5.4 percent in 1969. The share received by the top fifth declined from 45.9 percent to 41.6 percent of the total.[13] While the distribution of income has remained largely unchanged, as income levels have generally risen, the proportion of the population receiving poverty incomes has declined sharply. Accepting the Federal Government's estimates of the poverty population (i.e., the number of persons in families with incomes less than the equivalent of $3721 for a four-person family in 1969), there were 39.5 million persons with sufficiently low family incomes to be included in this group in 1959. By 1969, this number had declined to 24.3 million, a drop from 22.5 to 12 percent of the population.[14]

The Federal Government and, to a lesser extent, state and local governments influence the disposable income and therefore, the consumption of the low-income population through their tax policies and expenditure programs. For example, Federal individual income-tax payments in 1972 were estimated to make up one-half of 1 percent of personal income for taxpayers in the under $3000 income class. By contrast, the effective tax for tax-

[12] U.S. Office of Management and Budget, *Special Analyses: The Budget of the United States Government, Fiscal Year 1974*, p. 160.

[13] Derived from U.S. Department of Commerce, Bureau of the Census, *Income in 1969 of Families and Persons in the United States*, P-60, No. 65, December 14, 1970. The term "households" in this context refers to families and unrelated individuals, and it is identical with the concept of "consumer units."

[14] *Statistical Abstract, 1972*, p. 329. For a further discussion of changes in the size of the poverty population see Chapter Five and Appendix Table C-3.

payers in the $50,000 to $100,000 income bracket amounted to 22 percent of their income and to over 30 percent for wealthy persons receiving even larger incomes.[15] State and local tax systems frequently make the income distribution after taxes more unequal because of reliance on measures such as the sales tax, measures that exact a larger percentage of income as family income decreases. On the expenditures side, the Federal Government adds to the income and consumer expenditures of target groups, mainly low-income groups, through its income security programs. As far back as the middle 1960's, public income-transfer payments made up more than 40 percent of the money incomes of poor persons and the proportion has probably increased since.[16] The Federal outlays of $79 billion for cash benefit income security programs in the 1973 fiscal year added more than $70 billion to total personal consumption expenditures in that period. The cash benefit outlays were supplemented by income-in-kind programs amounting to $19 billion. The largest in-kind program was for the provision of health care, but these programs also included such measures as the Food Stamp and school lunch programs.[17]

Much of the questioning of the traditional emphasis on high and rising levels of personal consumption stems from the belief that growth in affluence has added to "ill-fare" as well as to welfare. The side effects of many personal consumption expenditures in contributing to illness or to reduced life expectancy, to accidents, or to pollution are frequently ignored by the producers and consumers of the products because the side effects are seldom included in the costs of the products to producers or the prices paid by consumers.

The uncompensated social costs arising from such sources as cigarette smoking or the pollutants given off by automobiles can be partially accounted for by translating them into the estimated dollar values for the medical care, property damages, or loss of earnings due to the shortened life expectancy or greater incidence of illnesses brought about by these types of consumption. A more complete appraisal of the costs would also allow for side effects that are difficult to translate into dollar equivalents, for example, human suffering because of automobile accidents. This kind of accounting would also allow for side effects that added to welfare as well as to "ill-fare." The benefits that the community, rather than the individuals concerned, derives from family expenditures to provide higher education for

---

[15] C. L. Schultze, *Setting National Priorities: The 1973 Budget,* 1972, p. 441.

[16] C. Green, "Income Security Through a Tax-Transfer System" in S. A. Levitan, et al., (eds.), *Toward Freedom from Want,* 1968, p. 169.

[17] *Special Analyses, The Budget of the United States Government, Fiscal Year 1974, op. cit.,* p. 165.

their young is an example. The costs in terms of dollar outlays for the negative side effects of personal consumption can be illustrated by smoking and alcoholism and by the contribution of automobile travel to accidents and air pollution. The estimates are summarized for a recent year in which the information is available (1968) in Table 2–2.

Table 2-2.   Estimated Costs of Selected Side Effects of Smoking, Alcohol Consumption, and Automobile Use in 1968[a]
(in millions of dollars)

Activity and Effects	Estimated Cost in 1968
Smoking	$ 1,983
Work days lost	1,900
Fire loss	83
Alcohol consumption	3,350
Work days lost, accident and training costs, and medical care costs[b]	3,350
Automobile use	18,500
Accidents	11,300
Air pollution	7,200
Total	$23,833

[a] C. K. Park, *Consumer Expenditures and Issues in the 1970's,* National Planning Association (unpublished), 1970; P. J. Cicurel, *External Effects to be Subtracted from GNP and NNP,* National Planning Association (unpublished), 1970.
[b] Accident, training, and medical care costs refer to costs to industry.

The instances cited are illustrative of a large group of side effects that could include much of congestion, litter, urban sprawl, or the excessive use of drugs such as barbiturates or amphetamines. The $24 billion total for the side effects of consumption listed in Table 2–2 would have added slightly more than 4 percent to personal consumption expenditures in 1968 if these costs had been included in the prices charged for tobacco, alcohol, or automobile use. The underlying reasoning in the estimates is that the individual who, for example, smokes "buys" a greater probability of illness and reduced life expectancy than nonsmokers. For instance, 58 percent of the deaths connected with arteriosclerosis and heart disease and 85 percent of those related to cancer of the respiratory system are associated with smoking. The shorter life expectancy because of smoking is illustrated by the report that a smoker of 20 cigarettes a day has a 10 percent chance of dying before age 62 as a direct result of his habit.[18]

The costs to society of the negative side effects of consumption can also be illustrated in terms of their impact on human capital, that is, on the nation's stock of human resources. Economists such as John Kendrick have estimated that as much as one-third of the national wealth of approximately $6 trillion in 1966 was represented by human capital.[19] The reduction in human capital because of the negative side effects of smoking, to cite an illustration, can be expressed as the present value of the earnings loss over time for the persons in the labor force in the late 1960's attributable to their reduced life expectancy or greater incidence of illness caused by smoking. Allowing for the effects of productivity increases on future earnings and discounting dollars earned in future years (in constant dollars) at 5 percent annually, the estimated value in 1969 of the earnings loss caused by smoking over an anticipated average future working life for the 1969 labor force amounting to 33 years is estimated at $77 billion. This earnings loss represents the equivalent of slightly more than 1 percent of the national wealth in 1966.

The negative side effects of private consumption figure among the major causes of the widespread demands for greater services from Federal, state, and local units of government. As families come to consume more frozen and prepackaged foods and more soft drinks or beer, more packages, bottles, and cans are discarded and local governments are called on to collect more trash. An increase in automobile use involves larger public outlays to control pollution and congestion and to provide parking space. Measures taken by government to minimize the contributions of private consumption to "ill-fare" include a law recently enacted by the State of Oregon, and under consideration in other states, requiring a deposit on all beer and soft drink containers to be reclaimed on the containers' return. They also entail an estimated outlay of $5.6 billion in 1969, largely borne by local governments, for solid waste disposal.[20] As private consumption expenditures increase in the 1970's, public outlays for environmental and urban development goals, to cite two important instances, are also expected to grow to cope with the undesirable side effects of the greater private affluence.

[18] S. H. Preston, "The Age-Incidence of Death from Smoking," *Journal of the American Statistical Association,* September 1970.

[19] J. W. Kendrick, "Total Investment and Growth of the U.S. Economy," Paper presented at annual meeting, American Statistical Association, December 30, 1967. The $6 trillion estimate is a measure of national wealth in 1958 prices. The equivalent of the $6 trillion in 1969 prices would have amounted to approximately $7.5 trillion.

[20] See Chapter Eleven, Table 11-1.

III

Private capital outlays are a means for achieving specific goals, and they contribute to economic growth and to full employment of the work force. Private outlays, especially for equipment, have represented a vehicle for translating advances in science and technology into the new processes and products and into the greater productivity that sustains growth. The slow pace of productivity growth in the United States during much of the recent past has led to concern that shifts in values and priorities in American society may diminish the impact of greater capital outlays in adding to productivity in the next decade.

All told, in 1969, private outlays for plant and equipment amounted to $99 billion, or to slightly more than a tenth of the GNP. Unlike personal consumption expenditures, spending for plant and equipment frequently flucauates markedly from year to year. For instance, business fixed investment, after adjusting for price increases, actually declined in 1970 and 1971 and then rose by 10 percent between 1971 and 1972.[21] While manufacturing industries account for close to a third of all private fixed investment, about four-fifths of the growth in business outlays for new plant and equipment between 1969 and 1973 took place in nonmanufacturing industries, especially in public utilities, communications, and commercial enterprises.

A number of factors have been significant in determining the volume of private spending for plant and equipment in the past decade. They include changes in the economy's overall output level and in the percentage of capacity at which individual industries operate, the rate of corporate profits, and the Federal Government's policies affecting corporate taxes, depreciation charges, and the cost and availability of credit. The rapid and sustained growth in private capital outlays between 1961 and 1966, for example, was stimulated by steady increases in demand by consumers and government for goods and services, by the introduction early in the decade of the 7 percent tax credit and accelerated depreciation guidelines, and by the enactment in 1964 of reduced corporate and personal tax rates.

[21] *Council of Economic Advisers,* 1973, *op. cit.,* pp. 20, 240; *ibid.,* 1971, p. 210. Current revisions in the national income accounts revise the private plant and equipment estimate downward to $98.5 billion; *ibid.,* p. 208.

Changes in national priorities also can play an important part in encouraging business investment by creating or expanding markets for the output of many industries or by bringing about the introduction of legislation or government programs creating new requirements for plant and equipment. The effects of the space exploration programs in the 1960's for capital outlays in the aerospace and electronics industries or the consequences of the pollution control legislation for capital outlays in a number of industries in the early 1970's are instances. Capital outlays by business for pollution abatement facilities, according to the McGraw-Hill Economics Department, grew from $1.7 billion in 1969 to $3.3 billion in 1972, and the planned investment in 1973 was estimated to reach $4.9 billion.[22] Most of this investment has taken place in response to the more stringent standards for the reduction of air and water pollution introduced in the early 1970's. Similarly, the complex of factors entering into the "energy crisis" in the 1970's, factors often stemming from the national search for "clean energy" sources as well as from shortages of petroleum from abroad, has been an important element in the rapid growth in capital outlays in the public utilities industry in the recent past.

Investment in new equipment often serves to introduce productivity-increasing technological improvements, frequently by incorporating laboratory discoveries into the mainstream of production. There has been a long-term tendency to concentrate capital expenditures more heavily on equipment than on plant. As far back as 1929, slightly over half of all spending for business fixed facilities was made up of outlays for plant, and less than half was spending for equipment. By the end of the 1960's, investment in plant had declined to about 30 percent of the total while equipment expenditures had risen to 70 percent.[23] These shifts probably reflect, among other considerations, the greater national R & D effort together with the decrease in the average number of years elapsing between the time of the establishment of the technical feasibility of an innovation and the time when the innovation is first introduced as a commercial product or process.[24]

[22] McGraw-Hill Publications, Economics Department, *Annual McGraw-Hill Survey of Pollution Control Expenditures*, 1971, 1972.

[23] A. Al-Samarrie, *Goals Largely Pursued Through the Private Sector*, National Planning Association (unpublished), 1971, p. 31.

[24] The National Commission on Technology, Automation, and Economic Progress has estimated, from a study of 20 major innovations, that the number of years elapsing diminished from an average of 37 years for the innovations in the 1885 to 1919 period to 14 years for those in the 1945 to 1964 period. National Commission on Technology, Automation, and Economic Progress, *Technology and the American Economy*, 1966, p. 4.

There has been considerable concern in the United States with the slowing down of productivity growth in the second half of the 1960's, and with the lesser rate of productivity increase in this country than in a number of other non-Communist advanced industrial economies such as Japan or West Germany. Apprehension over the slow rate of productivity growth was evident in 1970 when the Administration established a National Commission on Productivity to assess the problem of renewing productivity growth. The changes in productivity responsible for this concern are illustrated by Table 2–3.

Table 2-3 **Average Annual Growth Rate in Output per Man-Hour in the Private Economy, 1948 to 1970**[a]

Time Period	Average Annual Growth in Output per Man-Hour
1948–1970	3.2%
1960–1970	3.0
1965–1970	2.3

[a] National Planning Association *Revised National Economic Projections to 1980, Report No. 71-N-2*, 1971, p. S8. See also Appendix Table C-4.

In the last two years of the decade, from 1968 through 1970, the increase in output per man-hour for the entire economy was less than 1 percent.[25] Similarly, the average growth of productivity in the United States since 1950 has been less than in the industrially advanced nations in Western Europe and substantially less than in Japan. The average rate of increase in the United States, including the government sector, between 1965 and 1969, for example, was 1.7 percent. The comparable rates for the Western European nations were 4.5 percent and for Japan the rate was 10.6 percent.[26] Offsetting the higher rates of productivity growth in these other nations, American workers, on an average, continue to produce 20 percent or more output per hour of work than in nations such as Japan.

The significance of higher or lower rates of productivity growth is emphasized by the estimate that an increase of 0.1 percent in the 1971 productivi-

[25] *The Wall Street Journal,* October 16, 1971, p. 1.

[26] U.S. House of Representatives, Committee on Science and Astronautics, *Hearings, Science, Technology, and the Economy,* No. 7, 1971, p. 12. The West European nations referred to were Italy, Germany, France, Belgium, the Netherlands, and the United Kingdom.

ty growth rate would have added about $1 billion to the Gross National Product in that year.[27] Slow productivity growth contributes to the deficits in the trade balance by making American products less competitive abroad, it frequently makes it difficult to offset the cost increases contributing to inflation at home, and slow growth reduces the additional output available for higher living standards or for the pursuit of other goals.

Many factors contribute to growth in productivity including such developments as the rising educational attainment and skill levels of the work force as well as changes in the quantity and quality of tools, equipment, and organization with which they work. Over short time periods, productivity is more likely to be growing rapidly when the economy is moving out of a recession than during boom periods when many industries are experiencing bottlenecks in obtaining adequate supplies of manpower and materials. With the acceleration in economic activity late in 1971, the pace of productivity growth rose and became more pronounced than in other recent recoveries. This change suggests that the decrease in productivity in the second half of the 1960's could represent a temporary aberration. Other developments raise the possibility that changes in the structure of the economy, together with what *The Wall Street Journal* describes as "a shift in values and priorities in American society," may be diminishing the impact of greater capital outlays or rising educational and skill levels in adding to productivity growth.[28]

For another consideration, the most rapidly growing sector of the economy—the services sector—is characterized by low rates of productivity growth insofar as productivity can be measured in industries such as education or health. The share of the national product originating in agriculture, a high productivity growth industry, has been declining for many years, and this decline, like the growth in the service industries, is expected to continue during the next decade. Similarly, outlays for pollution abatement equipment by industry, spending to remove pollutants from waste water, for example, would typically be regarded as reducing productivity by the accounting standards used to measure the Gross National Product because these outlays add to capital expenditures without creating a product possessing a market value. More generally, the growing reluctance to accept technological advance as synonymous with human progress has eroded public support for the R & D that in the past has frequently directly or indirectly become translated into capital outlays for new equipment or processes leading to higher productivity. In the past generation, the computer and the jet air-

[27] *The Wall Street Journal, op. cit.*
[28] *Ibid.*, February 15, 1972, p. 18.

plane have provided the classic instances. Within industry, a special task force reporting on "Work in America" to the Secretary of Health, Education, and Welfare in 1972 concluded that the "alienation and disenchantment" with their work of significant numbers of American workers was retarding productivity growth by affecting "absenteeism, turnover rates, wildcat strikes . . . and a reluctance by workers to commit themselves to their work tasks."[29]

Private outlays for durable equipment and nonresidential structures have grown more slowly in the United States in the 1960's than in many other industrially advanced nations. This fact together with the lesser percentage of the American GNP devoted to capital outlays indicates that the gap in productivity growth between the United States and the other nations has long-term foundations that are unlikely to disappear in the next few years. These developments are summarized in Table 2–4.

Table 2-4 Private Investments in Nonresidential Structures and in Durable Equipment, Selected Nations, 1950 to 1969[a]

Country	Average Annual Growth Rate in Investments, 1950 to 1969	Fixed Asset Investments as Percent of GNP	
		in 1959	in 1969
United States	4.3%	11.9%	10.7%
United Kingdom	4.8	12.7	13.5
France	6.3	14.9	18.4
West Germany	8.1	17.7	19.1
Japan	14.9	22.7	29.6

[a] U. S. House of Representatives, Committee on Science and Astronautics, *Hearings, Science, Technology, and the Economy,* No. 7, 1971, p. 15.

The significance for the achievement of goals in the 1970's of the slow productivity growth in the recent past, or of the lesser ratios of business fixed investment to the GNP in the United States, is little more than suggestive of problems and potentials in the decade ahead. The low productivity growth, in part, comes about because of difficulties in measuring productivity or from the absence in the national economic accounts of an allowance

[29] U.S. Department of Health, Education, and Welfare, *Work in America, Report of a Special Tast Force to the Secretary of Health, Education, and Welfare,* 1972, pp. x, xi.

for the value of socially desirable advances such as the abatement of pollution. The international comparisons imply that recurring balance of payments problems, and the inflationary pressures that often accompany them,
are likely to become more of a consideration in assessing the priorities to be
assigned to domestic social goals in the next decade than in the past one.
Recent experience also suggests that a more heavily service-oriented economy, and one faced with pervasive questioning of the desirability of economic
growth and technical advance, will face more formidable barriers in according a high priority to productivity growth and the capital outlays that facilitate this growth than in the past.

IV

Spending for personal consumption and for private plant and equipment absorbed slightly more than seven-tenths of the economy's output in 1969 and
1972. With the $1.4 trillion GNP anticipated in 1980 on the basis of recent
trends, over four-fifths of the economy's output would be absorbed in attaining the two private sector goals—household consumption and private plant
and equipment. These increases in requirements in the private sector in the
1970's would be competing with an array of claims for greater resources to
pursue economic, environmental, and social goals largely financed through
the public sector. The pursuit of many of the goals financed by government
would affect the private sector by adding to individual purchasing power
and consumption expenditures. Attaining the objectives included in the social welfare goal, for example, is estimated to add over $36 billion to the
personal consumption expenditures projected for 1980 on the basis of the
assumed economic growth.

Average household consumption expenditures are projected to increase to
nearly $11,000 by 1980 because of economic growth, an increase of close to
one-fourth greater than in 1969 (in 1969 dollars). The estimate assumes
that most Americans will maintain their commitment to higher levels of personal consumption by continuing to spend slightly more than nine-tenths of
their disposable personal income for consumer goods and services. The
changes in personal consumption expenditures anticipated in this framework
are described in Table 2–5.

Table 2-5   Estimated Consumer Expenditures,
1969 and Projected 1980, Growth Estimate
(in 1969 dollars)

Item	in 1969[a]	Projected 1980	Percent Change, 1969 to 1980
Personal income (in billions)	$ 750.5	$ 1,160.0	55%
Personal taxes (in billions)	116.0	214.0	85
Disposable personal income (in billions)	634.0	946.0	49
Personal consumption expenditures (in billions)	579.6	866.5	50
Consumption expenditures as percent of disposable income	91.4%	91.6%	—
Average consumption expenditures per household	$8,837	$10,929	24

[a] See Table 2-1 and Appendix Table C-5.

The projection of a nearly constant ratio of personal consumption expenditures to disposable income could be disturbed by continuing inflation, a factor tending to increase consumer spending, or by increases in the unemployment rate that could cause many families to postpone purchases of costly durable goods. The estimates assume a savings rate ranging between 5 and 7 percent of disposable income during the second half of the 1970's, a rate consistent with experience in the 1960's. The percentage increase in personal tax payments (about five-sixths) is substantially greater than the comparable increase for consumption expenditures. The average household would be paying $2700 in personal taxes in 1980, an increase of over $900 dollars beyond 1969 and $800 more than in 1972 (in 1969 dollars).[30]

The greater purchasing power available to most households in the next decade will be spent in even larger measure for services and durables than in the recent past, accounting for 60 percent of all consumer outlays in 1980 as compared with 57 percent in 1969 (in 1969 prices). Allowing for the more rapid price increases for services would increase the weight of services

[30] The estimates assume that with the present tax schedule the effective tax rate would go up from an average of 15.5 percent of personal income in 1969 to 18.5 percent by 1980.

in this total further. Spending for recreation, for example, is projected to rise by nearly three-fourths, again in 1969 prices, amounting to over $63 billion by 1980. In part, the growth in spending for personal services such as recreation or travel will arise out of the increase in leisure, an increase expected to represent the equivalent of an additional week and a half a year in leisure time in 1980 as compared to 1969. In consumer durables, about half of the total purchases in 1980 are estimated to stem from purchases of automobiles and parts.[31] In the late 1960's, about five-eighths of the households with annual incomes of $15,000 or greater owned two or more cars.[32] By 1980, the average income of American households is expected to reach $14,600. Continuation of present patterns of automobile ownership, accordingly, would mean a large increase in the number of multiple-car-owning families. All told, by 1980 the number of automobiles owned by Americans is projected to reach 120 million, 35 million more than in 1969.

The economic growth responsible for the substantial increases anticipated in average household income and consumption in the next decade would also reduce the size of the poverty population. Allowing for a modest increase in what is regarded as the upper limit to poverty income, an increase at half the rate of growth in average household income, the poverty cut-off income for a four-person family, would rise from the government's estimate of $3721 in 1969 to $4220 in 1980. The population in the poverty group would decline by an anticipated 6 million in this period, from 24.3 million persons to 18.3 million. The incidence of poverty would drop more sharply as the size of the poor group fell from 12 percent of the population in 1969 to 8 percent in 1980. Many poor persons in 1980 would be in families headed by a woman with little or no participation in the labor force while others would be in households headed by a person (usually a male) employed on a full-time year-round basis in a variety of unskilled occupations yielding poverty incomes to those who work at them. An income support program in the place of the present public welfare assistance system could eliminate the poverty income gap remaining in the next decade and provide incentives to poor persons to increase their earnings from work at an estimated cost of approximately $21 billion in 1980.[33]

The volume of consumer spending in 1980 can be projected, as in Table 2–5, on the basis of the anticipated annual average GNP increase, in constant dollars, of slightly under 4 percent, and the assumed personal tax and

---

[31] U.S. Economic and Demographic Projections: 1972–81, op cit., p. 41.

[32] A. Al-Samarrie, op. cit., p. 13.

[33] For a discussion of the income support program, the poverty income gap and program costs, see Chapter Five and Appendix Table C-3.

savings rates derived from recent experience. Higher levels of consumer expenditure would be necessary if a priority were given to attaining specific goals whose achievement either depended heavily on increases in consumer spending or that added to personal income and, therefore, to consumption expenditures. The impact of the pursuit of individual goals for personal consumption expenditures can be illustrated by the social welfare goal, the goal with the largest single potential for increasing consumer spending. Continuation of the social welfare programs similar to those already in existence at the end of 1972, allowing for continued expansion in wage levels, built-in increases provided for in present legislation, and growth in the population of beneficiaries, would increase cash benefit payments to individuals to an estimated $142 billion by 1980. The largest item in this total are the OASDHI (Social Security) income transfer payments to the aged, their survivors, and the disabled.[34] Since the benefit payments are typically received by low-income individuals, they are very largely spent. If 95 percent of the additions to income from this source were spent, nearly $135 billion of the $867 billion total listed for personal consumption expenditures in 1980 in Table 2–5 (about 15 percent of all personal consumption expenditures) would originate in social welfare cash benefit payments from public and private sources. Attaining the standards for the social welfare goal would call for larger cash benefit payments to the aged, the dependent, the disabled, and the unemployed than would be expected from a continuation of the present types of programs in a growing economy. The additional outlays would largely be attributable to increases in average retirement benefits from public and private sources to approximate the Department of Labor's estimated income requirement in the early 1970's for a "modest" living standard for an elderly couple in urban areas—about $4200—by the addition of income protection insurance in the event of illness for the entire labor force, and by a family assistance program to provide a nationwide floor to income for low-income families by 1980, including the working poor (see Chapter Five). These improvements are expected to add over $38 billion to the cash benefit payments to individuals projected for 1980 from the continuation of the present types of programs. The larger benefit payments would add an estimated $36.4 billion to personal consumption expenditures in that year. Nearly three-fifths of the additional consumer outlays are expected to represent greater spending for food and for housing and household operation.

An emphasis on the attainment of other goals such as health care, education, environmental quality, or housing would also involve increases in

[34] The health services component of OASDHI is included in the expenditures listed for the health goal rather than the social welfare goal.

consumer expenditures beyond the levels projected for 1980 because of higher family incomes and population increase. The dollar outlays listed for the household consumption goal take these increments of expenditure into account. In addition, an allowance should be included for national, state, and local consumer information and protection services to supply consumers with information about the quality of the products offered to them, to provide legal services for consumers, and to work with other government agencies and with industry to define and implement health, safety, and effectiveness standards for consumer products. If the equivalent of one-tenth of 1 percent of personal consumption expenditures were utilized for these purposes, outlays for consumer information and protection would amount to approximately $900 million a year by 1980. The different items that enter into the household consumption goal are summarized in Table 2–6.

**Table 2-6   Estimated Expenditures for the Household
Consumption Goal in 1980[a]
(in billions of 1969 dollars)**

Item	Projected Expenditures in 1980
Personal consumption expenditures, growth projection	$866.5
Additional consumer expenditures from other goals	63.8
Education	5.4
Environmental quality	2.2
Health	15.6
Housing	2.9
Manpower training	1.0
Social welfare	36.4
Other	0.3
Total, personal consumption expenditures	930.3
Consumer information and protection services	0.9
Total, household consumption goal	931.2
Personal consumption expenditures as percent of the GNP	66.5%
Personal consumption expenditures in 1969	$579.6

[a] See Appendix Table C-7.

The projections for the household consumption goal make up a scenario for a high-consumption economy. As a percentage of the GNP, personal consumption expenditures would rise from the approximately 62 percent spent in 1969 and 1972 to 66.5 percent of the $1.4 trillion GNP projected for 1980. The negative side effects of these massive increases in consumer outlays in the 1970's would be responsible for much of the growth in spending by government and business, as well as by consumers, for the environmental quality, health, urban development, and other goals. Part of the increase in consumer expenditures, therefore, as in the case of spending for health, would represent an effort to offset the undesirable consequences of other types of consumer spending, for example, for the ill effects of cigarette smoking. To cite another instance, solid wastes of the types handled by sanitation departments were reported to amount to an average of 5.7 pounds per person daily in urban areas and to 3.9 pounds in rural areas in the late 1960's. As household income and consumption levels rise in the next decade, one of the by-products of this growth is expected to take the form of an increase in the overall generation of solid wastes by 1980 to a daily average of 8 pounds per person in all areas.[35] Disposal of this larger volume of solid wastes is estimated to require an increase of $3.2 billion in annual outlays for solid waste disposal, largely in spending by local governments, a growth from the $5.6 billion spent in 1969 to $8.8 billion a year by 1980.

V

The private plant and equipment outlays listed for 1980 represent part of the costs of growth, both the overall growth needed to maintain high levels of employment and consumption, and the additional growth in productive capacity required in specific industries to achieve different goals. Creating a sufficiently dynamic economy to absorb the expected increase of nearly 19 million persons into the labor force while reducing unemployment to close to a 4 percent rate is projected to involve an increase in private capital outlays of about two-thirds, from $99 billion in 1969 to $164 billion in 1980. The larger volume of productive capacity required to attain all of the goals considered would involve private capital outlays reaching as high as $208

[35] R. U. Ayres, *National Goals as Related to Environmental Quality,* National Planning Association (unpublished), 1971, p. 31. See also Chapter Ten, Table 10-4.

billion by 1980. A critical assumption in making these estimates is that productivity growth per worker, conventionally measured in terms of output per man-hour, will rise substantially above the low 1965 to 1970 increases.

The projected private capital outlays are related to the pursuit of goals in several ways. As one example, spending for plant and equipment represents the setting aside of resources that could otherwise be utilized to satisfy current private and public needs and employing these resources in uses that are expected to yield increased output for greater satisfaction of needs in the future. The $164 billion listed for private capital outlays in 1980 symbolizes a sufficient quantity of resources set aside for growth. The resources set aside each year to expand and modernize the economy's productive capacity make it possible to more effectively pursue goals in education, health, urban development, private consumption, or in other areas after the additional capacity is in operation. However, these increases would fall short of providing the capacity required to attain the standards considered for the individual goals. Attaining the urban development goal, to cite a leading instance, would involve nearly $20 billion more in private capital outlays for industrial and commercial plant, public utilities, and recreational and other leisure facilities than would otherwise be anticipated because of economic growth.

Past experience regarding changes in the relationship of capital stock to output in different industries supplies a basis for estimating the private outlays for plant and equipment needed to produce the $1.4 trillion GNP projected for 1980. This increase in GNP, in constant prices, implies an annual average growth rate for the overall 1969 to 1980 period of 3.8 percent a year, a pace of economic growth slightly greater than the overall 1948 to 1970 rate. The estimates take into account the high rate of obsolescence for existing plant and equipment, and they also allow for the long-term tendency to concentrate capital expenditures more heavily on equipment than on plant. The estimates for the growth projection are summarized, by industrial sector, in Table 2–7.

The manufacturing sector is expected to continue as the source of about a third of all plant and equipment outlays with the more rapid increases taking place in the durable than in the nondurable goods industries. The largest percentage increases are listed for the transportation, communications, and public utilities industry groups. Rapid growth in demand for electricity and other energy, together with growing concern for the safety of nuclear power plants and for measures to reduce the pollutants they generate, explain the large increase listed for public utilities. In communications, the rapid expansion in investments in business fixed facilities are expected to take place in the telephone and telegraph industry—the dominant communications subgroup. Major developments leading to greater capital outlays are likely to in-

Table 2-7 Estimated Private Plant and Equipment Expenditures Required to Achieve Economic Growth, 1969 and Projected 1980[a]
(in billions of 1969 dollars)

Sector	Actual Expenditures in 1969	Projected Expenditures in 1980	Percent Change, 1969 to 1980
Manufacturing	$32.6	$ 53.7	68%
Durable	16.2	29.0	80
Nondurable	15.8	24.7	56
Mining	1.9	3.1	63
Transportation	6.0	11.4	92
Communications	8.2	16.4	99
Public utilities	11.4	20.6	80
Trade, service, finance, construction	16.3	27.5	69
Agriculture	5.1	7.2	42
Nonprofit organizations	5.4	8.3	54
Other	13.0	15.4	16
Total	99.3[b]	163.5	65
Total as percent of the GNP	10.7%	11.7%	

[a] Derived from National Planning Association, *Revised National Economic Projections to 1980, Report No. 71-N-2,* 1971.

[b] Current revisions in the national economic accounts would reduce this total in 1969 to $98.5 billion. See *Annual Report, Council of Economic Advisers,* 1973, p. 208.

clude widespread use of picture phones by 1980 and improvements in existing teletype exchange services and data transmission facilities. The more than $9 billion listed for private nonprofit organizations in 1980 represents spending for the construction of churches, schools, hospitals, museums, and similar facilities.

The projections for private nonresidential fixed investment in Table 2–7 show that private outlays for plant and equipment are expected to make up 11.7 percent of the 1980 GNP, an increase of one percentage point from the 10.7 percent in 1969. Partially because of this increase, productivity growth in the private economy, as measured by increases in output per man-hour, is expected to go up from the 1965 to 1970 average of 2.3 percent a year to an annual rate of 2.8 percent during the 1969 to 1980 period. This increase implies a recovery of productivity growth—but a recovery to levels below those in the first half of the 1960's and to slightly less than the 3.2 percent annual increase for the overall post-World War II years. A more rapid increase in total private capital stock and in capital stock per employee is expected to be required between 1969 and 1980 to obtain this relatively slower growth in productivity than was the case between 1962 and 1969. These anticipated relationships in the private economy are summarized in Table 2–8.

Table 2-8   Estimated Average Annual Growth in Productivity, Private Capital Stock, and Capital Stock Per Worker, 1962 to 1969 and Projected 1969 to 1980[a]

	Average Annual Growth Rate	
Item	1962 to 1969	Projected 1969 to 1980
Output per man-hour, private economy	3.3%	2.8%
Private capital stock	4.2	4.6
Employment in private economy	1.8	1.3
Capital stock per employee in private economy	2.3	3.3

[a] National Planning Association, *U.S. Economic and Demographic Projections: 1972–81,* Report No. 72-N-2, 1973, pp. 4, 44, 58; and unpublished NPA data. See Appendix Table C-4.

A more rapid increase in private capital stock, or in capital stock per employee, is projected to accompany a slower pace of productivity growth in the next decade than in the past one for several reasons. One reason is that the high rates of increase in private capital outlays in the 1970's are expected to take place in the durable goods industries and in transportation, communications, and public utilities. These are capital intensive industries, that is, industries characterized by a high ratio of plant and equipment per employee. Part of the business investment, especially in public utilities, will be directed at reducing pollution. While the investments will lead to the socially desirable result of improving environmental quality, this consideration is overlooked in the national economic accounts and in the productivity measures derived from them. However, to an increasing extent in the next decade, business investments in pollution abatement facilities will come about in ways that do show up in the standard productivity measures. This will occur as concern with pollution accelerates the introduction of new technology that increases productivity while also possessing the desirable side effect of diminishing pollution. The pelletizing and continuous-casting processes in the steel industry constitute instances.

Aside from these concerns, the projected recovery in productivity growth from the low 1965 to 1970 levels suggests that the apprehensions in the early 1970's that changes in social values and priorities were posing new barriers to productivity growth will have been largely resolved in the next decade. So, the projections imply that a work force largely made up of high school graduates or persons with college education will continue to accept the discipline of the work place in automobile assembly plants, steel mills, large corporate office staffs, or in service facilities such as metropolitan hospital centers. As in the past, a combination of higher wages and rising consumption levels, together with longer vacations, will facilitate this acceptance. In other instances, the substitution of teams of workers participating in many aspects of the production or assembly of a finished product for the present highly specialized division of labor may lead to a similar result. Specific changes aside, the maintenance of a high rate of productivity growth is dependent on the skills, attitudes, and expectations of the individuals who make up the work force as well as on the growth in the stock of capital.

The $164 billion projection for private capital outlays in 1980 assumes an emphasis on the pursuit of goals involving substantial private nonresidential fixed investments such as urban development, environmental quality, or transportation. For instance, the Council on Environmental Quality estimates that private and public investments amounting to a total of $93 billion during the 1971 to 1980 period would be required to implement the pollution control standards in the legislation in force at the beginning of 1972.[36] These investments would be an important factor in maintaining the economy's growth in the coming decade. However, the standards for the individual goals frequently entail a considerably greater volume of private spending for plant and equipment than is embodied in the outlays required to support growth. The additional consumer expenditures that would be generated by a high priority for the achievement of some goals, especially the social welfare goal, would also lead to requirements for additional productive capacity to produce this greater output of consumer goods. Taking into account the additional fixed investment required to achieve all of the goals considered would involve private outlays for plant and equip-

[36] Council on Environmental Quality, *Environmental Quality*, 1972, p. 277.

ment in 1980 estimated to amount to $208 billion. The projections allowing for the larger requirements to attain the individual goals are listed in Table 2–9.

**Table 2-9   Estimated Private Expenditures for Plant and Equipment
Required to Achieve Goals in 1980
(in billions of 1969 dollars)**

Item	Projected Expenditures in 1980
Private plant and equipment outlays, growth projection	$163.5
Additional private plant and equipment requirements specified by	
Environmental quality goal	3.8
Health goal	0.9
Transportation goal	4.6
Urban development goal	19.8
Other individual goals	0.4
Greater output level to attain other goals	14.8
Total, additions to growth projection	44.3
Total, private outlays for plant and equipment to achieve goals	207.8
Private capital outlays as percent of GNP	14.9%
Private plant and equipment outlays in 1969	$ 99.3

The largest single increase in the projections are the additional require-ments to attain the urban development goal. A high priority for rebuilding the cultural and commercial facilities of the downtown areas, while also pro-viding the suburbs and new towns with the additional public utilities, mass transit, industrial parks, shopping centers, churches, recreational centers, and similar facilities could add close to $20 billion to the private capital out-lays otherwise anticipated in 1980. The additional capital expenditures list-ed for the transportation goal include $2 billion for improving the roadbed, rolling stock, and other facilities of the nation's railroad to make it possible to utilize high-speed railroad passenger trains with rights-of-way and equip-ment adequate to permit speeds of up to 200 miles an hour, and potentially higher speeds, in the close to a dozen urban corridors with sufficient population density to support this alternative to automobile and short-haul air travel.

The projections for the private plant and equipment goal point to a "high investment" economy in the next decade in much the same way that the estimates for the consumer expenditures goal suggest a "high consumption" economy in 1980. The projections for private outlays for plant and equipment in Table 2–9 would represent an increase from the 10.7 percent of GNP figure in 1969 to 14.9 percent in 1980. While the high rate listed for 1980 is less than similar ratios for such nations as Japan or West Germany during the 1960's, it would be greater than the historical ratios of private nonresidential fixed investment to the GNP in the United States in any year in the past generation. The cost of this high investment economy for the United States in the 1970's would be a lesser growth in public outlays for a variety of purposes that could include national defense programs, environmental quality measures, human resources development, or a modest slowing down in the increase in private consumption.

Chapter Three

GOALS CONCERNED WITH COMMUNITY DEVELOPMENT: URBAN DEVELOPMENT AND HOUSING

I

Two goals are directly concerned with community development. One is the goal of providing adequate housing to all Americans, both in the urban and in the rural areas. The other is urban development, a goal that provides a framework for integrating all of the requirements for physical facilities that contribute to creating viable urban communities.

The atmosphere of crisis that engulfed so many of the nation's large cities in the 1960's had largely disappeared by the early 1970's. In the middle 1960's, as James T. Lynn, Secretary of the Department of Housing and Urban Development, pointed out, "there were cities on fire. There were riots. There was destruction."[1] While the large-scale civil disorders have become history, many of the underlying problems that fostered them and strengthened the barriers to more effective solutions remain. For one important consideration, the division of the metropolitan areas between central cities largely made up of low-income, elderly, young, and a nonwhite population, and suburbs composed very largely of middle-income white families influences virtually all efforts to make the large metropolitan centers more livable and more governable communities. The social and physical disorganization and the ghettos that have come to symbolize many of the large central cities such as Cleveland, Detroit, Los Angeles, Newark, or St. Louis have their counterparts in the more prosperous suburbs in a way of life characterized by one authority on urban problems, Wilfred Owen, as "cars without community."[2]

Demographic shifts, along with changes in labor participation and lifestyles, are expected to constitute a major force for change in urban arrangements in the next decade. The decline in average family size during the 1960's from an approximately three- to a two-child family is probably the most far-reaching change. For example, only a third of the young married women in the 18- to 24-year age group responding to a survey in 1955 reported that they expected to have two or fewer children. Seventy percent gave this response when the survey was repeated in 1972. Declining family

[1] *White House Press Release,* March 8, 1973.
[2] W. Owen, *The Accessible City,* 1972, p. 111.

size is associated with a greater propensity for women to seek work. Between 1947 and 1971, for instance, the adult female population grew by 40 percent. The number of women in the labor force almost doubled during this period, increasing from 16.7 million to over 32 million.[3] A considerably larger number of two-child and two-career families would stimulate the demand for smaller homes located reasonably close to urban or semi-urban workplaces, for second "vacation" homes, and for child-care facilities. Low birth rates would result in a larger proportion of older persons in the population in the next decade, a change reflected in a preference for smaller housing units situated close to shopping and recreational facilities.

The demographic developments point to a renewed burst of urban growth, residential construction, and community formation in the next ten years. The population in the 25- to 34-year age group, the group that creates the bulk of the new households, is projected to increase by nearly 12 million between 1970 and 1980. This is roughly five times as large as the comparable increase in the preceding decade.[4] With urban growth of these dimensions, the nation will be faced with choices at many points as to whether to assign a high priority to rebuilding the central city slums and downtown areas, or whether to give primary emphasis to developing new towns, satellite cities, and other more livable suburban developments on the periphery of the present metropolitan areas. Export of the problems of the inner city to the suburbs—the drug culture, racial conflicts, high crime and delinquency rates, and congestion—may diminish the pull of the forces encouraging the exodus of middle-class families to the suburbs. Sharply rising prices for gasoline will raise the cost of commuting to the urban center from the more distant suburbs. Renewal of the central cities may also be facilitated by an influx of younger middle-class college-educated persons for whom the values represented by homeownership in a physically safe and wholesome, if sterile environment, could loom less large than the freedom, the cultural advantages, and the anonymity of the urban centers. Rising land and construction costs, on the other hand, may make it economically infeasible to replace or rehabilitate the dilapidated and abandoned houses in many of the central city slums. Resources on a large scale will be utilized both for reconstruction of the urban centers and for suburban development. However, the choice of priorities, the planning to implement them, and the commitments of resources have largely yet to be made.

[3] *Manpower Report of the President,* 1973, pp. 61, 65.

[4] *Ibid.,* 1973, p. 219. The estimates for 1980 are series E projections—the intermediate fertility projections.

II

Developments during the past decade have continued—and frequently speeded up—the extensive urbanization and suburbanization that has taken place since World War II and earlier. Considerable progress was made during the 1960's in reducing the prevalence of substandard housing. In many other areas, the existing physical facilities were less adequate in serving urban needs at the end of the decade than at the beginning. The experience with urban mass transit is an instance.

Almost five-sixths of the nation's population growth between 1960 and 1970 took place in the metropolitan areas, with about two-thirds of the increase occurring outside the central cities of the metropolitan areas. Significantly, less than a tenth of the urban growth took place in the large cities, in the urban centers of a million or more population. The demographic shifts that figure in defining the character of so many of the nation's urban problems are summarized, for the 1960's, in Table 3–1.

The population growth outside of the central cities in the metropolitan areas in the 1960's was more than four times that of the central cities. While the white population in the central cities continued to outnumber the Negro population by a wide margin, the black population in the urban centers grew by three million and the white population remained stationary. Outside the central cities in the metropolitan areas, in the suburbs, the black population increased by over a fourth, by 800,000. Yet approximately 20 whites were added to the suburban population in the 1960's for every additional black person. While in-migration from the rural areas was a relatively minor factor in the growth of the large metropolitan areas in the past decade, the migration of Negroes out of the South continued in the 1960's at about the same levels as in the 1950's, an average net out-migration of 147,000 a year in both decades. This movement contributed to the decline in size of the black population in the nonmetropolitan areas. However, in explaining the rapid increase in the Negro population both in the central cities and in the nation in the past decade, considerable allowance must be made for a considerably higher birthrate among blacks than whites.[5] Negroes have come to

[5] The birthrate for whites in 1970 was 15.5 live births per 1000 population. The corresponding rate for Negroes and other nonwhites was 25.2. *Statistical Abstract, 1972,* p. 50.

Table 3-1 Population Changes by Residence and Race, 1960 to 1970[a]
(in millions)

Component	1960	1970	Percent Change, 1960 to 1970
Total	179.3	203.2	13.3%
Standard Metropolitan Statistical Areas	119.6	139.4	16.5
Central cities	60.0	63.8	6.3
Outside central cities	59.6	75.6	26.8
Nonmetropolitan areas	59.7	63.8	6.9
White	158.8	177.7	11.9
Central cities	49.4	49.4	0
Outside central cities—in SMSAs	55.7	71.1	27.6
Nonmetropolitan areas	53.7	57.2	6.5
Negro	18.8	22.6	20.2
Central cities	9.9	13.1	32.3
Outside central cities—in SMSAs	2.8	3.6	28.6
Nonmetropolitan areas	6.1	5.8	−4.9

[a] U.S. Bureau of the Census, *U.S. Census of Population, 1960 and 1970,* Vol. I. Figures presented exclude Alaska and Hawaii and nonwhites other than Negroes.

make up two-fifths or more of the population in such northern cities as Detroit, Washington, Newark, or Gary, Indiana. As this growing black population has been added to the low-income white population remaining in the central cities, the tendency observed in the middle 1960's for "the old, the poor, and discriminated against"[6] to become concentrated in the inner cities was typically more true in the early 1970's than a decade earlier.

The problems stemming from the bifurcation of the metropolitan areas along social and racial lines have been accentuated by the more rapid growth in employment in the suburbs than in the central cities in many metropolitan areas. For example, in one recent survey of the growth in employment in 10 metropolitan areas between 1959 and 1967, more than three-fourths of the employment increase in manufacturing and retail trade within the SMSAs and over two-thirds in wholesale trade took place outside of the central cities.[7] The cities themselves accounted for a majority of the em-

[6] President Johnson's 1965 *Message on the Cities.*
[7] *Manpower Report of the President,* 1971, pp. 89–90.

ployment growth in service occupations, often in poorly paid jobs such as hospital and parking-lot attendants, and also in many of the better-paid white-collar jobs in finance, corporate headquarters, government, or the communications industries. These white-collar positions were frequently held by middle-class white persons who commuted from the suburbs to the city.

The decline of urban mass transit during the 1960's made it more difficult for the low-income and often nonwhite population in the central cities to gain access to jobs in the suburbs for which they might possess entrance qualifications or acquire them through skill training programs. Rides per capita on all types of urban mass transit facilities decreased from 75 in 1960 to 49 in 1970, thereby continuing a decrease that has been going on for several decades.[8] Rapid rail transit suffered from a concentration of demand during the two peak periods of the rush hours of commuting to and from work and from underutilization of facilities at other times. The net result has been a series of increases in transit fares, curtailed services, and further declines in transit patronage. Mass transit in many cities has become the mode of travel of the poor, the old, and the very young. This social basis of mass transit patronage is underscored by the fact that as recently as the middle 1960's over half (57 percent) of the households with incomes below $3000 did not own an automobile.[9] Accordingly, except in a few of the older and larger urban centers such as New York City, automobile travel has achieved a practical near-monopoly of transportation within the metropolis other than for low-income groups, the old and the young, and for trips to and from the central business district. Programs to enlarge and improve mass transit facilities, therefore, can serve to lessen racial tensions and poverty along with relieving congestion and pollution.

The exodus of the middle-class population and of many business firms to the suburbs has eroded the tax base of the cities at the same time that the pressures for more public services requiring greater expenditures have multiplied. As one aftermath of this exodus, the dependent population of the very young, the aged, and families receiving public welfare assistance has come to make up a larger share of the population in many central cities. Local governments also find themselves called on to provide more police, fire, street maintenance, and pollution control services—services required, in part, because of the presence of large numbers of suburban commuters who contribute little to the revenues of local governments. As the real-estate tax base of the urban centers has grown less rapidly than their expenditures, the property tax has come to provide a smaller proportion of the required reve-

[8] American Transit Association, *Transit Fact Book*, 1970–1971, p. 6.

[9] U.S. Bureau of the Census, *Series P. 65, No. 18,* August 11, 1967, p. 1.

nues, falling from nearly 35 percent of city governments' revenues in 1960 to 28 percent by 1969.[10] The needs of the cities for additional revenues from other sources make up one of the major reasons for the rapid growth of Federal grant-in-aid programs and also for the current drive for general revenue sharing by the Federal Government with state and local governments. While there has been considerable questioning of the Federal Government's role in urban development in the recent past, the government's spending for urban public facilities has continued to grow. In the 1973 fiscal year, the Federal Government's spending for facilities within the metropolitan areas included in the urban development goal is estimated at $7.5 billion, largely in the form of grants-in-aid to state and local units of government.[11] Spending for community development and housing by the national government in the 1969 through 1972 period was approximately one billion dollars a year greater, on an annual average basis, than in the preceding four years.[12]

If the cities have been burdened by the departure of much of the middle class and of industry, the suburbs have been faced with shortages of power, sewer and water facilities, congestion, and ugly and sterile housing developments. The suburbs have sprawled into being, to quote the National Policy Task Force of the American Institute of Architects, "without the armature of public utilities and services that make the difference between raw development and livable communities."[13] Frequent brownouts and power failures during the 1960's, both in the suburbs and the cities, have served as an indication that the growth in requirements for electrical power from home air conditioning and other sources had come to exceed the construction of additional facilities for generating electricity. The slow growth in the number of nuclear plants for generating electricity has contributed to the chronic power shortages in the large urban centers.

The division between central cities and suburbs has intensified the fragmentation of authority found in nearly all the metropolitan areas. For instance, there are about 16,000 independent authorities concerned with some aspect of urban development. The suburban population has typically been reluctant to join with the cities in common governmental units endowed with authority since much of the reason for the move to the suburbs was a desire to escape the poor schools and public services, the fear of crime and civil

[10] *Statistical Abstract, 1971*, p. 415.

[11] Derived from the U.S. Office of Management and Budget, *Special Analyses, The Budget of the United States Government, Fiscal Year 1973*, 1972, p. 248.

[12] *Address by the President on Urban Affairs*, White House Release, November 1, 1972. This comparison is in current dollars.

[13] The American Institute of Architects, *A Plan for Urban Growth: Report of the National Policy Task Force*, 1972, p. 2.

disorders, and the rising political power of the nonwhites in many of the urban centers. Yet problems of transportation, pollution control, water and sewer facilities, and more general issues of zoning and urban development transcend the boundaries of the central cities and of individual suburbs, and, as in the New York metropolitan areas, they often encompass several states. Thus, the social and racial divisions within the metropolitan areas add both to the problems of urban development and they introduce formidable barriers to arriving at more workable solutions.

III

The importance of adequate housing for community development has been recognized in legislation since at least 1949, when Congress adopted the Housing Act pledging as a goal "a decent home in a suitable living environment for every American family." More recently, the Housing and Urban Development Act of 1968 established targets for national goals in housing that, as initially stated, called for the construction or rehabilitation of 26 million housing units in the 1969 to 1978 period.[14] However, the criteria of adequacy in housing are as much economic and social criteria involving considerations of income and neighborhood as they are questions of the anticipated requirements for housing units in the decade ahead.

The nation's housing stock grew during the 1960's by considerably more than the overall population, by 18 percent for housing as compared with 13 percent for population. The increase in requirements for dwelling units has reflected new household formation, rural-urban and central city-suburban population shifts, higher living standards generated by rising incomes and, especially for low-income groups, the impact of national housing policy. The changes in the housing inventory are summarized in Table 3–2.

Nearly 20 million units were added to the housing inventory between 1960 and 1970. Substandard housing, defined as the absence of plumbing facilities or overcrowding, fell off sharply. The percentage of houses lacking full plumbing facilities, for example, declined by more than half. By the late

[14] The 1968 goals, as subsequently interpreted, provide for 25 million new units plus the publicly subsidized rehabilitation of 1 million existing units.

Table 3-2 Changes in Housing Inventory, 1960, 1968, and 1970[a]

Item	1960	1968	1970
Number of year-round housing units (in millions)	58.3	65.6	67.6
Percent of total			
With 1.01 or more persons per room	11.5%	—	8.2%
Lacking plumbing facilities	16.8	8.4%	6.9
Deteriorating, with full plumbing	7.8	7.4	—

[a] Peter Wagner, *Housing and Community Development,* National Planning Association (unpublished), 1971, p. 43.

1960's, inadequate housing, according to these criteria, had become largely a rural and a Southern problem. Well over half of all substandard dwelling units were in the South, and nationally close to two-thirds were outside of the metropolitan areas. Over half, 52 percent, of the poor households living in rural areas in the middle of the last decade were housed in substandard dwellings.[15] The low-income population are primarily renters rather than homeowners, and they spend a considerably larger proportion of their incomes for rent than the more affluent families. Negroes in the central cities, for example, rented nearly two-thirds of the housing units they occupied in 1970. Only 2 percent of the purchases of new homes insured by the Federal Housing Administration and 6.5 percent of the purchases of existing homes in 1970 were made by families with incomes of $7000 or less.[16] Half or more of the families with incomes of $4000 or less in the late 1960's spent more than a fourth of their incomes, depending on age and income, for rent and household utilities. For all income and for age groups other than the elderly, the proportion spending over a fourth of their income for rent and utilities was slightly more than a fifth in the central cities and less than a fifth in other urban areas.[17]

Rising land and construction costs, together with severe gyrations in the availability of mortgage credit and in the interest rates on home mortgages have made it more difficult for the low- and often moderate-income families to become homeowners. The interest rates paid on home mortgages insured by the Federal Housing Administration, for example, fluctuated in the past

[15] C. L. Schultze, *Setting National Priorities: The 1972 Budget,* 1971, p. 291.
[16] L. H. Keyserling, *The Coming Crisis in Housing,* 1972, p. 50.
[17] *Setting National Priorities,* 1972, op. cit., p. 292.

decade from an average of 5.5 percent in 1965 to slightly more than 9 percent in 1970,[18] and equally high rates have become evident in 1973.

Many persons concerned with housing, in and out of government, have looked to innovations in residential construction as the most likely source for the cost-reducing improvements that would make more adequate housing available to low- and moderate-income families. However, innovations in residential construction have been slow to gain acceptance, although the experience in the recent past points to an increased receptivity to change. On an average, about 17 years have elapsed between the first commercial utilization of an innovation in housing and its general acceptance in everyday use as a standard state-of-the-art option or practice.[19] Modular construction, mobile homes, and relaxation in building codes illustrate changes likely to influence the character of residential construction in the next decade. Modular construction involves, as a minimum, the factory production of panels of standard sizes that are then assembled on the construction site. Less frequently, it entails the production in factories of entire housing units. In the early 1970's, only about 7 percent of the newly constructed homes included some form of modular construction. The producers of modular housing claim they can reduce construction costs by 15 to 25 percent if quantity production of these units can be sustained.[20] To facilitate modular construction, 12 states had passed laws by 1971 providing that modules passing state inspection were not subject to local building codes.

Mobile homes are another innovation that has received considerable acceptance. Production of these homes has grown from approximately 100,000 units in 1960 to nearly 500,000 units by 1971.[21] Mobile homes have appealed particularly to low-income families outside the central cities, to married-student households, and to highly mobile workers such as construction employees. The introduction of more complex and more fully equipped units has pushed up the cost of these homes, but their prices, including standard appliances and air conditioning, still compare favorably with conventional units. While recent changes in FHA regulations have considerably eased the financing of mobile homes, their attractiveness has often been diminished by a lack of suitable home sites offering widely desired amenities. The growth of mobile homes in the coming decade will be affected by the cost of the more conventional housing, including the extent that

[18] Statistical Abstract, 1971, p. 445.

[19] P. Wagner, Housing and Community Development, National Planning Association (unpublished), 1971, p. 77.

[20] Ibid., p. 75.

[21] Statistical Abstract, 1972, p. 683.

modular construction methods have taken hold and reduced construction costs for the less-expensive houses.

The Federal Government has been a major force in housing since the 1930's. The government has directly financed the construction of housing for low-income families and military personnel, and it has acted to reduce the cost of housing to low-income families by providing them with rent supplement subsidies and subsidies to reduce the cost of mortgage payments for low- and moderate-income home purchasers. The Federal income-tax deduction for real-estate taxes and interest payments on home mortgages provides an additional subsidy, in the form of reduced tax payments, to homeowners, largely to middle-income families, which amounted to $4.5 billion in 1969.[22] In the 1972 fiscal year, Federal programs supplying direct outlays for housing were expected to assist in the completion of over a million units of new or substantially rehabilitated housing. The direct outlay programs, together with the insurance loan activities of the FHA and the mortgage market activities of government enterprises such as the Federal National Mortgage Association, are estimated to affect decisions by private investors in housing involving some $22 billion in 1972 and $38 billion in 1973.[23]

The publicly financed or subsidized housing programs that gained acceptance as far back as the 1930's as part of the nation's program for the third of the population whom President Franklin D. Roosevelt described as "ill-housed, ill-clad, ill-nourished" have encountered considerable skepticism in the 1970's. Homes built in central-city slums with Federal assistance have, in many instances, been abandoned by their landlords who found this course of action preferable to paying local property taxes or making the repairs needed to meet local housing regulations. Massive multi-storied public housing projects built in earlier periods have often turned into crime-ridden slums. In St. Louis, an entire public housing development was demolished as uninhabitable. By the early 1970's the Federal Government owned over 90,000 subsidized housing units whose owners had defaulted on mortgage payments.[24] The government, to cite an example, owned 5000 single family homes in Detroit's inner city.[25] The Federal urban-renewal program, ac-

[22] The National Urban Coalition, *Counterbudget: A Blueprint for Changing National Priorities,* 1971, p. 150.

[23] *Special Analyses, The Budget of the United States Government, Fiscal Year 1972, op. cit.,* 1971, p. 217; *Ibid., Fiscal Year 1973,* 1972, p. 207.

[24] *Community Development Section of the President's State of the Union Message,* March 4, 1973.

[25] *The New York Times,* January 2, 1972, p. 44.

cording to the Urban Coalition, has resulted in "a net loss of housing."[26] To President Nixon, experience with the Federally supported housing programs shows that "the time has come to recognize the errors of past Federal efforts to support community development."[27]

There is less controversy concerning the anticipated requirements for housing in the next decade than about the role of the Federal Government in financing their construction. Goals for housing for the 1969–1978 period, as needs for housing units were conceived in the early 1970's, are summarized in the *Annual Report on National Housing Goals* required by the Housing and Urban Development Act of 1968. The anticipated requirements and their sources are described in Table 3–3.

Table 3-3   Estimated Requirements for Housing, 1969 to 1978[a]
(in millions of units)

Source	Projected Requirements, 1969 to 1978
New household formation	13.5
Increase in vacant units	3.5
Replacements for all dilapidated units	5.3
Replacements for losses of nondilapidated units	2.0
Replacements for losses of mobile homes	1.2
Rehabilitated substandard units	2.7
Total, new and rehabilitated units	28.2

[a] *Message from the President of the United States, Second Annual Report on National Housing Goals,* 1970. Estimates refer to fiscal years 1969 to 1978. This estimate differs from the target in the 1968 Housing and Urban Development Act largely because of the inclusion of 1.7 million substandard units that are expected to be rehabilitated without public subsidy.

The estimates take into account population growth and shifts, and they allow for increases in standards including the replacement or rehabilitation of all substandard and dilapidated housing during the decade. To set limits to increases in rents and home-purchase costs induced by shortages of housing, the estimates include sufficient housing construction to allow for as many as 3.5 million more vacant units by 1975. However, growth in the number of new households is the major source of the anticipated housing needs accounting for over half of the requirement for new housing units.

The cost estimates for the housing goal in 1980 are derived from the projections of housing requirements in the 1969–1978 period. The estimates

[26] *Counterbudget, op. cit.,* p. 137.
[27] *President's Message on Community Development,* March 8, 1973.

for the housing goal allow for continued population growth and for more extensive changes in standards, such as the incorporation of central air conditioning in virtually all homes built in 1980. Increases in vacancies are projected at less than half the *Annual Report on Housing Goals* estimates, while the demand for second (mainly vacation) homes is expected to more than double during the 1970's, amounting to 1.5 million housing units during the decade. Many more housing units will have special facilities to serve the needs of the aged and of handicapped persons, and many more will be designed to minimize maintenance chores in families in which both parents regularly work. Construction costs of single family dwellings, excluding mobile homes, are expected to rise to $24,000 by 1980 (in 1969 prices).[28] The estimates for the housing goal arrived at on this basis are summarized in Table 3–4.

Table 3-4   Estimated Starts and Expenditures for Housing Goal, 1969 and Projected 1980
(dollar totals in millions of 1969 dollars)

Item	Starts and Expenditures in 1969[a]	Projected Starts and Expenditures in 1980
New housing starts (in thousands)	1,912	2,961
Rehabilitated substandard units (in thousands)	—	300
Substandard housing units as percent of total	6.9%	0.0%
Expenditures for new residential construction	$24,640	$60,300
Expenditures for additions and alterations	5,580	13,900
Expenditures for maintenance and repair	5,200	11,200
Total, expenditures for housing goal	35,420	85,400
Expenditures as percent of GNP	3.8%	6.1%

[a] The U.S. Department of Commerce, *Construction Review,* September 1971; Mobile Home Manufacturers Association (unpublished). Estimates for 1969 and 1980 exclude land costs.

[28] This estimate of construction costs includes an increase of 3 percent a year in construction costs, in 1969 dollars, to allow for improvements in housing standards such as central air conditioning, the elimination of dilapidated housing, and new designs to serve the needs of families in which both parents are pursuing careers.

All told, outlays to attain the housing goal would involve more than a doubling of expenditures for housing, an increase from $35 billion in 1969 to an estimated $85 billion by 1980. An approach to housing goals in these terms, in housing starts and the rehabilitation or replacement of substandard units, would provide the entire population with a minimum of physically adequate housing as it was defined in the early 1970's. It would also allow for the demand for more elaborate housing or for second homes expected to arise from higher family incomes and the demand for more housing stemming from population growth. However, the criteria of adequacy in housing extend beyond the physical character of housing units. Considerations of the adequacy of housing also involve the adequacy of the community facilities in the neighborhood, the police and fire services, the schools and libraries, and the public transportation and recreational facilities. To nonwhites confined in central city ghettos, freedom to move to any section of the metropolitan area without encountering the barriers of segregation would also be a major factor in housing goals. Housing goals, therefore, involve many aspects of community development which extend beyond the number and adequacy of housing units.

IV

Experience in the past decade shows that there is no specific national policy that can be identified as "urban policy." Urban development policy is essentially one aspect of many national policies concerned with growth and development including policies dealing with population growth and distribution. A variety of public and private actions affect urban growth and development, and they often create their effects as an unintended consequence of actions undertaken for other purposes.

In assessing the Federal Government's role in urban development, Patrick Moynihan, formerly Counselor to the President on Domestic Affairs, speaks of the government's "hidden urban policies." There is hardly an agency of the national government, Moynihan points out, "whose programs do not in some way have important consequences for the life of cities, and [for] those who live in them." Agency executives are, "to their minds, simply building highways, guaranteeing mortgages, advancing agriculture, or whatever.

. . . [Yet] they are simultaneously redistributing employment opportunities, segregating neighborhoods, or desegregating them, depopulat-
ing the countryside, or filling up slums, etc."[29] In the same vein, the private
entrepreneurs who build shopping malls or who purchase land on the out-
skirts of the metropolis for later development into real estate subdivisions
are seldom concerned with the indirect consequences of their actions for the
cities.

Although residential construction is responsible for the largest single item
in the expenditure estimates for the urban development goal, spending for
transportation facilities is probably the most critical single element affecting
the viability of the cities. The alternatives available in transportation significantly influence patterns of land use, the concentration or dispersion of the
urban population, the growth or decline of central business districts, the
availability of jobs to the low-income population in the central cities, and
even public health. As the urban centers have expanded outwards in un-
planned and, frequently, chaotic growth, greater expenditures for transportation, especially the transportation provided by automobiles, has typically
become the remedy called upon "to make the disorder viable."[30]

In the coming decade, automobiles, rapid-rail transit, commuter railroads, and bus travel are all expected to figure in the improvements in metropolitan transportation. For travel to and from the central business district, and for other uses where traffic density is heavy, rapid-rail mass transit
is indispensable in the larger cities. The decisive advantage of rapid-rail
transit is that a single rapid-rail lane supplies a carrying capacity for 40,000
persons per track per hour in trains made up of 10 cars with 90 seconds
headway between them. Automobiles carrying passenger loads somewhat
greater than the present average load in the trip to and from work would require a 16-lane expressway for this purpose.[31] However, for most Americans, the convenience and flexibility of their private automobiles, in spite of
frequent congestion and pollution, were of sufficient weight for motor vehicle registrations to increase during the 1960's by more than three times the
rate of increase for population. This preference reflects the absence of attractive alternatives to auto travel in many metropolitan areas.

While urban mass transit is often identified with subway and surface-
rail transit, bus transportation often plays a critical role in areas where the
density of population makes subways an economically questionable enter-

[29] D. P. Moynihan, "Toward a National Urban Policy," *Appalachia*, August 1969, pp.
3–4.

[30] Owens, *op. cit.,* p. 53.

[31] Wagner, *op. cit.,* p. 138.

prise. Similarly, commuter railroads supply an important form of urban transportation serving a special market, one typically built around the more affluent middle-class communities providing from 200 to 2000 passengers daily for longer distances than rapid-rail urban transit can be expected to serve. Urban mass transit must also allow for transport from downtown and suburban centers to metropolitan area airports, often by systems using special bus lanes or, as in Cleveland, by subway transport, to reduce the frequently lengthy delays in commuting to and from airports. These delays, in some cities, can consume more time than the time spent airborne on a 500 to 600 mile trip by jet plane.

While the technical means to create new types of mass transit systems (e.g., monorails) have existed for several decades, few such systems have gained acceptance in everyday use on any scale. Some of the most striking innovations have come about from the utilization of computerized and automated traffic control and train movement systems, as in the BART system in the San Francisco area. Other innovations, as yet largely untried, offer potentials for contributing to the solution of urban transport problems that are sufficiently striking to make it appear reasonable to anticipate that they will receive greater recognition in the decade ahead. Use of the walk-on, walk-off sidewalk conveyor belt system in downtown areas is an illustration. The "moving sidewalks" offer savings in time and greater convenience than walking or traveling by automobile in many central business districts. Their everyday use would go far toward making it possible to convert many downtown areas into pedestrian malls from which automobiles were barred, at least during the day. So far, the conveyor belts have received limited use in special circumstances, as in the Los Angeles airport.

Recent developments suggest that important steps are under way to reverse the continuous decline in urban mass transit since World War II. The Urban Mass Transit Act of 1970, for example, proposes a Federal commitment of $10 billion over a 12-year period for capital outlays and research and development for urban transit facilities. In addition, in enacting the 1973 Highway Trust Fund bill, funds have been made available from this source, for the first time, for urban mass transit. These are supplementary to $3 billion in general revenues to be used for urban transit in the next three years.[32] The prospects for expanding urban mass transit are highlighted by the fact that in 1970 there were 33 metropolitan areas with over a million inhabitants. Only five areas had rapid transit systems and another two cities had systems under construction. Ten rapid-rail systems were in the construction or planning stage in the early 1970's. The total investment required to

---

[32] *The New York Times,* August 14, 1973, p. 17.

complete these systems was estimated at $15.5 billion in terms of the prevailing construction costs at the time.[33]

The solution to accelerating urban transportation needs, according to one authority, S. S. Taylor, "lies in discovering that complementary system of streets, freeways and transit lines which most effectively promote . . . a truly functional pattern of land use."[34] Both mass transit and the private automobile can be expected to figure as essential components in this complementary system in the next decade with the issues centering on the desirable mix of urban transit facilities. Prohibitive land costs, more costly and sometimes unavailable gasoline supplies, concern with pollution, and opposition to displacing people from their homes or dislocating cultural and recreational facilities are likely to slow down new highway construction in the urban areas other than near new suburban developments. Widening existing highways (frequently by adding lanes) and eliminating sharp turns and steep grades are responsible for the bulk of the outlays for urban streets and highways included in the cost estimates for 1980 in the urban development goal. Many large cities are expected to restrict auto use in the heart of the city by converting streets to walks, parks, and playgrounds, essentially pedestrian-oriented clusters, with circulatory systems provided by moving sidewalks, escalators, minibuses, elevators, and underground terminals located on the edges of the pedestrian clusters for parking facilities. Others will seek to limit auto use by coupling more attractive alternatives in mass transit with new taxes and related charges levied on automobile commuters from the suburbs to the central business district. However, after allowing for these efforts to limit auto use, spending for city streets and urban highway construction and maintenance in 1980 is projected to outweigh the capital outlays for urban mass transit by close to a 7 to 1 margin, by approximately $17 to $2.5 billion.

V

The new urban structures built each year in the United States involve the equivalent of constructing a city about the size of Philadelphia.[35] The

---

[33] Wagner, *op. cit.*, pp. 138, 142.
[34] Quoted in L. Lecht, *Goals, Priorities, and Dollars—The Next Decade,* 1966, p. 98.
[35] Owen, *op. cit.*, p. 53.

projections for the urban development goal in 1980 assume that in the mass of construction undertaken in the next decade urban growth and regrowth will proceed together with the choices centering on the priorities for each. Renewal of the older and more densely populated neighborhoods in the inner city is expected to go hand-in-hand with the building of new communities on vacant land on the edge or outside of the metropolitan areas. In many of the larger cities "new towns in town" containing approximately 25,000 people will provide a focus for integrated structures of apartments, town houses, shops, schools, and other facilities for attracting and retaining people who would prefer to live in a neighborhood within the city.

A high priority in the next 10 years for new types of cities representing a sharp break with present arrangements would add substantially to the anticipated capital outlays for transportation and other urban physical facilities. Instances would include the proposed Minnesota Experimental City, a plan to create a new city of 250,000 persons in what is currently a rural area in Minnesota, or the "linear cities" planned around new high speed transportation technologies. While many innovations can be anticipated in urban design in the 1970's, and even more by the year 2000, urban arrangements that imply a low priority for rehabilitating the central cities in the next five or 10 years also imply a massive disinvestment in existing housing, schools, office buildings, museums, and other public and private facilities within the urban centers.

Aside from transportation and housing, schools, hospitals, industrial and commercial buildings, public utilities, sewer and water systems, churches, recreational facilities, and a variety of government buildings contribute to the physical facility needs that enter into the urban development goal. Since most of these facilities also figure as part of the requirements for other goals such as health or education, many goals contribute to making the cities more viable places in which to work, move about, and play. Requirements for urban facilities in the 1970's and 1980's would increase substantially even if there were no improvements in standards or major departures from present urban arrangements. Population growth and shifts, including new household formation estimated to add an average of 1.3 million households a year to the population during the 1970's, would provide a major source of requirements for additional capital outlays. Replacement needs will constitute another major source of capital requirements since much of the urban physical plant, especially in the central cities, will be approaching an end to its useful life, a useful life often dating back to the early years of the century. Close to three-fifths of the expenditures listed for the urban development goal in 1980 represent outlays preempted to meet requirements arising from these sources.

The standards including the "improvements" listed for urban development are derived from several sources. In many instances, for example, education or health, the estimates are based on the proportion of the projected capital outlays listed for these goals that are expected to represent outlays in metropolitan areas. In housing, to cite another instance, it is assumed on the basis of recent experience and the distribution of housing units between urban and rural areas that approximately five-sixths of the outlays will take place in the urban areas. The estimates also take into account projections of facility needs from other sources such as the Joint Economic Committee of Congress' report, *State and Local Public Facility Needs and Financing.*[36] However, the projections have been adapted to reflect the assumptions about demographic changes, economic growth, and similar strategic variables in this report. In general, the private outlays for urban facilities such as shopping centers are related to the projections of changes in residential construction, personal income, and average income per household. The outlays for the separate items that enter into the urban development goal in 1969 and the projected requirements in 1980 are summarized in Table 3–5.

Transportation facilities, probably the most critical single element in planning for urban growth and change, account for about a ninth of the anticipated 1980 outlays. The $2.1 billion listed for mass transit facilities, about 1 percent of the total, includes as its largest item the annualized cost of providing all metropolitan areas currently with a million or more population with a rapid-rail system by 1990. Expenditures for sewer, water, and solid waste disposal systems are projected to nearly quadruple. The magnitude of this increase stems both from the greater concern with pollution and also from the critical role of water and sewer facilities as a prerequisite for the growth of new communities within the metropolitan areas. Overall, the estimates for the urban development goal imply an increase in spending for urban facilities from slightly less than a tenth of the GNP in 1969 to more than an eighth by 1980.

Dollar estimates for urban development are incomplete representations of the requirements for creating viable urban centers because the planning and the organization with which the dollars are used are as important as the volume of dollars expended. In the absence of adequate planning by metropolitan-wide units of government, more dollars spent for highways, for instance, would primarily add to the congestion, pollution, and sprawl that now diminish the attractiveness of so many urban areas. The estimates are again incomplete because they pertain to physical facilities. Since the overriding

[36] U.S. Congress, Joint Economic Committee, *State and Local Public Facility Needs and Financing,* December 1966.

concern of urban renewal is the quality of life in the nation's cities, outlays for physical facilities make up only one part of the costs of providing the public and private services essential to urban communities. Virtually all of the nation's domestic goals contribute to urban development.

Table 3-5   Estimated Outlays for Urban Development Goal, 1969 and Projected 1980 (in millions of 1969 dollars)

Item	Expenditures in 1969[a]	Projected Expenditures in 1980
Urban construction excluding transportation	$80,145	$174,700
Residential construction	26,055	64,600
Industrial and commercial buildings	16,170	33,600
Public utilities	5,435	12,700
Sewer, water, and solid waste disposal systems	2,245	8,500
Health facilities	2,925	4,100
Educational facilities	6,445	8,900
Recreational facilities	880	1,800
Other government buildings	4,690	7,200
Churches, private institutional facilities, and miscellaneous	2,270	5,700
Maintenance and repair	13,030	27,600
Urban transportation systems	9,780	21,300
Urban street and highway construction	6,740	13,500
Highway maintenance	1,900	3,800
Mass transit facilities	580	2,100
Airport facilities	560	1,300
New urban transportation technologies	—	400
Converting streets to pedestrian ways, parks, and playgrounds	—	200
Total, expenditures for urban facilities	$89,925	$196,000
Expenditures as percent of GNP	9.7%	14.0%

[a] Peter Wagner, *Housing and Community Development*, National Planning Association (unpublished) 1971, Table 4.

Chapter Four

GOALS CONCERNED WITH AMERICA'S ROLE IN WORLD AFFAIRS: NATIONAL DEFENSE AND INTERNATIONAL AID

I

Goals concerned with international affairs—national defense and international aid—have received a lesser priority during the past decade. Measured by the GNP yardstick, spending for the two goals declined from 10.7 percent of the GNP in the early part of the decade to 9.3 percent by 1969. Outlays for these goals in the 1970's can be expected to reflect the extent that the Vietnam experience and the thawing of the Cold War lead Americans to redefine the nation's participation in world affairs.

Spending for national defense has figured prominently in the discussions of changes in national priorities, particularly as national priorities are expressed in the Federal Government's budget. In these debates, the level of spending for national defense rather than the function the expenditures are intended to serve has typically emerged as the object of concern. While increases in spending to build more hospitals or schools are regarded as desirable because of the improvements in health or education that are expected to result from the greater outlays, growth in expenditures to add military installations, equipment, or personnel are only a means to another objective —peace and national security. Continuation of the recent signs of lessening international tensions, developments symbolized by the Strategic Arms Limitation Talks (SALT) agreement and by President Nixon's visits to mainland China and the USSR could make it possible to attain peace and security in the next 10 years while devoting a substantially smaller proportion of the nation's resources to national defense.

Conflicts over objectives, together with changes in the climate of opinion within American society, help to explain the low priority accorded aid to the developing counties. In the recent past, the Federal Government's foreign assistance programs have been more concerned with national security considerations than with long-term development objectives. The decline in public development aid has been partially offset by greater American private investment in the nations seeking to industrialize, an effort often assisted by the Federal Government through public guarantees against losses from measures such as expropriation. A high priority for long-term development objectives in the next decade could lead to a near-tripling of outlays for the international aid goal, and to a search for new directions in the use of aid resources including large-scale regional development projects as in the proposed Mekong Basin project.

Because of the scale of the outlays, spending for national defense goals influences employment opportunities and business prospects at home as well as America's international posture. In 1969, for example, more than 7.5 million, and in 1970 nearly 7 million persons were employed in the public and private sectors because of expenditures for national defense and the frequently-related atomic energy programs.[1] Barring a major deterioration in relations between the United States and the USSR and mainland China, defense-related expenditures are projected to account for a considerably smaller proportion of the nation's output and employment in 1980 than in 1969 or 1970.

II

While outlays for national defense have been increasing in the recent past as a percentage of the GNP, expenditures for national defense, by virtue of size alone, occupy a strategic position in discussions of changes in national priorities or in the analysis of shifts in business conditions and in employment within the United States. The impact of defense spending is evident in the Federal Government's budget, in manpower utilization, and in the nation's effort to advance the frontiers of science and technology through research and development.

Outlays for national defense amounting to $81 billion in 1969 and $78 billion in 1971 loomed less large expressed as a percentage of the GNP than the $52 billion level of defense spending in 1962 (in current dollars), 7.4 percent of the GNP in 1971 as compared with more than 9 percent in 1962. However, defense purchases at the end of the 1960's were sufficiently large to account for the employment of nearly a tenth of the labor force and for the utilization of about half of the Federal Government's spending for research and development. The role of defense expenditures in the economy is summarized by the indicators in Table 4–1.

[1] This estimate includes both civilian and military government personnel. *Manpower Report of the President*, 1972, p. 284.

Table 4-1   Selected Indicators, Role of Defense Expenditures
in American Economy, 1962, 1969, and 1971[a]

Item	1962	1969	1971
Defense expenditures (in $ billions)	$ 51.7	$ 81.0	$ 78.0
Defense expenditures as percent of GNP	9.2%	8.7%	7.4%
Defense expenditures as percent of Federal budget outlays	47.4	42.5	35.2
Defense R & D expenditures (in millions)[b]	$6350	$7550	$7800
Defense R & D expenditures as percent of all Federal R & D spending[b]	57.0	50.0	50.6
Armed forces (in millions)	2.8	3.5	2.8
Civilian employment attributable to defense spending (in millions)[c]	4.0	4.1	3.3
Percent of labor force employed because of defense spending	9.4	9.0	7.0

[a] *Special Analyses: The Budget of the United States Government, Fiscal Years 1971, 1972, 1973, 1974; Annual Report, Council of Economic Advisers, 1971, 1972, 1973; Manpower Report of the President, 1972; Statistical Abstract, 1971.*

[b] Refers to expenditures for the conduct of research and development.

[c] Includes civilian employment in private industry, government, and government enterprises attributable to spending because of national defense and atomic energy programs.

The indicators show a diminishing role for defense outlays in the economy. As a claim on the Federal Government's budget, spending for defense objectives declined from 47 percent of total budget outlays in 1962 to 35 percent in 1971.[2] The defense purchases that were responsible for the employment of nearly one out of every 10 persons in the labor force in the early 1960's accounted for the jobs of one out of every 14 labor force participants in the early 1970's.[3] While the Federal Government's R & D effort

[2] Derived from *Annual Report, Council of Economic Advisers,* 1972, pp. 270–271.

[3] Derived from *Manpower Report of the President,* 1972, pp. 157, 284.

continues to be dominated by defense-related considerations, the rapid rates of increase in expenditures in the past decade have taken place in the non-military aspects of research and development.

Allowing for these changes, the effects of defense spending are evident in many areas. Changes in defense expenditures, according to a recent report, have played an important part in helping to start or to stop three of the five recessions in the United States since the end of World War II.[4] The stationing of large numbers of American troops outside of the United States has been responsible for a major contribution to the deficits in the international balance of payments in the early 1970's. At home, as the war in Vietnam tapered off, cutbacks of defense purchases and, therefore, in employment were a significant element in the growth in unemployment in 1970 and 1971. For example, civilian employment in the private economy attributable to defense purchases declined by 1.2 million between 1968, the peak of the Vietnam War effort, and 1971.[5] The impact of these cutbacks were magnified in the areas where defense procurement is concentrated, the Pacific Coast, for instance. More than a third of the reduction in defense-based employment in manufacturing between the end of 1967 and the middle of 1970 took place in one state—California.[6]

The factors that are likely to influence outlays for national defense objectives in the 1970's can be assessed in terms of four sets of forces that have shaped defense expenditures in the past decade. They are foreign policy objectives, defense policy, manpower and technological considerations, and domestic politics. In the past four or five years, the effect of three of these factors—foreign policy objectives, defense policy, and domestic politics—has been to keep defense outlays from rising. The thrust of the fourth element—manpower and technology—has been to increase them.

President Nixon's visits to the USSR and China and the withdrawal of American opposition to the seating of the Chinese People's Republic in the United Nations symbolize a shift from a period in which Cold War considerations dominated foreign policy to one in which the major powers approach their differences more and more in terms of national interests rather than ideologies. The results are evident in the SALT agreement and the continuing talks for their extension, and they are also apparent in a number of treaties to which the United States and the USSR are cosignatories. These include the Nuclear Test Ban Treaty, the treaty banning military activities in Antarctica, and the treaties prohibiting the orbiting of weapons of mass de-

[4] C. L. Schultze, et al., *Setting National Priorities, the 1973 Budget*, p. 166.

[5] *Manpower Report*, 1972, *op. cit.*

[6] *Annual Report, Council of Economic Advisers*, 1971, p. 47.

struction in space or the establishment of military installations on celestial bodies. At home, the United States has ended the production of biological weapons. President Nixon has summed up the significance of these developments as indicating that "we have been moving . . . from a period of continued confrontation and arms competition to a period of negotiation and potential arms limitation."[7]

The thawing of the Cold War has been accompanied by changes in what are perceived as the scope of the "threat" against which an armed defense is required. The Administration's defense policy during the middle 1960's was influenced by the "two-and-a-half war strategy." This was explained by the then Defense Secretary, Clark Clifford, as the maintenance of a capability "to meet simultaneously two major contingencies (one in Europe and one in Asia) and one minor (or "brushfire") contingency as well as a War at Sea."[8] As the differences between the Soviet Union and the Chinese People's Republic have come to be revealed as a deep-seated cleavage with long-term implications, the two-and-a-half war strategy has been reappraised and transformed into a one-and-a-half war strategy. The drift of this reappraisal, according to President Nixon, is that "we will maintain in peacetime General Purpose Forces that are adequate for simultaneously meeting a major Communist attack in either Europe or Asia, assisting allies to cope with non-Chinese threats in Asia, and in addition meeting contingencies elsewhere."[9]

So far as nuclear weapons are concerned, the Nixon Administration has adopted the term "sufficiency" to describe its strategic defense policy. The operational content of this policy is similar to the Johnson Administration's emphasis on maintaining an "assured destructive capability" and a "damage limiting capability." A critical element in the "sufficiency" policy is an emphasis on redundancy in nuclear weapons systems to deter hostile surprises by assuring that at least one nuclear system would survive an attack and launch a retaliatory strike. For this reason, the United States currently maintains three independent nuclear deterrents, an underwater deterrent based on the Polaris submarines and their more powerful successors, land-based Minutemen missiles, and B–52 and FB–111 bombers. An increase in international confidence levels sufficient to lead to acceptance of two separate systems or a single (probably underwater) system could lead to a sizable reduction in defense expenditures in the next decade.

[7] *State of the Union Message,* January 20, 1972, p. 12.

[8] Quoted in *Fiscal Year 1971, Defense Program and Budget,* Senate Armed Services Committee and Senate Subcommittee on Department of Defense Appropriations, February 20, 1970, p. 53.

[9] *Ibid.,* p. 10.

The improved climate of international relations and revisions in strategic policy emphasize the prospects for protecting national security with lesser outlays for defense purposes in the 1970's. Manpower considerations and the sharply rising costs of new weapons systems point to elements that can be expected to limit the decreases or to translate them into increases. For instance, total manpower employed by the Department of Defense, civilian as well as military, was reduced by 1.5 million between fiscal years 1968 and 1973. However, military personnel costs went up by $10 billion in this period. Pay legislation alone, according to the Brookings Institution study, *Setting National Priorities: The 1973 Budget,* has increased the defense budget since 1968 by an amount almost equal to the budgetary savings realized by the withdrawal from Vietnam.[10]

The increases in military personnel compensation stem partially from comparability pay legislation enacted to bring Federal salary levels, including military salaries, up to what is regarded as their equivalents in the private sector. The steep rises in compensation levels are also attributable to the emphasis on incentive pay increases in order to encourage movement toward the goal of an all-volunteer armed force. The President's Commission on an All-Volunteer Armed Force has recommended the utilization of financial and other incentives to attract volunteers suitable in number and in caliber to end conscription. The Commission estimates that a 10 percent pay increase is required to increase enlistments by 12.5 percent.[11] Since the Administration has adopted the volunteer army as one of its major goals in defense policy, the incentive payments required to achieve this goal are likely to make for sizable increases in military personnel compensation during the 1970's.

New weapons are typically more complex and sophisticated than their predecessors. For this reason alone, aside from inflation, they would add to defense expenditures. To cite an instance, the Army's new transport helicopter, on the drawing boards at the end of 1971, is estimated to cost $800,000 to $900,000 per unit. This compares with $270,000 for the older Huey helicopter, the workhorse of the Vietnam War. Similarly, fighter aircraft now being developed for procurement in the middle 1970's will cost five to six times more than the comparable aircraft at the beginning of the 1960's.[12] Inflation and the cost overruns accompanying the production of many of the complex new items of military equipment, such as the C–5A plane, accentuate the increases in costs for the advanced weapons systems.

[10] *Setting National Priorities: The 1973 Budget, op. cit.,* pp. 37, 61.

[11] *Ibid.,* p. 148.

[12] *The Wall Street Journal,* December 27, 1971, p. 1.

Domestic political considerations have also served to restrain increases in expenditures for national defense. Outlays for national defense in 1970 were estimated to account for as much as 65 percent of that part of the Federal budget that is controllable, that is, subject to discretionary changes in annual budgets without changes in existing legislation.[13] The total controllable portion of the Federal budget amounts to about half of the total. Reductions in defense spending, therefore, appear to many persons as offering a source for financing significantly larger outlays for civilian priority areas such as urban development or mass transit. Advocates of high levels of defense spending contend that "our ability to build a stable and tranquil world—to achieve an arms control agreement, for example—depends on our ability to negotiate from a position of strength."[14] Critics of the priorities embodied in the current defense budget, for instance, the Urban Coalition, argue that "current defense forces are unnecessarily large in relation to the purposes they serve."[15] As an example of this costly excess capability, the Coalition cites the maintenance of a three-tiered nuclear deterrent with each component by itself sufficient to assure the destruction of Soviet or Chinese society in a retaliatory strike.

The debates over the priority to be accorded national defense center on "how much" within a relatively restricted range. The President's proposed 1973 defense budget calls for an $80 billion level of defense expenditures, an estimated 6.4 percent of the GNP.[16] The critics who urge a lesser priority for defense objectives, such as the Urban Coalition or Senator George McGovern, have proposed defense budgets in the $50 to $55 billion range.[17] The $25 to $30 billion difference in these proposals is approximately equivalent to the estimated Federal outlays for health care in the same year. However, with a GNP of $1.15 trillion in 1972 and one somewhat higher after discounting for inflation in 1973, the range of difference between the advocates of a high or a low priority for national defense is roughly between 4.5 and 6.5 percent of the GNP.

---

[13] See C. M. Roberts, "The Nuclear Years," 1970, pp. 56–57, *The Los Angeles Times,* November 8, 1970, p. F-3. This proportion has been reduced since 1970 to closer to half.

[14] *State of the Union Message,* January 20, 1972, p. 14.

[15] National Urban Coalition, *Counterbudget: A Blueprint for Changing National Priorities,* 1971, p. 254.

[16] *State of the Union Message, op. cit.,* p. 13.

[17] The Urban Coalition's recommended defense budget for 1973 is $49 billion. *Counterbudget, op. cit.,* p. 273.

IV

Estimates of the expenditures required to attain national defense objectives five or 10 years from now are surrounded, of necessity, by a considerable margin of uncertainty. This is the case because the choices involve imponderables such as the size and makeup of the programs that the nation should undertake to insure against remote contingencies (e.g., the outbreak of a nuclear war) when the cost of being uninsured could be catastrophically high. Similarly, the choices require decisions as to the desirable spending levels for new weapons systems still in the process of development that are often regarded as worth adopting primarily because they create "bargaining chips" offering incentives for the other side to engage in negotiations for reductions in armaments. In addition, the projections of defense expenditures depend on developments in other nations, developments that can often be influenced by American policies although they are beyond our control. Estimates of defense outlays in the next decade, therefore, essentially stem from scenarios reflecting different assumptions about these developments, and especially about the future relations between the United States, the Soviet Union, and the Chinese People's Republic.

Events in the early 1970's provide a reasonable basis for anticipating improved relations between the United States, the USSR, and China, and an interest on the part of all three nations in reducing the burden of defense for their economies. These expectations provide the essential ingredient for a projection of future defense expenditures assuming as a scenario partial disarmament. Disarmament of the kind envisaged could come about as part of a second round of negotiations stemming from the recent SALT agreement, or the arms reduction could be initiated unilaterally by either party without a formal agreement and continued as the other parties responded with favorable countermoves of their own. A second scenario reflecting recent experience, the arms stabilization alternative, assumes a situation in which each nation abstains from the introduction of new weapons that could endanger the survivability of the nuclear deterrents of their potential adversaries. Defense expenditures in this scenario are maintained at close to the level of the early 1970's. A third and less optimistic projection, the arms buildup scenario, anticipates a competitive race among the great powers to introduce new strategic weapons and to enlarge stocks of existing ones following a lapse of the SALT agreements. The projected outlays for the national defense goal consistent with each of the three scenarios are summarized in Table 4–2.

**Table 4-2   Estimated Outlays for National Defense Goal
Assuming Alternative Defense Scenarios in 1980
(in millions of 1969 dollars)**

Item	Expenditures in 1969[a]	Projected Expenditures in 1980		
		Partial Disarmment Alternative	Limited Arms Stabilization Alternative	Arms Buildup Alternative
Miliary personnel[b]	$24,850	$23,300	$27,300	$29,100
Operation and maintenance	21,850	12,700	21,200	24,800
Procurement	21,525	6,300	16,900	28,700
Research and development	7,550	8,900	11,000	13,400
Military construction	1,875	1,100	1,500	2,700
Foreign military assistance	750	1,000	1,000	1,000
Atomic energy (military)	2,450	1,400	1,800	2,500
Civil defense	100	100	100	500
Other	75	100	100	200
Total	81,025	54,900	80,900	102,900

[a] Derived from *The Budget of the United States Government, Fiscal Year 1971*, p. 82, *ibid., Fiscal Year 1972*, p. 86.
[b] Includes retirement pay.

The estimates for defense outlays in 1980 range between $55 and $103 billion, depending on the particular scenario selected. All three alternatives assume an all-volunteer army in the place of the present draft system. To attract sufficient volunteers, military pay scales are projected to increase by an average of close to 3 percent a year after allowing for inflation. The major differences in the three estimates are those listed for procurement, and for operation and maintenance. The elements that enter into the three estimates are summarized below.

Partial Disarmament

The first objective in a mutually acceptable reduction of defense outlays is to maintain a high degree of stability in the strategic balance in order to constrain threats to the survivability of the retaliatory forces of each of the powers. A second purpose is to contain the arms competition so that both international tensions and the costs of maintaining an adequate national defense are reduced. To achieve these objectives, the nations participating in the arms reduction would agree to put aside the further development of new weapons such as the multiple nuclear warhead packages (MIRVs), a weapon that multiplies the power of individual intercontinental ballistic missiles. Similarly, the nations involved would prohibit continuous tracking of missile firing submarines by surface ships as well as submarines. The two ABM sites allowed the United States and the USSR under the Moscow Treaty would be eliminated. The success of this type of nuclear disarmament would involve agreement on some form of international inspection or sufficient improvement in satellite surveillance capabilities to make an international inspection agreement unnecessary.

With greater confidence in the prospects for easing tensions, there could be a shift in reliance for "survivability" from three to two independent nuclear deterrents, and then perhaps to one deterrent. The inventory of land and seabased missiles would be reduced by half and manned bombers would be completely eliminated from the nuclear weapons inventory. Aircraft carriers approaching obsolescence would not be replaced. The other major cost reductions in this scenario would arise from the decline in the size of the armed forces from 3.5 million in 1969 to an anticipated 2 million by 1980. As the size of the armed forces fell and the numbers and types of nuclear deterrents were cut back, expenditures for military procurement would decline by about seven-tenths from the 1969 level, a level considerably influenced by the requirements for the war in Vietnam. With fewer military personnel and weapons and equipment, operation and maintenance expenditures would also decline, but less so than procurement outlays since the more complex military equipment in use in 1980 would be more costly to operate and maintain.

Even with partial disarmament, spending for military research and development would fall little, if at all, and for some time it would be likely to increase. A high volume of defense-related R & D would serve to maintain an advanced technological base as a hedge against possible future arms build-ups and also to provide "bargaining chips" in negotiating further reductions in armaments. So, R & D would probably continue on the undersea long-range missile system (ULMS) as a follow-up to the Polaris and Poseidon submarine force. Development of the ULMS, its adherents contend, could serve as a counter force to induce the USSR to agree to further limits on land and submarine based nuclear deterrents.

Limited Arms Stabilization

This alternative illustrates the anticipated implications of a continuation of the present relations between the superpowers and of roughly constant spending levels for national defense. The underlying presupposition here is that the two superpowers, the United States and the USSR, will refrain from introducing new types of nuclear weapons to avoid destabilizing the existing balance of forces and thereby bringing about an arms race. Accordingly, the projections assume a quantitative although not a qualitative freeze in strategic missile systems development by 1980. The major changes in this version of the future would take place in procurement, operation and maintenance, and in the size of the armed forces. Block obsolescence of the large nuclear carriers built between 1955 and 1960 would be offset by building one nuclear carrier a year between 1979 and 1985. Troop levels would be maintained at 2.5 million, 500,000 more than in the partial disarmament alternative.

With stabilization rather than partial disarmament, military research and development would concentrate more heavily on the development of new weapons systems such as the B–1 long-range strategic bomber. Development of the ULMS would be accelerated so that it could be rushed into production in the early 1980's if the Soviets were found to be successfully developing antisubmarine weapons that threatened the survival of the successors to the Polaris submarines, the Poseidons. Efficiency in the procurement of the new weapons resulting from R & D would be maintained by a "fly before you buy" policy, that is, by the development of a number of working test models and their demonstration in use before a commitment was made to purchase them on a regular production basis. The United States would continue to maintain three nuclear deterrents.

Arms Buildup

The arms buildup alternative represents a less optimistic alternative than either of the other two. This version of the future could come about through a resurgence of Soviet "hard-line" policy in Europe accompanied by a revival of a Cold War mentality within the United States, reversals probably implying such major changes as the reestablishment of close relations between the USSR and the Chinese People's Republic. One of the casualties of this kind of arms buildup would probably be the recent arms limitations measures such as the SALT agreement.

A critical ingredient in this scenario is an "action-reaction" pattern that becomes difficult to arrest in midcourse. For instance, knowledge that the

USSR had developed radically advanced antisubmarine detection technology that could threaten the survival of the Poseidon submarines could lead the United States to rush into large-scale production of the ULMS undersea long-range missile system. Lapse of the SALT agreement, perhaps following information obtained through aerial surveillance indicating that the Soviets were expanding the number of their missile sites, could lead the United States to expand the full antiballistic missile system to 12 sites and to production, rather than development and testing, of the B–1 long-range bomber. As the buildup of new and more advanced nuclear weapons continued, the presently inactive civil defense program, including shelter construction, would be revived.

The additional costs of a renewed arms race would show up in greater expenditures for procurement and in larger operation and maintenance costs. Since the buildup would center on strategic weapons, the size of the armed forces would increase only slightly beyond the level assumed in the arms stabilization projection, 2.7 million as compared with 2.5 million. However, the full gamut of defense-related technologies and weapons would be represented in the nation's military effort. Work would be resumed, for example, on the Manned Earth Orbiting Laboratory (MOL), an effort that was set aside as part of the R & D budget cutbacks in the early 1970's. Other activities might include the development of new transport systems to improve the mobility of ground forces, for example, surface-effect ships, advances in electronic and chemical warfare, and in the applications of laser technology to national defense.

Which of the three alternatives will emerge as the closest approximation to reality is presently difficult to discern. However, a reversion to an arms race would constitute a more far-reaching break with the recent past than the two other options considered. Changes of the dimensions implied by this scenario would be unlikely to occur without far-reaching political changes within the United States.

V

Spending for aid, including capital supply for the poor nations, like spending for national defense, has received a diminished priority in the past decade. As the nation's approach to the developing countries comes to be less influenced by national security considerations, a renewed emphasis on development assistance, assistance often channeled through international financial organizations, could lead to a substantially higher priority and larger outlays in pursuit of aid goals in the 1970's.

The assistance to the developing nations that enters into the concept of international aid includes many and diverse elements. It includes direct loans and grants for development projects made by the United States Government to other governments. American foreign aid also embraces technical assistance for such purposes as improving crop yields, stamping out contagious diseases and providing the food and agricultural raw materials made available under Public Law 480, the Food for Peace program. Another part of the Government's aid is made up of contributions to international nonfinancial organizations (e.g., the World Health Organization) and to international financial organizations such as the World Bank agencies that make "hard" or "soft" loans to the less-developed nations. In addition to the Government's aid, private capital investments from the industrial nations to the less-developed countries, investments undertaken in the expectation of the profits to be earned, can also contribute to economic growth and the development of a more highly skilled and better-paid labor force. These aspects of international aid are economic. Part of foreign assistance is made up of military equipment and supplies made available to the nonindustrial nations. The bulk of the economic and military assistance in recent years has gone to Southeast Asia and, to a considerably lesser extent, to Latin America.

One of the by-products of the war in Vietnam and the Cold War perspectives from which this conflict emerged has been a substantial increase in the role of national security considerations in the foreign assistance programs. These considerations have prompted the direct provision of military equipment and supplies and also the expansion of supporting assistance programs, that is, military-related economic aid, to help countries such as South Vietnam bear the cost of fighting a war. The estimated distribution of the U.S. Government's aid between the security assistance, welfare and emergency aid as in famine relief, and development assistance in 1964 and 1972 is summarized in Table 4–3.

The security-related Government economic aid approximately doubled between 1964 and 1972, accounting for nearly all of the increase in the doller volume of the public aid between the two years. In keeping with this emphasis, the United States in the early 1970's was spending more than $3 billion annually on military and supporting assistance to the nations of Southeast Asia.[18] In terms of American defense policy, the security assistance,

[18] The estimate refers to aid provided to Vietnam, Laos, Cambodia, and Thailand. C. L. Schultze, et al., *Setting National Priorities: The 1972 Budget*, p. 123.

Table 4-3 Distribution of U.S. Public Foreign Assistance Funds by Function, 1964 and 1972[a] (in millions of dollars)

Category	1964		1972[b]	
	Amount	Percent of Total	Amount	Percent of Total
Security assistance	$2064	39.0%	$4393	58.0%
Welfare and emergency relief	569	10.5	450	6.0
Development assistance	2678	50.5	2711	36.0
Total	5311	100.0	7554	100.0

[a] C. L. Schultze, et al., *Setting National Priorities, The 1972 Budget,* 1971, p. 131. The data pertain to fiscal years 1964 and 1972.
[b] Estimate.

military and economic, serves as a substitute for more direct military participation involving the utilization of American military forces abroad.

In the next few years, now that the war in Vietnam has ended, the Federal Government's foreign assistance programs can be expected to become more concerned with reconstruction in war-damaged areas and with seeking long-term solutions to the gaps between the per capita incomes, living standards, and life chances in the industrially advanced and the less-developed nations. Much of the postwar reconstruction aid in Southeast Asia is likely to take the form of regional development projects organized around river basins. One such project, first proposed by President Johnson, envisages a billion-dollar American contribution for regional development of the lower Mekong River basin in Vietnam. The Mekong Basin Project is intended to provide food, water, and cheap power as part of an all-encompassing regional development plan including flood control, highway and bridge construction, and improved educational facilities for the population.[19] Similar development projects have been proposed for the Jordan River Valley and for the Indus River Basin.

The regional development projects seek to channel energies and interests of rival nations and ideologies into a commonly shared objective. Otherwise, the Government's economic aid to the developing nations in the 1970's is

[19] F. P. Huddle, *The Mekong Report: Opportunities and Problems of Regionalism,* Science Policy Research Division, Congressional Research Service, Library of Congress, 1972.

likely to stress a greater separation of the development from the political and military objectives. As part of this separation, international financial institutions such as the International Development Association will become the focus for much of the public development effort financed by the United States. These institutions account for one-third of the total world development lending on terms involving special concessions, such as reduced interest rates, and even more if the large volume of World Bank loans at roughly market rates of interest are allowed for. Part of the appeal of the international financial institutions is their ability to provide a means for pooling the efforts of many countries into an integrated series of programs with a development rather than a political perspective.

In spite of rapid economic growth in the developing nations, it still remains true that "two-thirds of the world's population . . . lives in conditions of poverty, disease, and hunger."[20] Between 1960 and 1969, the Gross National Product in the developing nations, after adjusting for price changes, rose by 60 percent. This was slightly ahead of the 56 percent growth reported in the more industrialized nations. However, the apparent gain was offset by much more rapid population increase in the poor countries. Accordingly, per capita output grew by only 28 percent in these nations since 1960, while in the richer countries it rose by 41 percent. The gross product per person at the end of the 1960's amounted to more than $2600 a year in the advanced nations, 10 times as much as the $250 level reported in the poor countries.[21]

Growth targets for the developing nations can be assessed in terms of the requirements for reversing the process by which income levels in these countries continue to fall behind the comparable levels in the advanced countries. This goal could be attained by an average GNP growth rate of about 6 percent a year during the 1970's. Allowing for the rapid population increase in the developing nations, a 6 percent pace of economic growth could provide the basis for an increase in per capita output estimated at slightly more than 3.5 percent a year.[22] Sustained growth of these dimensions would add to pollution in the large cities and hasten the uprooting of the rural and, typically, poverty-stricken population from their traditional way of life. It would also expand employment opportunities for a growing labor force and increase the resources available for coping with shortages of public facilities of many kinds in education, health, housing, and other areas.

---

[20] *The Foreign Assistance Program, Annual Report,* 1971, p. 1.

[21] "Foreign Economic Aid in the 1970's," *The Conference Board Record,* November, 1970, p. 40.

[22] C. K. Park, *International Aid: Objectives and Requirements,* National Planning Association (unpublished), 1971, p. 42.

Aid requirements for attaining the growth targets can be approached in several ways. One is in terms of the "savings gap," the excess of the capital investment needed to achieve the targets over the anticipated domestic savings. A second approach is in terms of the "foreign exchange gap," or the excess of import requirements to attain growth goals over export earnings. These target-type approaches should be modified to allow for the fact that economic development is more than a question of obtaining more capital or foreign exchange. The absorptive capacity of these countries (i.e., their capacity to employ additional resources) is frequently limited by social rigidities, shortages of skilled personnel, change-resistant attitudes, and ineffective governments.

If the estimated 1960–1975 growth rates in the exports and imports of the developing nations are extended to 1980, a GNP growth target of 6 percent a year would imply a trade gap of close to $40 billion by 1980 in dollars of 1969 purchasing power. Vigorous pursuit of policies in the developing countries that increased domestic savings and accelerated exports might reduce the gap by an estimated 20 percent, to $32 billion by 1980.[23] This $32 billion gap could be filled if the advanced industrial nations were to transfer 1 percent of their GNP to the developing nations in the form of capital supply from public and private sources. The 1 percent target has been adopted by the United Nations in their Decade of Development program and by a number of official and unofficial organizations including the Organization for Economic Cooperation and Development (OECD) and the Committee for Economic Development in the United States.

The flow of private capital and Government economic aid from the United States to the developing countries in the early 1970's, including the security-related economic aid, amounted to about one-half of 1 percent of the American GNP. Doubling this proportion would increase the flow from approximately $5 billion in 1969 to close to $15 billion by 1980. Taking into account the rapid growth in the private component in the supply of capital and other economic aid from one-fifth of the American total in the early 1960's to three-eighths by the end of the decade, private capital is projected to make up close to half of the total by 1980. This increase in the role of private capital is more likely to be welcomed in the developing nations if it is concentrated to a greater degree than in the past in manufacturing, public utilities, and trade rather than in the traditional extractive industries. Aside from the economic aid, military assistance is projected to continue at a level of approximately $700 million annually to reduce demands for the involvement of American forces by increasing the capability of the nations receiving the assistance to assume their own defense.

[23] *Ibid.*, pp. 46–47.

The estimated expenditures for the attainment of the international aid goal by 1980, together with the actual outlays in 1969, are summarized in Table 4–4.

Table 4-4   Estimated Expenditures for International Aid Goal,
1969 and Projected 1980
(in millions of 1969 dollars)

Item	Expenditures in 1969[a]	Projected Expenditures in 1980
Public economic aid	$3,330	$7,805
Bilateral	3,000	3,975
Food for Peace	970	1,000
Other	2,030	2,975
Multilateral	330	3,830
Private capital supply	1,320	6,920
Total, public economic aid and private capital supply	4,620	14,725
Military assistance	725	725
Total	5,375	15,450

[a] *Development Assistance, 1970 Review,* OECD, 1970, pp. 176–77; *The Budget of the United States Government, Fiscal Year 1971,* pp. 91–92; *ibid, Fiscal Year 1972,* p. 96; *Statistical Abstract, 1971,* p. 759.

The projections for the international aid goal point to three major concerns in the relationship of the United States to the poor nations. One is the need for a change in priorities within the United States if the development needs of these nations are to receive more extended consideration in the next decade than in the past one. A second is the far larger role anticipated for government economic aid provided through multilateral channels rather than on a bilateral, government-to-government basis. The projections assume that by 1980 most of the long-term development assistance would be supplied by international financial organizations, frequently by World Bank affiliates. Technical assistance, Food for Peace, other humanitarian and emergency relief, and military and security-related economic aid would continue to be made available on a government-to-government basis.

A third element in the projections centers on the relationship between "aid" and "trade." The estimated foreign exchange gap of $32 billion listed for 1980 could be considerably reduced if the aid-giving nations removed trade barriers and opened their markets to the exports of the poor nations.

The aid made available could be utilized more effectively if the aid-receiving nations were free to make their purchases with the aid funds in the cheapest markets rather than being restricted by the tie-in clauses in the aid agreements requiring them to utilize the funds to purchase goods in the United States. In 1970, for instance, 98 percent of the expenditures for commodities under the billion-dollar foreign assistance program administered by the Agency for International Development represented purchases from the United States.[24]

VI

The projections for the two goals directly concerned with international affairs—national defense and international aid—indicate offsetting expectations. A high priority for the international aid goal would about double the proportion of the economy's resources used for public economic aid, private capital supply, and military assistance to the developing nations. A high priority for national defense, even with the arms buildup option, is projected to reduce this share.

The effects of the spending for the nation's international objectives on the domestic economy are apparent in the weight of the outlays as a share of the GNP, in the proportion of the labor force they employ, and in the importance of the expenditures in shaping the development of science and technology. These consequences are more readily observable in the case of the national defense goal since the outlays projected for this goal in 1980, depending on the particular option involved, are expected to range between 3.5 and 6.5 times as large as those required to attain the international aid goal. The impacts considered are summarized in Table 4–5.

The impact indicators point to an economy that would be considerably less defense-oriented in 1980 than in 1969. In 1969, for example, 9 percent of the labor force was employed in civilian jobs or in the army because of defense expenditures. The comparable proportions in 1980 are estimated to vary between 4 and 6.7 percent. This projection reflects the more rapid growth of other employment in an expanding economy, the reduction in the size of the armed forces, and the influence of productivity increases in di-

[24] *Statistical Abstract, 1971*, p. 762.

Table 4-5   Indicators of the Impact of Spending for the National Defense Goal, 1969 and for Projected Outlays in 1980

	Estimate for 1969[a]	Projections for 1980		
		Partial Disarmament	Limited Arms Stabilization	Arms Buildup
Total expenditures (in millions of 1969 dollars)	$81,025	$54,900	$80,900	$102,900
Expenditures as percent of GNP	8.7%	3.9%	5.8%	7.4%
Defense R & D expenditures (in millions of 1969 dollars)	$7,550	$ 8,900	$11,000	13,400
Defense R & D as percent of total Federal R & D[b]	50.0%	35.0%	41.5%	48.5%
Size of armed forces (in millions)	3.5	2.0	2.5	2.7
Civilian employment due to defense spending[c] (in millions)	4.1	2.0	3.1	4.0
Defense-related employment as percent of labor force	9.0%	4.0	5.6	6.7

[a] See Table 4-1.

[b] Based on ratio of defense R & D expenditures to total Federal outlays for the conduct of R & D to attain the research and development goal in 1980 (see Table 9-4). Half of the changes in defense R & D spending in 1980 in the three alternatives is assumed to be reflected in changes in the Federal total.

[c] Refers to civilian employment in government, in government enterprises, and the direct and indirect employment generated by defense purchases in the private economy.

minishing the manpower required in the private sector for each billion dollars of defense purchases of goods and services. Similarly, defense considerations are expected to loom less large in the Federal Government's research and development effort by the end of the 1970's. As the proportion of R & D resources (or of the GNP) utilized for defense declined, the resources no longer utilized for this purpose could be devoted to coping more effectively with civilian society problems such as environmental pollution, making health care more readily available, or the development of new sources of energy to meet burgeoning demands. How, and to what extent, these prospects materialize would depend partly on how changes in defense outlays influenced changes in spending elsewhere in the economy. A decline in defense spending of the magnitude envisaged in the projection for the partial disarmament alternative, for example, could lead to a slowing in the pace of economic growth and to sizable increases in unemployment, if it were unaccompanied by other changes such as increases in nondefense Government spending or tax reductions.

There are few comparable indicators, other than the GNP yardstick, for assessing the impact of growth in outlays for the international aid goal for the economy. The projected near tripling of expenditures to attain this goal indicates that a substantial increase in employment would result from a high priority for international aid abjectives. How large these effects would be would depend on the types of commodities purchased with the aid funds and the proportion of the aid used for purchases in the United States. Current moves to allow the aid-receiving countries greater freedom to purchase goods in the cheapest markets would probably reduce the share of the American aid directly leading to spending and the creation of employment in the United States. It is reasonable to anticipate that a billion dollars spent for international aid objectives in the United States generates about the same number of jobs in the private economy as a billion dollars spent for national defense. If two-thirds of the public aid funds and private capital supply included in the international aid goal were utilized for purchases within the United States, on this basis it could be estimated that the spending would generate 550,000 to 650,000 jobs in the private sector in 1980.[25]

There has been considerable discussion in the recent past of the connection between spending for national defense and the discretionary resources available to the Federal Government for new program initiatives. The resources available for this purpose in the 1970's will reflect many considerations other than the requirements for national defense. These include legislative commitments to existing programs, population growth, the tax structure, and the impact of economic growth. At present, there is no way of knowing what defense requirements will be five or 10 years from now. However, the consequences of the defense outlays for the economy will depend as much on these other factors, and especially on the rate of economic growth, as they will on the particular level of defense spending.

---

[25] See *Manpower Report of the President,* 1972, p. 284. The estimates of the manpower impacts of pursuit of the international aid goal assume a 2.7 percent annual average productivity increase during the 1970's.

Chapter Five

GOALS CONCERNED WITH INCOME ADEQUACY: SOCIAL WELFARE AND MANPOWER TRAINING

I

Two elements predominate in the transfers of income to the aged, the dependent, the disabled, and the unemployed that make up the substance of the social welfare goal. The larger element is composed of social insurance benefits, primarily benefits for the aged and their survivors. The other is represented by public welfare assistance, mainly assistance for dependent children in poor families headed by a female. Concern with rapidly growing public welfare rolls and high unemployment rates, especially among the young in the central cities, has led to a renewed emphasis on the Federal manpower programs as social programs intended to increase the employability and earning capacity of low-income persons who are, or who could be, in the labor market.

The great expectations that accompanied the introduction of the "War on Poverty" in the middle 1960's have been followed by widespread skepticism about the possibility of devising workable and politically acceptable programs for dealing with poverty and with the dependency that is so frequently associated with it. There has been general public support for the social insurance programs, support manifested, for instance, in the periodic increases in retirement benefits for the aged provided through the Social Security System. There has been general dissatisfaction with the public welfare assistance programs because of inequities in benefits, large and unanticipated increases in expenditures, and built-in penalties discouraging the recipients of the frequently meager benefits from increasing their incomes by working. So, according to President Nixon, "the present welfare system has to be judged a colossal failure . . . It breaks up homes. It often penalizes work. It robs recipients of dignity, and it grows."[1]

The search for alternatives to the current public assistance programs suggests that the theme "work and welfare go together" is likely to characterize the nation's approach to programs and objectives for coping with poverty and dependency in the decade ahead.[2] Income supplements can be expected

---

[1] *Message to Congress on Welfare Reform,* August 11, 1969.

[2] See S. A. Levitan, et al., *Work and Welfare Go Together, Policy Studies in Employment and Welfare Number 13,* 1972.

to provide the basic public assistance for dependent families with limited employment prospects for the family head and probably for the working poor. Manpower training programs are expected to constitute the major programs for poor persons who could earn sufficient incomes from work to escape poverty if they were provided with more adequate job skills and with supporting assistance such as child care.

Measured in terms of dollar spending, the goals concerned with income maintenance have received a high priority in the past 10 years. Outlays for social welfare, for example, increased during the 1962–1969 period, in 1969 dollars, about 50 percent more rapidly than the growth in the Gross National Product. The percentages are 53 percent for social welfare and 37.5 percent for the GNP. In the 1972 fiscal year, Federal spending for cash benefit and in-kind food programs, together with the spending for manpower programs, amounted to nearly as much as the expenditures for national defense, almost $76 billion for the social programs as compared with slightly more than $78 billion for national defense.[3] The costs projected for attaining the social welfare and manpower training goals would increase expenditures to over $197 billion by 1980. The most costly element in these outlays would be the expenditures to enable most retired persons to attain by 1980 the equivalent of a "modest" standard of living for an elderly couple as defined by the Department of Labor toward the end of the 1960's.

II

As a nation, we have pursued three major routes for coping with poverty and dependency. One has been the route of promoting economic growth, and thereby promoting opportunities for individuals at all income levels. A second has involved providing income transfers to families without incomes or with inadequate incomes. A third, represented by the Federally supported manpower training programs, has concentrated on increasing the earning capacity of low-income persons through programs intended to upgrade their job skills.

[3] U.S. Office of Management and Budget, *Special Analyses, The Budget of the United States Government, Fiscal Year 1973,* p. 180; *Annual Report, Council of Economic Advisers,* 1973, p. 269.

Economic growth, in the past, has been the most important factor in reducing the size of the low-income population. Growth largely accounts for the decrease in the poverty population, according to the Federal Government's estimates, from 39.5 million in 1959 to 24.3 million in 1969. The reverse effects of a slowing down of economic growth were apparent as the pace of growth slackened in late 1969 and in 1970. With this slackening, the number of poor persons increased by nearly 1.3 million between 1969 and 1970.[4]

Economic growth contributes to the reduction of poverty because it increases the demand for labor. Persons who had previously been unemployed, or who have part-time or poorly paid jobs, obtain employment, work more hours, or move into better paid jobs in periods of "tight" labor markets. Formal credentials such as a high school diploma, or discriminatory barriers based on race, sex, or age become less important in hiring and upgrading when employers are faced with labor shortages. The role of economic growth was of sufficient weight during the prosperity years in the 1960's to convince the Council of Economic Advisers at the end of the decade that, if the reduction of the number of poor persons that took place during the 1961–1968 prosperity period (about two million a year) could be maintained, "poverty would be eliminated entirely in about ten years."[5] In spite of this optimistic expectation, there are substantial reasons for anticipating that, even with rapid growth, the presence of a large population of persons with little or no earned income will still figure as an important problem for public policy in the coming decade. Since growth reduces poverty because it increases opportunity in the labor market, economic growth bypasses many individuals with a marginal participation in the labor market or who are unable or do not wish to enter it. These include the aged, the disabled and the severely physically and mentally handicapped, and many female heads of families with children of preschool age. So, during the period of rapid growth extending from 1961 to 1969, almost a million families and over 3.7 million individuals were added to the rolls of the Aid to Families with Dependent Children program (AFDC).[6]

The reductions in poverty due to the economy's growth have typically occurred in families whose heads were in the labor force, usually male family

[4] *Manpower Report of the President,* 1973, p. 245.

[5] *Annual Report, Council of Economic Advisers,* 1969, p. 159.

[6] *Social Security Bulletin,* December 1972, p. 62. This increase, of course, reflects liberalized eligibility requirements as well as growth in numbers of poor persons who were bypassed by the greater opportunities in the labor market.

heads. Yet, rapid economic growth has been compatible with the continued existence of millions of year-round jobs that yield poverty incomes to the persons holding them. In the late 1960's, for example, there were nearly 3.5 million persons who were poor, according to the Federal Government's criteria, who held year-round, largely full-time jobs.[7] As one indicator of the importance of poorly paid jobs in contributing to poverty, the President's Commission on Income Maintenance estimated that at the end of the 1960's there were 10 million jobs, including a number of state and municipal government jobs, that paid less than $1.60 an hour, then the Federal minimum wage.[8] The head of a family of four earning the minimum wage who worked full time throughout the year would have received a sufficiently low income to be included in the Government's count of the poor.

Income transfers constitute the major program in seeking to provide minimum standards of living for persons who are outside of the work force, who have a marginal attachment to it, or who are unemployed. These transfers include contributory social insurance programs as in the Social Security System (the Old Age, Survivors, Disability, and Health Insurance System), and they also include transfers in money and in kind, including food and limited social service assistance, provided on the basis of need. The income transfers have come to make up an important part of the incomes of the poor. As far back as the middle 1960's, for instance, public transfer payments made up somewhat over 40 percent of the money incomes of poor persons, and this proportion has probably increased since.[9] Income-in-kind programs have grown more rapidly in the past five years than the money transfers. By 1972, some 14.5 million persons were receiving assistance from the different Federal family food programs for the needy such as the Food Stamp program. This was double the number receiving these benefits in 1969.[10]

Benefits for the aged and their survivors have accounted for approximately three-fifths of all social welfare expenditures from public and private sources in recent years. Social welfare outlays in 1969 are summarized in Table 5–1.

[7] See C. K. Park, *Human Resources Development: Skill Training for the Poor,* National Planning Association (unpublished), 1971.

[8] The President's Commission on Income Maintenance Programs, *Poverty Amidst Plenty: The American Paradox,* 1969, p. 4.

[9] C. Green, "Income Security Through a Tax-Transfer System" in S. A. Levitan, et al. (eds.), *Toward Freedom from Want,* 1968, p. 169.

[10] *Special Analyses: The Budget of the United States Government, op. cit.,* 1973, p. 183.

Table 5-1   Estimated Social Welfare Expenditures in 1969[a]
(in millions of 1969 dollars)

Program Area	Expenditures in 1969
Retirement benefits	$30,570
OASDHI	17,698
Other public programs	7,012
Private programs	5,860
Survivors benefits	11,834
OASDHI	6,510
Other public programs	2,809
Private programs	2,515
Disability benefits	15,358
OASDHI	2,542
Other public programs	9,969
Private programs	2,847
Unemployment compensation	2,523
Public programs	2,423
Private programs	100
Public welfare assistance	7,275
Social service assistance	5,404
Public programs[b]	4,204
Private social service[c]	1,200
Total	72,964

[a] *Social Security Bulletin, Annual Statistical Supplement,* 1970, pp. 25, 29, 132; *ibid.,* January, 1971, p. 28; *ibid.,* April, 1971, p. 27; *Statistical Abstract, 1971,* p. 299.

[b] Over half of this total is made up of surplus food provided to institutions such as schools and hospitals by the Federal Government.

[c] Represents the allocation of funds raised through private philanthropy to welfare activities.

The data in Table 5–1 indicate that the American social welfare system is very largely a public system in which contributory programs regarded as a type of insurance predominate. Public welfare assistance expenditures amount to about a tenth of the total. Special veterans' benefits that enter into the estimates in the table, largely disability and retirement benefits, total nearly $6 billion. Income-in-kind in food benefits such as the Food Stamp or school-lunch programs account for nearly $3.7 billion in the total.

Retirement benefits are the most significant element in maintaining the standard of living for the aged. Nearly half (46 percent) of the income of persons aged 65 or older comes from retirement benefits, and close to nine-tenths of the aged receive some type of retirement benefit. Successive changes adopted by Congress have provided a basis for liberalizing benefits, usually by at least as much as the increase in the cost of living and frequently by somewhat more. In one recent change, in 1972, for example, Congress voted a general 20 percent increase in retirement and other benefits under the Social Security System, along with changes enabling individuals drawing the retirement pensions to earn up to $2100 a year without any reduction in benefits. So, the average monthly benefit paid to a retired worker amounted to $134 in August, 1972, an increase from $100 in 1969.[11] The changes in benefits, in the taxable wage base, and in the tax rates have resulted in a substantial loosening of the relationship between past contributions and the benefits paid to individuals. The net result, to quote a recent study of national priorities published by the Brookings Institution, is that there is "no way of avoiding the fact that each working generation supports the currently retired generation."[12] Yet, after allowing for the changes in Social Security benefits, one-fourth of the persons aged 65 and over in the early 1970's were receiving sufficiently low income from all sources to be included among the poor. This was double the rate for the entire population.[13]

Private pension plans in the United States have been largely confined to well-organized blue-collar workers and to the better-paid and more highly skilled white-collar employees, especially those in salaried managerial and professional positions. The private plans have come to cover nearly 30 million workers and their assets amounted to over $95 billion by 1970. While the private plans have been growing rapidly, only 5 percent of the income of aged persons in recent years has been received from private pensions as compared with over 40 percent from public sources.[14] Limitations on vesting rights frequently cause workers to lose pension benefits because they leave or are discharged from the employing unit to which the pension coverage is restricted before becoming eligible for benefits. By the end of the 1960's, however, more than three-fourths of the employees in private pension plans were in programs that included a vesting provision of some kind.

[11] *Social Security Bulletin,* December, 1972, p. 51.

[12] C. L. Schultze, et al., *Setting National Priorities: the 1972 Budget,* 1971, p. 208.

[13] National Urban Coalition, *Counterbudget: A Blueprint for Changing National Priorities,* 1971, p. 60; *Special Analyses, The Budget of the United States Government, op. cit.,* 1973, p. 180.

[14] *Social Security Bulletin,* April, 1970, p. 11.

Disability benefits to compensate for the loss of income due to illness or injury are the second largest element in the social welfare outlays. These include veterans' disability benefits, disability compensation paid through the Social Security System, Workmen's Compensation payments for occupational injuries, and public and private benefit programs to provide compensation for the income loss due to short-term illness. A comprehensive survey of disability in the late 1960's showed that there were 18 million disabled persons in the population, of whom six million were sufficiently disabled to be unable to work or to work regularly. Over half of the severely disabled had no public income maintenance support, and an estimated 1.3 million were receiving no benefits from any source including public assistance.[15] Compensation from public sources for nonoccupational short-term illness is provided by only four states and through the separate railroad social insurance system. In recent years, the benefits provided by all of the public and private plans including employers' leave arrangement and individual private insurance supplied protection for only about a third of the $15 billion income loss due to short-term illness.[16]

Like the Social Security benefits for the aged, unemployment compensation makes up another major element in the nation's social welfare system in which the insurance aspect is widely regarded as the basis for the payment of benefits. A combination of qualifying requirements (e.g., waiting periods before payments start and exclusions from coverage, such as the case of most farm workers) limit the payment of benefits, and the period for which they continue varies considerably from state to state. In 1970, for instance, the average weekly benefit ranged from approximately $33.50 in West Virginia to $60 in Connecticut. Nationally, the average weekly benefit has amounted to about three-eighths of the wage loss sustained during the total period of unemployment.[17] More generous benefits are available to employees covered in the separate Railroad Unemployment Insurance System while the Trade Expansion Act of 1962 and the Automotive Products Trade Act of 1965 make possible jobless benefits of 65 percent of weekly wages for workers who become unemployed as a result of government actions affecting international trade, such as a lowering of tariffs. In addition, recent legislation has expanded the benefits available through the public unemployment insurance systems. The Employment Security Amendments of 1970, for instance, provide up to 13 weeks of additional compensation to workers who have exhausted their regular benefits in periods during which the unemployment rate amounts to 4.5 percent or more.

[15] See *Social Security Bulletin,* May, 1968, pp. 14–21.
[16] *Statistical Abstract, 1971,* p. 283.
[17] *Ibid.,* p. 286.

In addition to the public unemployment insurance systems, there are about 700 supplemental private unemployment benefit plans established through collective bargaining. About half of the 2.5 million workers covered by the private plans are in the automobile and steel industries. Under the auto industry agreement in the early 1970's, employees with one year of seniority who were laid off would receive supplemental private benefits that, together with the public unemployment compensation, could provide them with 95 percent of their normal pay for as long as 31 weeks. Employees with seven or more years seniority would be entitled to similar compensation for up to a year.[18]

III

In addition to the social insurance programs requiring individual contributions, all levels of government provide welfare assistance to low-income persons based on need in money, in kind, and in professional welfare services. While public welfare assistance makes up only about a tenth of the total social welfare expenditures, the assistance outlays have made up the most rapidly growing and the most controversial element in the past decade.

Public attitudes with respect to the welfare assistance programs have shifted as the makeup of the beneficiaries has changed and as the population receiving the benefits has grown. The stereotype of the poor person requiring public assistance in the 1950's emphasized the blind person, the displaced coal miner, or the farm family eking out an existence in the pockets of poverty in states such as West Virginia. During the periods of economic growth in the 1950's and 1960's many poor families headed by a male moved out of the depressed regions and industries and found new jobs elsewhere providing them with more adequate incomes. By 1970, accordingly, fathers living at home who were not disabled made up only 5 percent of the family heads receiving the aid for dependent children (AFDC) assistance.[19] The popular stereotype of the poor families receiving public

[18] R. Munts, *Costs of Selected Income Maintenance and Social Service Goals in the Year 1980,* National Planning Association (unpublished), 1971, pp. 24–25.

[19] *Manpower Report of the President,* 1970, pp. 148–149.

assistance has increasingly become that of a family headed by a woman, frequently a nonwhite woman, living in a large urban center.

The population receiving the AFDC assistance more than quadrupled between 1950 and 1970, increasing from 2.2 to 9.7 million. More than half of this increase took place after 1965.[20] To a considerable extent, the welfare explosion has constituted a response to the civil disorders in the cities in the second half of the 1960's. The characteristics of the family heads in the AFDC program in 1972 are described in Table 5–2.

Table 5-2   Selected Characteristics of Family Heads Participating
in the AFDC Program in 1972[a]

Characteristic	Percent Distribution
Sex	
Male	18%
Female	82
Race	
White	49
Nonwhite	51
Residence	
Northeast	31
North central	19
South	27
West	23
Work experience during year	
Full-time all year	8
Some work experience	10
No work experience	82

[a] C. L. Schultze, et al., *Setting National Priorities: the 1972 Budget,* p. 177.

Over four-fifths of the family heads in the AFDC program in 1972 were women, about half were nonwhite, and close to three-fifths lived in the Northeast and the South. Only a small proportion, less than a fifth, were employed on either a full- or a part-time basis during the year. The overall portrayal of a group largely composed of families headed by a female with limited work experience continues to characterize the AFDC families in the early 1970's as it did in the 1960's.

Since public assistance is primarily a state-administered program, benefits vary widely from state to state. In Detroit, Michigan, for example, a family

[20] *Social Security Bulletin,* December, 1972, p. 62.

of four on welfare in the early 1970's would have received cash, food and medical care benefits amounting to $4894 a year, the equivalent of $5373 in income before income tax deductions. The same family in Atlanta, Georgia, would have been eligible for $2710 in benefits.[21]

For many heads of welfare families, obtaining a job in the place of receiving public assistance would mean very little increase, or an actual reduction, in disposable income. For one consideration, the 1967 amendments to the Social Security Act provide that the first $30 of income earned from work by welfare recipients and one-third of the remainder after deducting for work expenses would be disregarded in computing the monthly welfare benefits. Otherwise, benefits would be reduced by the amount of earnings from work. The implied tax rate on welfare recipients' earnings in the one-third rule is the equivalent, to quote Sar A. Levitan of George Washington University's Center for Manpower Policy Studies, of a "tax rate of 67 percent, applicable to the general population only at incomes above $140,000."[22] In addition, the in-kind benefits often become unavailable once a particular low-threshold income has been reached. For instance, in the early 1970's, a welfare mother in Chicago with three children earning $3000 a year from work would have a total income from work, AFDC payments, and the Food Stamp benefits of $5067. If her earnings from work rose to $5000 a year, her welfare benefits would fall and taxes would rise so that the total disposable income remaining after taxes would have increased only to $5310. If she earned another $1000 by working, her disposable income would decline since she would no longer be eligible for Food Stamp benefits.[23]

Successive amendments to the Social Security Act have stressed the goal of encouraging adults receiving welfare assistance to achieve economic independence by offering them job training along with supporting services such as child care. The Work Incentive Program (WIN) introduced by the 1967 amendments illustrates these efforts. Some 200,000 persons completed their enrollment in the WIN program through September 1971. About 40,000 of this group were considered to have left public welfare rolls after completing WIN. Most of those who completed the training did receive higher earnings, and the women's gains were larger than the men's. However, median hourly earnings for the female WIN graduate remained at under $2.00.[24] The lim-

---

[21] J. R. Storey, "Public Income Transfer Programs: The Incidence of Multiple Benefits and the Issues Raised by their Receipt" in Joint Economic Committee of Congress, *Studies in Public Welfare,* Paper I, 1972.

[22] *Work and Welfare Go Together, op. cit.,* p. 80.

[23] *Setting National Priorities: The 1972 Budget, op. cit.,* p. 181.

[24] *Work and Welfare Go Together, op. cit.,* pp. 103–104.

ited success with WIN and similar programs points to the absence of known, relatively inexpensive, and readily available measures for transforming large numbers of public welfare recipients into employed wage earners who are "taxpayers rather than tax eaters."

IV

The underlying assumption about the remedies for poverty in the income support programs is that "the poor lack money, and most of them cannot increase their incomes themselves."[25] This suggests as a solution that the government provide a minimum of income support to families in need. The manpower program route for dealing with poverty takes it for granted that large numbers of the poor suffer from handicaps that help to explain their poverty, for example, lack of work skills, inadequate education, physical or mental handicaps, absence of child care services, or discrimination on account of race, sex, or age. These are conditions that can frequently be remedied by public programs.

The Federally supported manpower programs, in effect, have become social programs aimed at increasing the employability and earning capacity of low-income persons who typically are in the labor force, although often unemployed, before entering training. The characteristics of the manpower program participants and of the overall civilian labor force in the early 1970's are described in Table 5–3.

Over three-fourths of the manpower program participants came from poor families in the early 1970's, and approximately a third were public assistance recipients. This is many times the comparable proportions in the overall labor force. Young workers and blacks, Puerto Ricans, and Mexican-Americans are more heavily represented among the manpower program enrollees than in the labor force generally. The percentage of high school "dropouts," that is, persons with less than a full high school education, was substantially larger among the manpower program enrollees. Although overall figures are unavailable, the manpower program enrollees are also considerably more unemployment prone. Over four-fifths of the trainees in the institutional programs conducted under the auspices of the Manpower De-

[25] *President's Commission on Income Maintenance, op. cit.,* p. 57.

Table 5-3   Selected Characteristics of Manpower Program Participants and of the Civilian Labor Force, 1970-1971[a]

Characteristic	Percent Frequency in	
	Manpower Program Participants, 1971	U.S. Civilian Labor Force, 1970
21 years old or less	36%	14%
Male	54	62
Less than a high school education	57	34
From poor families	76	7
Public assistance recipients	30	1
From minority races	39	11

[a] U.S. Office of Management and Budget, *Special Analyses; The Budget of the United States Government,* 1973, p. 148.

velopment and Training Act, for example, have been unemployed just before entering training.[26]

The Federally supported manpower programs fall into two major groups: structured training and work-experience programs. Structured training, as in the MDTA programs, involves formal training in a course or on the job, usually lasting a year or less, to impart skills leading to qualification for a specific occupation. Work-experience programs consist of activities that improve work attitudes and general skills by placing enrollees in a work environment under supervised conditions. To a considerable extent, these programs provide education and training to individuals from the disadvantaged groups in American society that most other Americans receive in high school, often in vocational education programs, in colleges and universities, or through experience at work. More recently, as unemployment reached levels of more than 5.5 percent for the entire labor force in 1972 and to over 10 percent for unskilled laborers, temporary public-service employment programs made available by Federal support for public service jobs in state and local governments, in activities such as hospital care, education, pollution control, and other public services, have emerged as a major manpower program.

The Federal Government's expenditures for its manpower programs, including the training programs and supporting services such as child care for working mothers, amounted to $2 billion in 1969. The $2 billion figure for

[26] *Manpower Report of the President,* 1972, p. 265. The programs formerly conducted under the auspices of the Manpower Development and Training Act and similar legislation have been largely decentralized to state and local authorities by the Comprehensive Employment and Training Act of 1973.

the manpower programs was less than a third of the public assistance out-lays under the AFDC and other programs. The major change since 1969 has been the expenditure in 1972 of close to $900 million for the temporary emergency public employment program.[27]

The strategic element in the manpower training programs is their poten-tial for joining the needs of low-income and unemployed persons for job skills to increase their earning capacity with the nation's continuing need for more production in many areas. In a study undertaken by the National Planning Association of the manpower requirements for achieving an illus-trative series of national goals in the 1970's, it was estimated that the total manpower input required to achieve the goals considered would exceed the civilian labor force projected for 1975 by 10 million persons. The expendi-tures to achieve goals in health and education, two of the major areas in-cluded in the study, were estimated to generate direct and indirect employ-ment for 17 million persons in the public and private sectors at widely varying levels of skills.[28] Making more effective use of individuals in the disad-vantaged groups in American society by upgrading their employment oppor-tunities (through job training, education, or the removal of discriminatory barriers) increases the pace at which the nation can pursue its goals without encountering inflationary pressures generated by manpower shortages.

These long-term perspectives presuppose an environment of vigorous eco-nomic growth and full employment. So the National Manpower Policy Task Force points out, the "manpower training programs are most successful in periods when employers are adding workers to do useful work at a wage that permits them to support their families."[29] The importance of growth is underscored by the experience in the early 1970's with the JOBS program, a program to subsidize a national effort by business firms to hire and provide on-the-job training for the "hard core" unemployed. As unemployment in-creased when the economy's growth came to a standstill in 1970, placements under the JOBS program fell off sharply. Cutbacks in automobile production in 1970, for example, prompted the Chrysler Corporation to cancel its $13.8 million program to train 4500 workers, the largest single contract in the JOBS program.[30]

The manpower programs stress the role of the work ethic as a remedy for poverty. Experience with these programs shows that they hold out both a

[27] *Special Analyses, op. cit., Fiscal Year 1971*, pp. 128, 130–148, *Fiscal Year 1972*, pp. 130, 134–148.
[28] L. A. Lecht, *Manpower Needs for National Goals in the 1970's*, 1969, pp. 10, 75.
[29] National Manpower Policy Task Force, *Manpower Policy and Programs: A Look Ahead, 1973*, 1972, p. 3.
[30] *Business Week*, May 16, 1970, pp. 29–30.

promise and a danger. The promise is that of increasing the income and career prospects of individuals otherwise excluded from economic opportunity. The danger is that too much may be expected from a program with a limited purpose without recognizing the condition that is necessary for its success—a dynamic economy.

V

Programs and objectives in social welfare are currently undergoing reexamination and change. Retirement pensions, unemployment compensation, and similar benefits are widely accepted as "insurance" available to the persons contributing as a matter of right. Much of the controversy over directions and objectives in the social welfare programs concerns the public assistance programs based on "need" as distinguished from the "insurance" programs.

Objectives for the social insurance programs are illustrated by the program offering the most comprehensive coverage to its target group, retirement benefits for the aged. As the present low birthrates continue through the 1970's, the proportion of the population made up of older persons will increase. By 1980, 24 million Americans are expected to be aged 65 or older, nearly 4 million more than in 1970.[31] Since Social Security benefits are currently received by seven-eighths of the aged, providing adequate retirement and survivors' benefits to this population through the OASDHI system is, far and away, the largest element in the projected expenditures for the social welfare goal in 1980.

There appears to be a "threshold" level of income that most people consider necessary to assure a reasonably adequate standard of living after retirement. This level, according to recent studies, is a close approximation to the Department of Labor's suggested income requirement in the early 1970's of $4200 to provide a "modest" living for an elderly couple in an urban area.[32] For another yardstick of adequacy, the International Labor Organization has recommended that the minimum pension for an aged couple should approximately equal at least 45 percent of their average earnings in

[31] *Manpower Report of the President*, 1973, p. 219.
[32] U.S. Department of Labor, Bureau of Labor Statistics, *Handbook of Labor Statistics, 1971*, p. 297.

the years prior to retirement, and that the minimum should increase to at least 55 percent in the wealthier advanced industrial nations.[33] These yardsticks provide a basis for assessing objectives for retirement benefits in 1980.

Average annual earnings are projected to increase commensurately with output per worker in the 1970's, by close to 3 percent a year after allowing for inflation.[34] If the average retirement benefit were to increase by less than double the annual growth in earnings, say by 5 percent annually, two-thirds of the elderly couples could be receiving incomes from public and private sources at or above the Department of Labor's "modest" budget level of $4200. Nearly three-fourths of the retired couples would be receiving at least 55 percent of their average income in the 5 years before retiring. The number of aged poor would drop to less than a million by 1980, a decrease from 4.7 million in 1970. These persons would be assisted by new income transfer programs. To expand the options of older persons to work or to retire, all retirement systems, public and private, would follow the practice in the 1972 amendments to the Social Security Act of allowing individuals the choice of retiring between 62 and 70 with progressively higher benefits, for instance, an increase of 1 percent a year, as age at retirement increased.

Attaining these relatively modest objectives in retirement benefits, together with growth in the population of older persons, is estimated to add $50 billion to the costs of retirement pensions by 1980. If benefits to surviving widows and other dependents were to increase correspondingly, an additional $15 billion would be added to social welfare outlays. These changes would very largely occur through the public, especially the OASDHI system, and they would require an increase in the taxable wage base for the Social Security System to $15,000, in 1969 dollars, by 1980. The major changes anticipated in the private pension systems, other than modest increases in coverage and benefits, are liberalizations of vesting provisions to provide employees generally, after a short qualifying period, with nonforfeitable pension rights vested in them.

The objective in disability insurance is to provide general standards and nationwide coverage in the place of the present programs that have grown up piecemeal in response to many different philosophies and approaches. New programs can be expected to concentrate on compensation for long-term disability since income losses from these disabilities are estimated at double or more the figure for short-term disablement. Total long-term disa-

[33] See R. Munts, *op. cit.,* p. 13.
[34] National Planning Association, *Revised National Economic Projections to 1980,* 1971, p. 7.

bility benefits including veterans' compensation, private and public group insurance, and aid to the blind and permanently disabled were estimated to amount to $9 billion in 1970, or to perhaps as much as 30 percent of the annual income loss.[35] Since persons suffering from disabilities that keep them from working do not incur work-related expenses, it would be unreasonable to expect full replacement of earning losses. If two-thirds of the estimated earnings loss from long- and short-term disability were reimbursed by public and private benefits, total outlays for disability compensation would increase from the $15 billion spent in 1969 to over $40 billion by 1980. National coverage for short-term nonoccupational illness could be attained by adding this insurance as a regular part of OASDHI in the place of the present programs.

The Department of Labor, successive administrations, organized labor, and students of income maintenance have been calling for reforms in unemployment compensation to establish national standards, expand coverage, and increase benefits. Complete coverage would involve adding many government, farm and private household workers to the three-fourths of the work force who were included in the unemployment compensation system in 1970. The Administration has called on the states to increase their weekly benefits to a maximum of two-thirds of the average wage in each state. Amendments to the employment security legislation in 1972 extended benefits, on a temporary basis, for as long as 52 weeks in periods when unemployment reached as high as 6 percent.[36] The objectives for unemployment compensation in the social welfare goal allow for a continuation of the changes implied by these developments. They include complete coverage for all wage and salary workers by 1980, weekly benefits of 65 percent of previous weekly earnings with a maximum benefit of two-thirds of each state's average weekly wage, and continuation of benefits, if no full-time job is available, for as long as 52 weeks. With these changes, the rationale for the private supplemental unemployment benefit plans would very largely disappear.

The costs for liberalizing the unemployment compensation system would depend both on the makeup of the changes and on the volume of unemployment. If the unemployment rate were to decline to a reasonable approximation of its minimum in the past decade—to the less than the 4 percent rates characterizing the late 1960's—the effect of the changes considered would be to increase unemployment compensation from the $2.5 billion paid out

[35] R. Munts, *op. cit.*, p. 35.

[36] *Special Analyses, 1972, op. cit.*, p. 179; *ibid., 1973*, p. 183.

in 1969, and the $4.4 billion public outlay as unemployment increased in 1970, to $6.6 billion by 1980. Persistence of the greater than 5 percent rates prevailing in 1971 and 1972 would add several billion dollars, depending on the volume of unemployment, to this total.

The social insurance components of the social welfare system, retirement and survivors benefits, disability benefits, and unemployment compensation, made up about six-sevenths of the social welfare outlays in 1969. Table 5–4 summarizes the social insurance benefits in 1969 and the projected benefits to achieve the social welfare goal by 1980.

Table 5-4   Estimated Public and Private Outlays for Social Insurance Benefits, 1969 and Projected 1980
(in millions of 1969 dollars)

Program Area	Expenditures in 1969[a]	Projected Expenditures in 1980
Retirement benefits	$30,570	$85,600
OASDHI	17,698	64,100
Other public systems	7,012	12,000
Private systems	5,860	9,500
Survivors and lump-sum benefits	11,834	27,100
OASDHI	6,510	18,100
Other public systems	2,809	4,900
Private systems	2,515	4,100
Disability benefits	15,358	40,500
OASDHI	2,542	9,200
Other public systems	9,969	23,300
Private systems	2,847	8,000
Unemployment benefits	2,523	6,000
Public systems	2,423	6,000
Private systems	100	—
Total, social insurance benefits	60,285	159,200

[a] See Table 5-1.

The projections for the social welfare goal assume increases in social insurance benefits amounting to nearly $100 billion a year in the 1970's. Over half of the increase ($55 billion) would represent larger retirement benefits for a growing population of older persons.

VI

A notable aspect of the public assistance programs throughout the past decade, to quote one authority in the field, "is the dissatisfaction expressed by all parties concerned . . . the applicants for and recipients of assistance, the rank and file public assistance staff, legislators, and the public at large."[37] The search for alternatives to the public assistance programs in the recent past has stressed the theme that income maintenance and manpower training programs are, to a large extent, complementary rather than alternative means for dealing with poverty.

Emphasis on employment as an alternative to the public assistance income transfers is evident in the provisions in the 1962 amendments to the Social Security Act stressing "rehabilitation rather than relief," and in the 1967 amendments to the Social Security Act setting up the Work Incentive Program to utilize training and supporting services to prepare family heads receiving welfare assistance for employment. President Nixon's proposed Family Assistance Plan (FAP) in the early 1970's constitutes the most far-reaching recent effort to reform the existing welfare system. The Administration's original proposal would have provided an income support of $2400 to a family of four with no other income. To strengthen work incentives, eligible family heads, already employed, could retain the first $720 of annual earned income together with half of the earned income beyond this amount until the total income for a four-person family reached $3920. This income limit is approximately equivalent to the Social Security Administration's cut-off point for poverty income for a family of four in 1970.

Recognition of a basic Federal obligation to provide a nationwide minimum family income to poor families is the most significant feature of the Family Assistance Plan. Integration of income supplements with manpower training was another essential ingredient. In the President's proposal, male family heads, or female heads who were not exempted for reasons such as family responsibilities, would lose their benefit payments by rejecting offers for training or employment. The working poor, including family heads with full-time jobs, would become eligible for the income supplements. To en-

[37]E. Schwartz, "A Way to End the Means Test," *Social Work,* July, 1964, p. 3.

courage female heads of families receiving AFDC support to embark on job training and employment, child-care services were to be made available to working mothers on a substantially expanded scale.

The Family Assistance Plan was accepted by the House of Representatives, but it was unable to receive favorable consideration from the Senate Finance Committee. However, FAP is important as illustrating a combination of income guarantees and job training as an alternative to the present public assistance whose main features have received widespread consideration in many different forms. FAP also illustrates some of the difficulties involved in devising an income support plan that seeks to encourage incentives to work. To preserve incentives, the income support allowances are reduced by only a fraction of the income earned from work. This means that the level of family income at which the benefit payments stop must be greater, often substantially greater, than the allowances for families with no income from work. For instance, with a $3600 income guarantee combined with a reduction of benefits of 50 percent for each dollar earned, benefits would continue until a family income of $7200 was reached. Much of the cost of the income supplement payments, therefore, would represent payments to families with low, but greater than poverty, incomes.

Where, and to what extent, the present public welfare system will be superseded in the next decade by programs combining income guarantees and job training is unknown at present. Proposals along these lines could emerge from considerations that "the guiding principle of welfare reform is the work ethic,"[38] or they could include extended consideration for the objective of providing female heads of poor families with a meaningful choice between working and remaining at home to care for their children. As one indication of potentials, the 1970 *Manpower Report of the President* indicates that 150,000 mothers receiving AFDC support reported a lack of marketable skills as the primary obstacle to their seeking work.[39]

The costs of the income support aspects of adopting a program combining income allowances and manpower training can be illustrated by taking into account the expected size of the poverty population, the income guarantee for families with no income from work, and the reduction of benefits because of earned income. Standards of what constitutes poverty change as overall living standards rise. If the poverty income cutoff for a family of four were to increase at one-half the projected percentage increase in average family income, the poverty line for a four-person family would increase from the Government's estimate of $3721 in 1969 to $4220 by 1980 (in 1969 dollars). On this basis, the poverty population would decrease from

[38] *Work and Welfare Go Together, op. cit.,* p. 111.
[39] *Manpower Report of the President,* 1970, p. 148.

24.3 million in 1969 to 18.3 million by 1980. There would be an estimated deficit of $8.4 billion between the incomes received by the poor and the incomes needed to move them out of poverty. An income allowance of $4220 for a family of four with no other income, together with a 50 percent reduction in benefits for each dollar of income earned from work, would mean that benefits would be payable to low-income families until the family income reached $8440. The total cost of the program is estimated at $21 billion in 1980, or about 1.5 percent of the projected GNP of close to $1.5 trillion. An income support program of this type would eliminate the poverty income gap in the sense that all families received an income at least equal to the anticipated cutoff income for poverty in 1980. However, over half of the income supports would represent payments to low-income families with incomes greater than the poverty level.

Future directions and objectives for the manpower training programs will depend on the character of the changes in the public welfare assistance programs. Continuation of the present welfare system would reinforce tendencies to maintain the manpower training programs as preparation for entry level jobs primarily for young unemployed workers, programs probably supplemented by public employment projects that expanded when unemployment increased. Adoption of measures similar to the Family Assistance Plan would expand the scope of training to include more female heads of families now receiving public assistance and also to include more upgrading training for the working poor. Expanding job training in this way would also involve a large role for the services that support training (e.g., child care) and a considerably greater involvement of the state employment services in counseling low-income persons and referring them to opportunities for training and employment.

The primary targets for the training programs in 1980 are expected to be the poor adults who are, or could readily be, in the labor force. In an earlier NPA study it was estimated that even with a GNP growth rate of 4.3 percent a year in the 1970's, there would still be nearly 5.5 million workers in full-time year-round jobs as hospital and parking lot attendants, domestics, or similar occupations.[40] If recent experience continues, allowance should also be made for an estimated quarter of a million "discouraged job seekers," persons outside the labor force who believe that lack of job skills or language barriers would keep them from finding or holding a job. With a substantial expansion of child-care facilities, it is expected that many more mothers from low-income families would become candidates for training and employment.

New enrollees in the Federally supported skill-training programs for

[40] C. K. Park, op. cit., p. 20.

adults amounted to 1.2 million in 1970 and to 1.3 million by 1971, or to approximately 1.4 percent of the labor force.[41] The dimensions of a high priority for these programs is illustrated by assuming that the proportion of the labor force in the training programs increased by half, or to 2.1 percent of the 100 million anticipated in 1980,[42] or a training level of 2.1 million persons. With this level of effort, a poverty target population of the dimensions projected for 1980 could all receive skill training in from three to four years, and close to half a million other enrollees could be drawn from low-income but nonpoverty backgrounds. Allowing for increases in the stipends paid trainees and in instruction costs per enrollee of 3 percent a year, expenditures for skill training in 1980 would total nearly $8 billion, or more than quadruple the 1969 outlays. Spending for the skill-training programs for adults in 1969, including supporting services and manpower research, and the projected expenditures in 1980 are summarized in Table 5–5.

Table 5-5 Estimated Expenditures for Manpower Training Goal, 1969 and Projected 1980 (in millions of 1969 dollars)

Program Area	Expenditures in 1969[a]	Projected Expenditures in 1980
Skill-training programs	$1756	$5969
Work-related adult basic education	53	106
Child-care services	100	1700
Other activities[b]	83	175
Total	1992	7950
Number of trainees (in thousands)	1202	2100

[a] *Special Analyses, The Budget of the United States Government, Fiscal Year 1971,* pp. 128, 130–148; *ibid., Fiscal Year 1972,* pp. 130, 134–148.
[b] Includes other supporting services and manpower research programs.

While the bulk of the increases listed are for skill training, the largest percentage increase is for child-care services to enable women from low-income families, often families receiving public assistance, to enter training or em-

[41] *Special Analyses, op. cit.,* 1973, p. 140.
[42] *Manpower Report of the President,* 1972, p. 254.

ployment. The cost of providing full-day child care to a preschool child in families receiving AFDC support has been estimated at $1600 by the Department of Health, Education, and Welfare, and other estimates run higher. After-school day care for school-age children is estimated at $400 per child.[43] For a low-income family with one preschool and two school-age children, child care costs would amount to $2400 a year or more. If economies of large-scale operation made it feasible to maintain these cost levels in 1980, over 700,000 low-income families headed by a woman would be receiving child care services to enable the family head to participate in training or work. Thus, encouraging female heads of low-income families with young children, families often receiving AFDC assistance, to receive job training would increase their options and their future contribution to the Gross National Product. However, this approach to poverty, if adequate child care is provided, is unlikely to be substantially less costly to the Federal Government than the family allowances for families with little or no income from work considered in connection with the social welfare goal.

The objectives included in manpower training, as in social insurance, welfare assistance, or social service assistance, make up a system of partially competing and partially complementary measures for coping with an absence of income or grossly inadequate incomes. Outlays for manpower training make up only a minor element in this system, less than a tenth of the total. The total outlays estimated for the two goals entering into this system, manpower training and social welfare, are described in Table 5–6.

The estimates for the two goals concerned with income adequacy refer to dollars, and, in terms of dollars of 1969 purchasing power, they indicate the changes in resource claims that would follow from assigning a high priority to attaining the objectives considered for remedying poverty and dependency in the coming decade. Utilizing the GNP yardstick, the expenditures to attain the two goals imply an increase from the 8 percent of GNP represented by the spending for social welfare and manpower training in 1969 to 14 percent of the far larger GNP anticipated in 1980. With slow economic growth in the 1970's, expenditures are expected to be larger than those shown in the projections, and the emphasis in programs would change. Public employment measures, with or without training, would become the major element in the manpower programs. The pace of economic growth, therefore, is a critical variable in assessing costs and programs for coping with poverty.

---

[43] U.S. Department of Health, Education, and Welfare, *Welfare Policy and its Consequences for the Recipient Population*, 1969, p. 75.

Table 5-6   Estimated Outlays for the Goals Concerned with Income Adequacy,
1969 and Projected 1980
(in millions of 1969 dollars)

Program Area	Expenditures in 1969[a]	Projected Expenditures in 1980
Social insurance	$60,285	$159,200
Income allowances for low-income families	7,275	21,000
Social service assistance	5,404	8,550
Total, social welfare goal	72,964	188,750
Total, manpower training goal	1,992	7,950
Total, social welfare and manpower training goals	74,956	196,700
Combined totals as percent of the GNP	8.1%	14.1%

[a] See Tables 5-1, 5-5.

Chapter Six

GOALS IN EDUCATION:
DIRECTIONS FOR THE 1970's

I

Education in the United States has had many of the characteristics of a secular religion. Widespread diffusion of educational opportunity has historically received a high priority as a means of diffusing social and economic opportunity, of enriching personal life, and of contributing the manpower needed in a technologically dynamic, service-oriented society. Objectives in education are being redefined at all levels in the 1970's in the light of the recession in school finances, changes in job markets, the slow pace of integration in the large cities, and the doubts concerning the effectiveness of many of the new programs adopted in the 1960's. Attaining objectives in education as they are conceived in the education goal is projected to increase expenditures from the $64 billion spent in 1969 to $124 billion by 1980. This would represent an increase of more than 90 percent in dollars of 1969 purchasing power.

Spending for education since World War II has constituted a steadily increasing claim on the economy's resources. In 1947, for instance, only 2.8 percent of the GNP was spent on education.[1] This proportion has risen to 5.1 percent by 1960, to 6.9 percent in 1969, and to approximately 7.5 percent by 1971. Growth in expenditures has been associated with a continuing rise in the level of educational attainment. From the late 1940's to the end of the 1960's the average number of years of schooling completed by persons 25 years of age or older increased from 10.6 to 12.2 years.[2] The proportion of persons in the employed civilian labor force with some college education grew from about a sixth to over a fourth.[3]

In spite of these signs of growth and progress, by the end of the 1960's the educational system at all levels was undergoing a crisis in credibility, in finances, and in objectives. Declining birthrates have diminished the growth in enrollments that provided much of the momentum for expansion in ele-

[1] U.S. Office of Education, *Digest of Educational Statistics,* 1970, p. 21.

[2] U.S. Department of Commerce, Bureau of the Census, *U.S. Census of Population, 1960, Vol. 1, Current Population Reports, Series P-20, No. 207,* 1970.

[3] *Manpower Report of the President,* 1972, p. 203.

mentary and secondary education in the past decade. More than 70 percent of new school bond issues were approved by the voting public in the 1958–1966 period. With the decline in public support for the schools, about half were turned down in 1971.[4] Studies such as the Coleman Report have cast doubt on the presupposition that larger expenditures for such traditional educational objectives as smaller classes become translated into improvements in students' academic performance. In higher education, student unrest in the 1960's followed by a worsening of the job market for college graduates, inflationary cost increases, and cutbacks in the Federal Government's R & D support have challenged the viability of the research and public service-oriented multiversity as the prototype for American higher education. By the early 1970's, educational theorists such as Ivan Illich were calling for a "deschooling" of society[5] while educational researchers such as Christopher Jencks were questioning whether education contributed in any significant way to reducing the social and economic inequalities fostered by a variety of other institutions.

Allowing for the "new depression" characterizing American education in the first part of the 1970's, it is apparent that new issues are emerging in education while many old ones continue to pose pressing problems. Efforts to diminish gross inequalities in the resources available to educate students because of reliance on local property taxes to finance the schools have received support in several courts. Recognition of the need to provide or pay for special education for more than a million students with physical, mental, and emotional handicaps sufficiently severe as to require services extending beyond the present scope of most school programs is gaining acceptance as a responsibility of the public schools. Greater awareness of the importance of the early years for later intellectual and personality development is expected to lead to a large-scale expansion of public education for three- and four-year olds in the 1970's. At the other end of the educational ladder, the current emphasis on "open admissions" and "universities without walls" reflects the continued commitment of blacks, adults beyond school-leaving age and others to higher education as an aid to social and economic mobility. While spending more money by itself is unlikely to assure that progress will be made toward attaining objectives in education, it is reasonable to anticipate that the choices made in expanding access to education for the very young, the handicapped, or persons from low-income backgrounds will entail considerably greater outlays in the 1970's than in the previous decade.

[4] C. L. Schultze, et al., *Setting National Priorities—the 1973 Budget,* 1972, p. 324.

[5] I. Illich, *Deschooling Society,* 1970.

II

The forces responsible for the mushrooming growth of the educational system in the first two-thirds of the 1960's were those linked with the "research revolution," the Cold War, the civil rights and black power movements, the Great Society programs, and the "manpower revolution." The decline in these forces toward the end of the decade, together with the decrease in

Table 6-1   Selected Indicators of Changes in Education 1960 to 1969[a]

Indicator	1960	1969	Percent Change, 1960 to 1969
Expenditures (in billions of 1969 dollars)	$33.3	$63.4	90%
Expenditures as percent of the GNP	5.1%	6.9%	—
Enrollment (in thousands) Elementary and secondary education	43,330	52,231	21
Higher education[b]	3,789	7,917	109
Median number of years of schooling, persons 25 and over	10.6	12.2	15
Number of bachelors' degrees awarded (in thousands)	479	990	107
Proportion of 18 to 24-year-olds enrolled in school	21.4%	31.5%	—

[a] U.S. Department of Health, Education, and Welfare, U.S. Office of Education, *Projections of Educational Statistics to 1978–79*, pp. 22, 86–87; *Digest of Educational Statistics, 1970*, pp. 25, 62, 66; "Preprimary Enrollment, October, 1969"; *Statistical Abstract, 1971*, pp. 103, 125; U.S. Bureau of the Census, *Current Population Reports*, "School Enrollment: October 1962," 1963; *ibid.*, "School Enrollment: October 1969," 1970.

[b] Includes both degree-credit and nondegree-credit enrollments.

birthrates, helps to explain the series of crises in the schools at the beginning of the 1970's.

By most indicators, the 1960's was a period of rapid growth in education. Some summary data highlighting the growth in enrollments, expenditures, and educational attainment are presented in Table 6–1.

While all of the indicators listed show growth during the decade, the most rapid increases were in expenditures, even after allowing for inflation, and in enrollments and degrees awarded in higher education. Enrollment in elementary and secondary education, for example, grew by about a fifth during this period. Enrollment in higher education more than doubled. School expenditures at all levels increased, in 1969 dollars, by more than nine-tenths.

Concern with the nation's leadership in world affairs has provided much of the impetus for growth and innovation in education in the past two decades. Legislation enacted following Sputnik in the late 1950's (e.g., the National Defense Education Act) expressed congressional determination to strengthen Federal aid to higher education in a variety of programs that could be related directly or indirectly to the nation's defense. Similarly, Federal support for research and development performed by colleges and universities, an effort largely concentrated in programs associated with defense or space objectives, tripled between 1960 and 1969, increasing from $770 million to $2.3 billion between the two years.[6] Innovations in school curricula, such as the new math, were encouraged by international comparisons of mathematical achievement indicating that students in the United States were performing rather poorly in comparison with the children in most of the 12 nations surveyed.[7]

The civil rights and black power movements also contributed to the pressures for change in education in the 1960's. To many Americans, white and nonwhite, the persistence of an unemployment rate for nonwhites double or more that of whites, like the far greater prevalence of poverty among nonwhites, was at least partially attributable to the gap in educational attainment between the two groups. Both the educational and the income differentials between the two groups diminished in the 1960's. In 1959, for instance, nonwhites in the labor force lagged by an average of 3.4 years behind whites in educational attainment. By 1969 and 1970, the difference had been reduced to about a year.[8] In the same period, the average Negro family income rose from 55 percent of the equivalent white income in 1960

[6] National Science Foundation, *National Patterns of R & D Resources, Funds and Manpower in the United States, 1953–1972,* 1971.

[7] T. Husen, ed., *International Study of Achievement in Mathematics,* 1967, Table 1.1.

[8] *Manpower Report of the President,* 1972, p. 203.

to 62 percent by the end of the decade.[9] While the gap in educational attainment was more substantially narrowed than the gap in income, the fact that both differentials diminished together suggested to many that the improvement in educational position, at least for younger Negroes, was one of the contributing factors in reducing the income gap.

The belief that greater equality of social and economic opportunity, and also of rewards, could be realized by improving access to education accounted for the introduction of a variety of Great Society compensatory education programs in the 1960's. The underlying assumption in these programs was that the absence in the home of appropriate stimuli for children in the "culturally deprived" low-income groups had the effect of depressing their educational achievement. Moreover, the differences in educational achievement increased with the time spent in school, indicating that the standard curriculum did little to overcome the initial disadvantage. To cite an instance, the median score of Negro students on verbal tests declined from over 85 percent of the comparable white median in the first grade to about 78 percent by the twelfth grade.[10] Project Head Start and Title I of the Elementary and Secondary Education Act were the major new programs seeking to provide compensatory education to children from low-income and, frequently, minority group backgrounds. In good part because of these measures, Federal support for education increased from under $4 billion in the 1963 fiscal year to an estimated $16 billion in 1973.[11]

Automation and the upgrading of the skills of the work force in the 1960's were widely regarded as constituting a "manpower revolution" intensifying the economic penalties for lack of sufficient education and training. Employment for professional and technical workers, the group with the highest level of educational achievement, increased by nearly half during the decade. However, employment growth for the less well-educated blue-collar workers amounted to only a sixth, and for the unskilled and poorly educated nonfarm laborers the increase was about 3 percent. These changes in the relationship between work, education, and employment, to quote the National Education Association, required an educational system preparing students for an economic environment in which "the whole labor force must be prepared for a change to higher and more complex levels of skills."[12]

---

[9] U.S. Department of Commerce, Bureau of the Census, *The Social and Economic Status of Negroes in the United States,* 1970, p. 26. However, this proportion had decreased to 59 percent by 1972. *The New York Times,* July 23, 1973, p. 17.

[10] *Statistical Abstract, 1971,* p. 119.

[11] U.S. Office of Management and Budget, *Special Analyses: The Budget of the United States Government, Fiscal Year 1973,* p. 117.

[12] National Education Association, *Financing the Public Schools, 1960–1970,* 1962, p. 11.

The "skills crisis" of the 1960's also supplied much of the incentive for the doubling of college enrollment, an increase from 3.8 million in 1960 to 7.9 million in 1969. Greater demands for services of many kinds in health and education increased opportunities for college-educated professionals, while economic growth and rapid expansion in spending for space vehicles and new weapons systems generated large requirements for scientists and engineers. As the supply of well-educated or better-educated persons increased in virtually all occupational fields, the greater availability of these persons to employers became an important factor in raising entrance requirements for many types of jobs. Accordingly, the college degree, like the high school diploma a generation earlier, came to be regarded by parents, school systems, and the public as the admissions credential for a secure middle-class status.

The influences that caused rapid expansion in the educational system lost their force by the late 1960's, or they were superseded by other developments that retarded rather than accelerated growth. Declining birthrates both among the poor and the nonpoor ended the rapid enrollment growth that had provided the basis for much of the expansion in elementary and secondary education. The fertility rate among women from families with annual incomes above $5000, for example, fell from 98 births per 1000 women of childbearing age between 1960 and 1965 to 81 between 1966 and 1970. The comparable rate among women in families with incomes of $5000 or less—the group with the large families—fell from 153 per 1000 to 121.[13]

By the early 1970's, the boom in the labor market for college graduates that characterized the 1960's came to a halt. For example, the Department of Labor estimated that some 50,000 to 65,000 scientists and engineers were unemployed in the middle of 1971,[14] the first time in well over a decade that unemployment loomed as a serious problem for these professionals. The National Education Association reported that, if the forces that were slowing down the growth in enrollments and expenditures in elementary and secondary education were to continue unchanged in the 1970's, there would be a surplus of 700,000 beginning teachers by the late 1970's.[15] The College Placement Council pointed out that several hundred corporations which hired some 70,000 college graduates in 1970 hired fewer than 50,000 persons from the 1972 graduating class. In keeping with these developments, the entering freshman enrollment in colleges and universities declined modestly by 1 percent in the 1971–1972 school year, one of the few declines

[13] *The New York Times,* March 3, 1971, p. 1.

[14] *Manpower Report of the President,* 1972, p. 121.

[15] *The New York Times,* November 29, 1971, p. 50.

since the end of the veterans rush to higher education after World War II. Freshman enrollment in colleges of education fell by 14 percent, and enrollment in colleges of engineering plummeted by 17 percent.[16]

Declining birthrates and a worsening of the job market for college graduates represent forces outside the educational system that were diminishing the prospects for growth within it. By the late 1960's, widespread skepticism had developed concerning the outlook for change within education, especially the changes associated with the compensatory education programs. Evaluations of programs such as Project Head Start reported that "the Head Start children cannot be said to be appreciably different from their peers in the elementary grades . . . with the exception of the slight but significant superiority of full-year Head Start children on certain measures of cognitive development."[17] Similarly, a recent analysis of the Title I compensatory education grants stated that less than one-fifth of the Title I participants achieved a significant gain in reading, roughly two-thirds showed no change, and the rest showed some loss.[18] The most far-reaching of these studies— the Coleman Report—indicated that differences in educational inputs as measured by differences in physical facilities, class size, or degrees held by teachers accounted for only a small fraction of the differences in pupil achievement.[19]

All of the studies were surrounded by unknown margins of uncertainty stemming from inadequacies in the original data, difficulties in statistical control of variables that frequently interacted with one another (e.g., I.Q. scores and socioeconomic status) and problems in interpreting the implications of the findings for policy. So, while several studies of Head Start showed that participation in the program was associated with only modest improvement in verbal or other achievement scores, it is unclear from the studies whether the programs themselves were defective or whether they were inadequately funded and, therefore, insufficiently intensive to produce the desired results. The net effect of the studies, however, cast doubt on the premise that spending more money for education produced more learning achievement, especially more learning achievement by the children from low-income and minority groups.

[16] *The Wall Street Journal,* February 8, 1972, p. 1.

[17] Westinghouse Learning Corp.—Ohio University, *The Impact of Head Start: An Evaluation of the Effects of Head Start on Children's Cognitive and Affective Development,* 1969.

[18] J. Froomkin and Dennis J. Dugan, *Inequality: Studies in Elementary and Secondary Education,* U.S. Office of Education, 1969, p. 4.

[19] J. S. Coleman, et al., *Equality of Educational Opportunity,* U.S. Office of Education, 1966, pp. 21–22.

While the often inconclusive findings of educational research questioned the effectiveness of the compensatory education programs, the research also showed that the most effective program for improving the educational achievement of minority group children was integration. Pupils' sense of control over their destiny, according to the Coleman Report, related more strongly to academic achievement than did the school quality indicators. For black students this sense of control was linked with the proportion of white pupils in the school they attended. Although the basic rationale for school integration rested on the long-term need to prepare young people for life in a multiracial society, even in the short run, to quote the Coleman Report again, "there is evident . . . an effect of school integration on the reading and mathematics achievement of Negro pupils."[20]

These findings were consistent with the court decisions in the 1950's stating that segregated school facilities were inherently unequal. Yet progress in integrating the schools proceeded at an uneven pace during the 1960's. The effect of the court rulings was to end the legally sanctioned separate school systems in the South without seriously affecting school segregation based on discriminatory housing and neighborhood patterns in the northern cities. So, between 1968 and 1971, the proportion of Negro pupils attending predominantly white schools in the South increased from 18 to 44 percent. The comparable proportion in the North and West remained constant at close to 28 percent.[21] As middle-income white families moved to the suburbs, the school systems in many large central cities came to be made up predominantly of black and other minority group students. School enrollment by white children in the 5 to 17 year age group in the central cities decreased by about 5 percent between 1960 and 1970. Enrollment by nonwhite children rose by 50 percent.[22]

The acculturation through education that had worked with such great success for the children of the immigrants from Europe in the nineteenth and early twentieth centuries was working with considerably less success in the 1960's for the children of the migrants from the rural South to the large cities. The apparent lack of success was accompanied by growing doubts about the extent to which the schools could be expected to change society by expanding opportunities for young people from low-income and minority groups. *The New York Times* editorialized that "the American people chronically expect too much of their schools."[23] These doubts came to en-

---

[20] J. S. Coleman, *op. cit.,* p. 29.

[21] *Setting National Priorities, 1973, op. cit.,* p. 336.

[22] *Statistical Abstract, 1971,* p. 106.

[23] Editorial, "Roots of Inequality," in *The New York Times,* Sunday, September 10, 1972, Section IV, p. 10.

compass the value of the heavy emphasis on educational credentials, for example, the high school diploma. One study questioned the widely held belief
that a high school diploma was a necessary insurance against a lifetime of
unskilled labor and poverty. "Dropping out," according to the author of the
study, Dr. Jerald G. Bachman of the University of Michigan, "was neither
good nor bad," and its significance depended on the academic motivations
and potentials of the students involved.[24] Other studies questioned the contribution both of the compensatory programs and of school integration in
improving the academic performance of minority group students. According
to Christopher Jencks of the Harvard Center for Educational Policy Research, eliminating all predominantly black schools would reduce the gap
between the scores of white and black students on standard achievement
tests by no more than from 15 points to about 12 points.[25] To others who
retained a belief in social progress through education, the antidote to the exaggerated expectations about the role of the schools in the early and middle 1960's was "not to declare them irrelevant, but to improve them."[26]

III

The budget crises, and the questioning of the effectiveness of programs and
approaches at many different levels, have prompted a reappraisal of goals
and priorities in education. The new priorities, along with the persistence of
many old ones, imply a continued commitment to the premise that the
schools can influence intellectual and personal development, and that
changes in the schools can make them a more effective means for economic
and social mobility.

The findings of the National Educational Finance Project, a large-scale
study of needs and finances in education, provide insight into priorities for
change in education in the 1970's as conceived by educators, educational researchers, and others. The Project's report includes a series of estimates of
the increases in the operating expenditures of elementary and secondary

[24] *The New York Times,* May 7, 1972, Sect. IV. See also J. G. Bachman, *Youth in
Transition,* Institute for Social Research, University of Michigan, 1970.
[25] *The Washington Post,* September 7, 1972, p. 1.
[26] *The New York Times, op. cit.,* Sunday, September 10, 1972.

schools required to meet a series of new or more pressing demands in education in the next decade. The estimates refer to the percentage increases needed beyond the 1969 current operating expenditures to achieve the demands by 1980. The demands and the estimated increases are listed in Table 6–2.

Table 6-2 Estimated Increases in Current Operating Expenses of Public Schools to Achieve Selected Demands for Change by 1980[a]

Item	Percentage Increase Required Beyond 1969 Operating Expenditures
I. Expansion in early learning programs	33.8%
A. Nursery school programs (enroll 6 million 3- to 4-year-olds)	18.1
B. Kindergarten programs (enroll all 5-year-olds)	12.5
C. Day-care programs (enroll 4.5 percent of population under 6)	2.3
D. Parent education programs (enroll one-third to one-half of all parents with children under 3)	0.9
II. Special and compensatory education programs	9.2
A. Special education for physically, mentally, and emotionally handicapped (100 percent increase in enrollment)	4.3
B. Remedial and compensatory instruction (targets vary in different parts of city)	4.9
III. Vocational programs (300 percent increase in enrollees)	6.0
IV. Improvements in instruction	14.0
A. Innovations in instructional programs	10.0
B. In-Service programs for professional staff (equivalent to half a year's leave for each six years of service)	4.0
V. Equilization of expenditures per pupil (increase per pupil expenditures in states below national average)	9.0
VI. Total, all categories	72.0
VII. Current operating expenditures in 1969 (in billions of 1969 dollars)	31.8

[a] National Educational Finance Project, Vol. 5, *Alternative Programs for Financing Education,* 1971, pp. 168–69. All estimates of increases in expenditures are based on 1969 prices. The estimates for nursery school programs are the "high demand" projections.

The National Educational Finance Project's estimates are derived from an assumed growth in level of services from what are often small current levels. The projections do not include the costs of many new demands such as those that could arise from several court decisions intended to more nearly equalize expenditures per pupil within states. All told, the current operating expenditures of the public elementary and secondary schools in 1969 were $31.8 billion.[27] A 72 percent increase would raise this total to $54.7 billion. The specific cost estimates aside, the projections underscore the fact that relatively modest changes in present educational institutions along lines currently receiving broad support by educators and others would entail major changes in outlays for education by the end of the decade.

Greater outlays for early learning programs are the largest single element in the Education Finance Project's estimates, and they are expected to figure as a major factor in defining objectives in education for the 1970's. Recent findings about the development of intelligence, like the earlier findings of psychologists and psychoanalysts about personality development, stress the importance of early learning for later intellectual and emotional growth. For example, research shows that as much of the growth in intelligence takes place in the first five years as in the next thirteen.[28] These findings suggest that the educational system, and especially the schools concerned with students from disadvantaged backgrounds, can make their greatest impact before students reach the first grade. Prekindergarten schools for 3- and 4-year-olds enrolled only about a tenth of the 7.8 million children in this age group in 1969.[29] Expansion of nursery school, kindergarten, and related day-care facilities would serve the needs of the children enrolled, and the greater availability of these facilities would also enable many women who wish to work or to obtain further education and training to do so.

Early learning programs for disadvantaged children can be expected to figure as part of an overall urban education effort including both preschool education and follow-up programs to retain the emotional and social as well as the intellectual gains made in the early years. A critical mass or threshold level of expenditures is probably required for these programs to take effect. Where resources have been spread too thin, as President Nixon has pointed out in the Administration's 1972 *Message on Education,* "they have been wasted or dissipated with little to show for their expenditures. Where they

[27] The estimate is an average of the 1968–1969 and 1969–1970 figures.

[28] Cited from *Education for the 1970's: Renewal and Reform, President's Message to Congress on Education,* March, 1970, p. 16.

[29] U.S. Office of Education, "Preprimary Enrollment, October, 1969," p. 11. Estimate refers to enrollment in programs with structured educational content.

have been concentrated, the results have been frequently encouraging and sometimes dramatic."[30] In a study of some 10,000 pupils enrolled in compensatory programs in California, for instance, 82 percent of the children in projects involving an additional expenditure of less than $150 per child showed little or no achievement gain. Where the additional outlays amounted to over $250 per pupil, 94 percent showed an achievement gain of more than one year of exposure to the program.[31]

The standard school programs seldom meet the needs of children with severe physical, mental, or emotional handicaps. Approximately 8 percent of the elementary and secondary school population, according to the National Education Finance Project, suffer from such handicaps, and the incidence of severe handicaps is estimated at 3 percent of the school population.[32] These children, and especially those with severe handicaps, require special remedial programs with small classes and large staffs of supporting professionals either in the public schools or in separate public or private institutions. Recent court decisions in the District of Columbia, in Pennsylvania, and elsewhere have set forth the principle that the states have the responsibility to provide adequate public school facilities for handicapped children or to pay the cost of their schooling in private institutions.

Special education or compensatory education constitute programs intended for specific groups of children whose needs are often bypassed in the regular school curriculum. The 1970's are also likely to witness renewed interest in vocational and career education intended for the majority of high school students who do not go on to a four-year college. Reluctance to embark on substantial new departures in vocational education in the past has often reflected a widespread opinion that vocational education is a program "designed for somebody else's children."[33] While vocational education has become more closely related to emerging career opportunities in the past decade, changes have taken place with many lags and inconsistencies. The annual program completions in such rapidly expanding fields as the nonprofessional health or the protective service occupations, to cite several instances, have recently amounted to about one-tenth of the anticipated annual job openings in these fields by 1980.[34] New departures in vocational education can be expected to include a larger role for work-study programs

[30] *Message to Congress on Education,* March 17, 1972, p. 13.

[31] *Ibid.*

[32] National Educational Finance Project, *Future Directions for School Financing,* 1971, p. 24, *Alternative Programs for Financing Education,* 1971, p. 140.

[33] *U.S. News and World Report,* October 13, 1968, p. 45.

[34] National Planning Association, *Policy Issues and Analytical Problems in Evaluating Vocational Education,* 1972, Part I, pp. 4–5.

in which the vocational instruction is provided by industry, and a greater emphasis on specialized occupational preparation in community colleges and other post-high school institutions. Career education before graduating high school will range from dissemination of occupational information in elementary school to providing high school students with sufficient training in a cluster of related occupations (e.g., the medical technologies) to equip them with the skills needed for entry level jobs or for further education and training after leaving high school.

Improvements in the effectiveness of elementary and secondary education, for disadvantaged children and for others, depend more on attracting and retaining competent teachers than on any other single factor within the schools. According to the Coleman Report, for example, the caliber of the teachers showed a stronger relationship to pupil achievement than did other school variables such as differences in physical facilities or curricula. Currently, many of the academically abler persons who enter public school teaching, especially males, tend to leave it. For instance, the National Research Council's Commission on Human Resources reported in a recent study that the average academic performance of the men who entered and then quit secondary school teaching was 1.68. For those who remained in the field the comparable index was 1.52.[35] Periodic sabbaticals and other opportunities for professional fulfillment, as well as higher salaries, will be necessary in the 1970's to recruit more able teachers and to slow down their exit out of teaching into administrative positions or other fields.

Nonschool agencies such as commercial television have probably become at least as important as the schools in the acquisition of basic verbal skills by young children. By the age of 16, a young person in contemporary American society has spent as many hours watching television outside of school as the total time spent in school.[36] The success of the recent Federally funded television production of the popular children's show "Sesame Street" represents an important first effort by the education authorities to influence the development of basic verbal and numerical skills through nonschool media. However, computer-assisted instruction organized around a time-shared computer connected with a number of student terminals has found only limited application in the elementary and secondary schools.

The high cost of computer assisted instruction or closed circuit television

[35] J. K. Folger, et al., *Human Resources and Higher Education, Staff Report of the Commission on Human Resources and Advanced Education,* 1972, Part I, pp. 4–5.

[36] J. S. Coleman, "Education in the Age of Computers and Mass Communications," 1969, quoted in *Toward Balanced Growth: Quantity with Quality, Report of the National Goals Research Staff,* 1970, p. 87.

in the past has been a formidable obstacle to the adoption of the new educational technology on more than a token basis. But the cost of utilizing computers in the schools has been declining rapidly, and cost considerations are unlikely to constitute the barrier to the use of this new technology in the next decade as in the past one. Once in everyday use, the new technology is inherently structured to facilitate innovations in the use of teaching personnel. Team teaching or the use of teachers' aides are instances. Closed circuit television, for example, requires the use of highly skilled and well-paid master teachers who would be responsible for the television performance. They would work together with other qualified but less well-paid teachers who would lead group discussions and provide individual instruction. Many of the persons on the new teaching teams would be teachers' aides, persons who would not normally be required to be college graduates or to have completed courses in education. The aides would relieve teachers of clerical and monitoring duties, and they would be responsible for the functioning of the teaching machines and for routine checking with students in the computer assisted instruction.

Attracting superior teachers to the schools, introducing innovations such as closed circuit TV, or team teaching might improve the academic achievement of students, including those from minority groups, and for these reasons they would fit in well with compensatory education programs. By themselves, such changes could be expected to do little to advance integration. While integration remains an important objective in education, the choices still have to be made as to the priority to be assigned to this objective in the large urban centers or the measures for achieving it. In some instances, compensatory education programs are likely to receive support as an alternative to more extensive integration, both from white groups that oppose resorting to school bussing to overcome *de facto* segregation and from militant black groups who assign a first priority to local community control of their schools. The advances in integration that will be sought can be facilitated by innovations such as the construction of educational parks consolidating existing schools at all grade levels into a single campus serving a sufficiently large area to draw on a student body with a heterogeneous racial and socioeconomic background. How far this kind of development will take place in the large cities depends on the progress made in implementing a number of goals affecting the institutionalized segregation of nonwhites including goals in urban development, transportation, and housing as well as education. It is apparent from the experience in the 1960's and early 1970's that the schools are unlikely to achieve a high degree of integration in an otherwise segregated society.

IV

Higher education in the 1960's basically changed by growing—by enrolling more students, enlarging facilities, and attracting ever increasing research support. Colleges and universities in the next decade are more likely to grow by changing. Much of the impetus for this change can be expected to come from efforts to make higher education available to those for whom access had been difficult before.

Approximately half the high school graduates in the United States now go on to some form of college or university, a proportion considerably higher than in other advanced industrial nations.[37] With such a large percentage of the high school graduates participating in higher education, colleges and universities have come to be widely regarded as institutions that promote equality of opportunity. Yet for the majority who do not pursue or complete higher education, lack of a degree or other appropriate educational credential perpetuates inequalities in employment and earnings, in socioeconomic status and, in the recent past, in prospects for military service. Nonwhites, older persons who missed receiving a good education when they were young, and individuals from low-income families are heavily overrepresented in this majority.

Until relatively recently, higher education has been predominantly the preserve of persons in the average and above-average ability levels from families in the upper half of the income distribution plus the more highly talented individuals from the lower half. Since World War II, especially in the past decade, there has been some shift in this pattern. The rapid growth of the two-year community colleges is an instance. While enrollment in the four-year institutions increased by four-fifths during the 1960's, enrollment in the two-year colleges tripled. The low cost, ease of admission, and convenience of the community colleges has enabled many young people from low-income families and often of modest academic abilities to take part in occupational training, general education, or the first two years of the four-year bachelors degree course in these institutions. The success of the com-

[37] In 1967–1968, for example, 44.5 percent of the 20- to 24-year-olds in North America were enrolled in higher education as compared with 16.7 percent in Europe and the USSR. *The New York Times,* October 2, 1972, p. 20.

munity colleges has been accompanied by a comparable development in four-year urban public colleges, largely commuter colleges, that provide low-cost higher education to students who in an earlier generation seldom went on to college.

Allowing for the expansion of educational opportunity stemming from the growth of the community colleges and the urban public universities, family socioeconomic status is still important in determining who shall go on to college. According to testimony before the Joint Economic Committee of Congress, if high school graduates from all socioeconomic groups were to go on to college in the same porportion as high school graduates in the same ability level in the top socioeconomic quartile, an additional 600,000 students a year would enter college within five years of high school graduation.[38] Motivation and the educational aspirations of young people, factors that also reflect socioeconomic background, are probably as important as finances in the decision to attend, or not to attend, college.

The recent unemployment among college graduates, and fears that the supply of college graduates may increase more rapidly than job opportunities in the next decade, raise questions as to whether a substantial increase in college enrollment, especially from the lower income groups, will continue to figure as an objective in education in the next decade. In 1969 nearly a million bachelor's degrees and first professional degrees were granted, more than double the number in 1960. Yet, employment in the occupational group in which college graduates were most heavily represented, the professional and technical workers, expanded by just short of half in the same time period, by 49 percent.[39] If this imbalance were to continue in the 1970's, many observers fear that a new type of "structural" unemployment would emerge in the United States, one indicating a built-in bias in the economy toward unemployment and underutilization of skills for the best educated and the highly skilled. Accepting this representation of the future, bright students from the central city schools, for example, would be more appropriately counseled to give first priority to TV repair or the building trades rather than to engineering or high school teaching.

While there is a likelihood that continued growth in the supply of college graduates will narrow the economic returns to a college education, a differential still exists that represents a substantial return to the investment in a college education. Unemployment rates are an example. The rates in selected occupational groups in 1972, and the level of educational attainment in each group, are summarized in Table 6–3.

[38] Testimony of R. W. Berls, *The Economics and Financing of Higher Education in the United States,* Joint Economic Committee of Congress, 1969.
[39] *Manpower Report of the President,* 1972, pp. 108, 171.

Table 6-3   Unemployment Rates and Level of Educational Attainment,
Selected Occupational Groups, 1972[a]

Occupational Group	Unemployment Rate in 1972	Median Number of Years of Schooling, 1972
Professional and technical workers	2.4%	16.3
Sales workers	4.3	12.7
Clerical workers	4.7	12.6
Craftsmen and foremen	4.3	12.2
Operatives	6.9	11.5
Nonfarm laborers	10.3	11.0
Service workers	6.3	12.0
Total labor force	5.6	12.4

[a] *Manpower Report of the President,* 1973, pp. 150, 180. Years of schooling estimates refer to persons in the employed civilian labor force, 18 years of age and over.

Although unemployment and underemployment for engineers or teachers have reached dimensions that have made them matters of public concern, the occupations in which a college degree is typically the prerequisite for admission are considerably less prone to unemployment than the labor force generally. The unemployment rate for professional and technical workers in 1972, for example, was 2.4 percent. This was less than half the rate for the entire labor force, 5.6 percent. Nonfarm laborers, the group with the highest unemployment rate, were also the occupational group with the lowest level of educational attainment.

Similarly, the income differentials favoring college graduates, while they are frequently exaggerated, are significant. In 1969, according to a recent Carnegie Commission report, the median family income of a college graduate with an advanced or professional degree, $13,100, was $1900 more than for a college graduate with only a bachelor's degree, and $4200 more than the earnings of high school graduates.[40] Not all of the differentials in earnings by level of educational attainment are caused by differences in exposure to education, since persons who attend college usually come from families with better than average socioeconomic status and IQ. Accepting the lack of a standard measure for distributing the differential between school

[40] *The New York Times,* October 8, 1971, p. 12.

and nonschool factors, the persistence of the higher earnings for persons attending college who come from different socioeconomic backgrounds suggests that much of it is probably attributable to education, both in the sense of what is learned and as a credential. In addition to the income differences, the economic returns to college education should allow for the fact that college-educated people hold jobs that generally expose them to fewer risks of accident than noncollege graduates. The jobs they hold also tend to depend less on physical capacity and thus are less affected by the aging process than most occupations. Aside from these economic considerations, changes in life styles in the 1970's among young people could lead to a greater concern with the nonmonetary returns to higher education and with its significance in encouraging community participation. Consistent with this anticipation, according to the Carnegie Commission's survey, college graduates were more satisfied with their jobs and more likely to vote and to participate generally in community activities.

The extent to which increases in the supply of college-educated persons will reduce the income and employment differentials currently favoring the college group is unknown at present. Schoolteachers' or engineers' salaries may rise less rapidly in the 1970's than in the 1960's, and less rapidly than the salaries of building trades workers, auto mechanics, or garbage collectors. Some persons with engineering degrees will probably be employed as technicians while Ph.D.'s in English or physics may be teaching in community colleges, and sometimes in high schools, rather than in four-year institutions or graduate schools. Offsetting these developments, rapid expansion in early learning, special education, or vocational education programs would soon encounter the obstacle of shortages of trained professional personnel. It has been estimated, for instance, that only 4000 to 5000 prekindergarten teachers are being graduated each year.[41] Beyond these possibilities in specific fields, changes in the pace of GNP growth and shifts in national priorities will have a critical bearing on the employment opportunities available to college-educated or other persons. Greater concern with energy shortages or the quality of the natural environment, for example, would generate many new positions for engineers, pollution control technicians, research scientists, public administrators, and other college-educated persons. A higher priority for urban development would create many new openings for architects and engineers and for building-trades workers in many crafts.

Recent developments suggest that the disadvantaged groups in American society are still committed to education, and especially to higher education,

---

[41] National Urban Coalition, *Counterbudget: A Blueprint for Changing National Priorities,* 1971, p. 91.

as a major channel for social and economic mobility. For this reason, black and other minority groups have been in the forefront of the demands for "open admissions" policies to ease admission requirements in the urban public universities. Women's groups have been pressing for admissions policies better adapted to the life patterns of women who must frequently leave the labor market for shorter or longer periods after their children are born and who then seek to return. Innovations to reach adults who cannot attend school on a full-time basis can be expected to accompany the movement to enlarge access to higher education. "Universities without walls," such as the Empire State College of the State University of New York, are instances. Teaching and learning in an off-campus setting by mail, tape, and television, coupled with periodic conferences with teachers, will play an important part in the mass education of the 1970's. It is changes such as these, rather than expansion in the established four-year, graduate, and professional schools, that will provide much of the growth in higher education in the coming decade.

V

Goals in education reflect the objectives of different groups that frequently reinforce and sometimes are inconsistent with one another. To cite a strong case, the objectives of the groups seeking to encourage integration by constructing educational parks differ from the aims of those who seek to encourage the neighborhood schools controlled by the local community. Yet, side-by-side with the differences, there is a broad core of agreement on the desirability of expanding prekindergarten programs, on the need for more and better special education and career education, and on the desirability of diminishing, if not eliminating, the influence of socioeconomic status and race on decisions to complete high school or to enter college.

The elements included in the education goal reflect the implications of current developments for education in the decade ahead. The projections for early-learning programs for 3- and 4-year-olds draw on and extend beyond congressional and Administration proposals for day care for preschool children such as those in President Nixon's Family Assistance Plan. The proposed outlays to equalize expenditures per student are derived from the recommendations of the President's Commission on School Finance. The construction estimates for higher education take into account the recommendation of the Carnegie Commission on Higher Education that community colleges should expand their physical facilities sufficiently to allow for more than a doubling of enrollment in the 1968–1980 period.

The costs of achieving goals in education can be expressed along many dimensions. These include the expenditures required to sustain enrollments at target levels, or the costs of providing more adequate special services to larger groups of students who require them, for example, special education for the handicapped, or the cost of innovations in teaching practice such as team teaching. Because of the limited understanding of the quantitative relationships between changes in dollar spending and in educational achievement, the cost projections for the education goal refer to inputs, to outlays for educational services or physical plant.

The objectives in terms of enrollment in the education goal for 1980 include the following:

1. The extension of free public education for 3- and 4-year-olds from the tenth of the population now being served in this age group to 60 percent.
2. The attainment of a four-year high school education or the equivalent by 95 percent of the population under 30.
3. Equalizing access to higher education by enrolling two million more students, primarily from the less-favored socioeconomic groups, than would attend on the basis of current enrollment-to-population ratios.

Enrollment ratios currently differ markedly from one age group to another stemming from differences in attendance ratios at different levels of education. Almost 95 percent of the 14- to 17-year age group are enrolled in school, reflecting the near attainment of enrollment goals in high school education. However, only a third of the 18- to 24-year age group are in school, generally in colleges and universities. Enrollment by educational level in 1969 and two estimates of enrollment in 1980 are presented in Table 6–4. One shows the growth in school attendance if the 1969 enrollment-to-population ratios were frozen to 1980. The other shows the larger enrollments anticipated because of the attainment of the education goal.

The projected decline in enrollment in the elementary grades stems from the anticipation of continued decline in birthrates in the low- as well as the high-income groups. If the trends in birthrates in the past decade were to continue in the next one, the population of 5- to 13-year-olds, an age group with an over 95 percent school enrollment rate, would decrease from 37.2

Table 6-4   Enrollment by Educational Level, 1969 and Projected 1980
(in thousands)

Educational Level	Enrollment in 1969[a]	Projected Enrollment in 1980	
		Constant Ratio Estimate	Estimate for Education Goal
Prekindergarten	778	911	5,376
Elementary, including kindergarten	37,524	34,150	34,740[b]
Secondary	14,707	14,775	15,020
Colleges and universities	7,917	9,800	11,760
Undergraduate	7,028	8,700	10,350
Graduate and professional	889	1,100	1,410
Total, all educational levels	60,925	59,636	66,896

[a] U.S. Office of Education, *Digest of Educational Statistics,* 1970, pp. 25, 33, 66; "Preprimary Enrollment, October, 1969," p. 11; *Statistical Abstract, 1971,* p. 125.

[b] The increase in enrollment projected for 1980 beyond the constant ratio estimate is largely made up of kindergarten enrollments.

million in 1969 to an estimated 34.7 million by 1980.[42] Population growth would be only a minor factor in the large projected increase in enrollment in prekindergarten education and, to a lesser extent, in higher education. If college enrollments were to continue to make up the same proportion of the 18- to 24-year-age group in 1980 as in 1969, the student population in higher education would amount to 2 million less than the 11.8 million estimate for the education goal.

Much of the growth in expenditures listed for the education goal is made up of the larger costs of providing more and better educational services to special groups of students who have largely been bypassed by the educational system in the past. Day-care and early-learning programs are instances. The cost of full day care for children under 6 is estimated at $1600 a year per child in the Administration's Family Assistance Plan proposal.[43] A

[42] This is the estimate in the Bureau of Census' Series C projection for 1980, the basis for enrollment projections in Table 6-4. The population in the Bureau of the Census' Series E projection for 1980 would be 32.9 million, 1.8 million less. U.S. Department of Commerce, Bureau of the Census, *Current Population Reports, Series P-25, No. 448,* August 1970, *No. 473,* January, 1972.

[43] *Business Week,* March 21, 1970, pp. 110–111.

combination of full day care and less intensive programs for 3- and 4-year-olds is expected to cost an average of $1000 per child in 1980. If 60 percent of the 3- and 4-year-olds were enrolled in these programs, total outlays for early learning would exceed $5 billion.

Adequate programs for the physically, mentally, and emotionally handicapped children in the next decade would involve expenditures of a magnitude comparable with the early learning programs. Handicapped children require small classes taught by teachers with special training working together with other professionals including school psychologists, social workers, psychiatrists, and vocational rehabilitation counselors. Costs per child for the severely handicapped in private institutions often run to $5000 a year or more. In 1966, the most recent year for which this information is available, one million handicapped children, other than those with speech handicaps, were in special programs including 127,000 in residential institutions.[44] If the 8 percent of the school age population that is handicapped were to receive special consideration in the schools, with extended consideration for the 3 percent reported to be severely handicapped, this total would rise to four million by 1980. Assuming that costs per pupil for the less severely handicapped were two-thirds more than the national average, and for the more severely handicapped two and a half times more, outlays for special education would reach a level of about $6 billion a year by 1980.

The basic requirement for improving the quality and availability of education for handicapped children or for others is a capable teaching staff. For many years, low salaries loomed large as the barrier to attracting and retaining competent teachers. However, since World War II, the salaries of elementary and secondary teachers have increased more rapidly than the average increases for all wage and salary workers. In 1947–1948, for example, the average salary per instructional staff member was $4034 (in 1969 dollars) as compared with $4115 for all wage and salary workers. By the end of the 1960's, these relationships had become reversed as salaries for the instructional staff members rose to an average of $8200 and for all wage and salary workers to slightly under $6800.[45] If elementary and secondary school classroom teachers' salaries were to continue rising in the next decade at the same rate as in the past one, approximately 3 percent a year after allowing for inflation, their average salary would reach $11,300 by 1980 (in 1969 dollars). As the teacher shortages of the 1960's come to be followed by teacher surpluses in many fields in the 1970's, increases in teacher supply will restrain salary increases in this profession. The growth in supply will probably also go far toward attaining the oft-cited goal of educational

[44] *Statistical Abstract, 1971,* p. 108.
[45] *Digest of Educational Statistics, 1969, op. cit.,* p. 38.

organizations such as the National Education Association of a pupil-teacher ratio of 20 to 1.

Considerations other than enrollment growth will provide the stimulus for most of the outlays for school construction in the next decade. The priorities assigned to school integration provide an illustration. The U.S. Commission on Civil Rights has described educational parks as the "boldest" of "all the plans that have been put forward for integrating urban schools."[46] Construction costs for educational parks to serve 15,000 students at all levels from kindergarten through the twelfth grade have been estimated at about $50 million.[47] If 40 educational parks were built each year during the 1973 – 1980 period, by the beginning of the 1980's over four million students would be enrolled in these integrated facilities. All told, the U.S. Office of Education has projected an annual level of new public school classroom construction amounting to 75,000 units during the 1970's.[48] Constructing these facilities, including the educational parks, plus the additional class-rooms for the projected influx of 3- and 4-year-olds and for the expansion of special education are estimated to involve costs increasing from $4.9 billion in 1969 to $5.9 billion a year by 1980.

While school bond issues provide much of the finances for school construction, the local property tax makes up the largest single source of funds to finance the operations of public elementary and secondary schools. Since the wealth of local communities varies widely, their tax base and, consequently, their resources to support the public schools also diverge markedly. For example, in the early 1970's Beverly Hills, California listed $50,885 in assessed valuation per pupil while nearby Baldwin Park commanded a meager $3706. Although the tax rate in Baldwin Park was more than double the Beverly Hill rate, $5.48 as compared with $2.38, the Baldwin Park public schools spent $577 per pupil, less than half the $1232 expenditure in Beverly Hills. Similar differences exist between states.[49] In the early 1970's, the five states with the highest net income per person spent an average of $1000 per pupil while the five with the lowest per capita income spent only $574.[50]

[46] U.S. Commission on Civil Rights, *Education Parks,* October, 1967, p. 1.

[47] T. F. Pettigrew, "The Metropolitan Educational Park," *Needs of Elementary and Secondary Education for the 1970's,* Committee on Education and Labor, U.S. House of Representatives, 1970, pp. 649 ff.

[48] U.S. Office of Education, National Center for Educational Statistics, 1970, unpublished estimates.

[49] *The Wall Street Journal,* March 2, 1972, p. 18.

[50] National Educational Finance Project, *Future Directions for School Financing, op. cit.,* p. 18.

Several recent decisions in California and elsewhere have outlawed reliance on the local property tax to finance the schools on the ground that the quality of education cannot be made to depend on the size of the local tax base. So in the landmark California case of *Serrano* v. *Priest* the courts have held that "the right to an education cannot be conditioned on wealth."[51] While these decisions have not been sustained by the higher courts on appeal, they reflect a widespread sentiment to narrow differences in expenditures per pupil within the same state between the schools in the wealthy suburbs and other communities. The President's Commission on School Finance has recommended as a target that the differentials in per pupil expenditures be kept to a 1.1 to 1 range within the same state.[52] The states, with the assistance of the Federal Government, according to the Commission, should take the lead in making it possible to eliminate larger differences in outlays by taking over much of the burden of financing public elementary and secondary education. Implementing the Commission's recommendations is estimated to cost $8 billion a year by the late 1970's. If an additional billion dollars were spent in making a serious beginning in reducing inequalities in expenditures per pupil between different states, the direct equalization outlays would amount to $9 billion a year by 1980. Total expenditures for prekindergarten, elementary, and secondary education, public and private, including construction outlays, operating costs, and the equalization expenditures, would double from the $42 billion spent in 1969 to $84 billion by 1980 (see Table 6–5).

Libraries, like classrooms and laboratories, are an important intellectual and educational resource, and, for this reason, they are included as part of the educational goal. Spending for local public libraries in 1969 amounted to about $3.40 per person, or a total of close to $700 million. If library expenditures per capita were to grow by 50 percent during the 1970's, by 1980 they would amount to $5.10 per person, or a total of $1.2 billion. A substantial part of this growth in spending would be concentrated on the 2700 public libraries that in 1970 reported annual incomes of less than $2000, or book funds of under $500.[53]

Implementing goals in higher education would mean concentrating resources on eliminating differentials such as those indicated by the fact that 11.6 percent of whites in 1970 reported four or more years of college attendance as compared with 4.5 percent for blacks.[54] Attaining the enroll-

[51] *The New York Times,* January 10, 1972, p. E-1.

[52] *Ibid.,* March 7, 1972, p. 1.

[53] *Statistical Abstract, 1971,* p. 131.

[54] *Statistical Abstract, 1972,* p. 112. These differentials are less in the younger age groups and for women.

ment goal in higher education would increase the student population from the 7.9 million enrolled in 1969 to 11.8 million by 1980, a growth of nearly half. This would represent a considerably lesser rate of increase than the more than 100 percent growth in higher education enrollments between 1960 and 1969. Expressing enrollment in colleges and universities in all ages as a proportion of the 18- to 24-year age group, the projections for the education goal imply an increase in enrollment from 33.5 percent of this age group in 1969 to 43 percent by 1980.

Projections of sizable increases in enrollment in higher education, although less sizable than in the recent past, run counter to current developments in the financing of higher education and the worsening job market for college graduates. In 1971, for example, the Carnegie Commission reported that about 1500 colleges and universities enrolling over three-fifths of the students were in severe financial difficulties or they appeared to be headed for them.[55] The financial difficulties for students seeking higher education in the next decade are likely to be eased, in part, by a concentration of the growth in enrollment in low-cost public institutions, especially the community colleges. Financial problems for students and for the schools will also be remedied by innovations in the financing of higher education such as deferred tuition payment systems.

The financial pressures that have caused private institutions to raise tuition to unprecedented heights are increasingly affecting public institutions as well. The average tuition charge in all four-year colleges and universities was $1375 in 1969. If tuition were to increase by 3 percent a year, a modest rise in light of the experience of the past decade, tuition charges alone would reach an average level of $1900 by 1980, a sizable expenditure for families in the lower- and middle-income groups. State and local governments in the 1960's provided close to half of the current revenues in public institutions of higher education.[56] Most of these state and local tax systems are regressive, that is, they demand relatively higher tax payment in relation to income from the poor than from the rich. Greater reliance on this type of funding is likely to encounter more opposition in the 1970's since the less affluent groups in the population, the groups that are underrepresented in higher education, would, in effect, be subsidizing the college education of young people from more affluent families.

Current proposals to remedy the financial crisis in higher education emphasize growth in support from the Federal Government and deferred tuition loans. Much of the increase in Federal support can be expected to stem from a resurgence of Federal funding for research and development, espe-

[55] *The New York Times,* January 10, 1972, p. E-2.
[56]*Ibid.*

cially for basic research. Most of the basic research in the United States and part of the applied research is performed by colleges and universities or by research centers affiliated with them. This R & D is projected to grow from $2.7 to $5.7 billion, about half made up of greater funds for basic research.

Student loans, as in the deferred tuition plans, have come to receive widespread support as a way of enabling colleges and universities to charge tuition rates more closely in line with their costs and also as a means of making it possible for more students from low-income families to attend college. President Nixon has proposed the creation of a National Student Loan Association to grant government-subsidized loans to low-income students and unsubsidized loans to other students. The Association would attract funds from insurance companies, banks, pension funds, and similar sources. Other proposals include an "Educational Opportunity Bank," an agency of the Federal Government, that would lend money to students to cover tuition and subsistence. The loans would be repaid from the borrower's future income with repayments estimated to average approximately 1 percent of gross income over a 30-year period for each $3000 borrowed.[57] Yale University, to cite one of several private institutions, has announced its intention to establish a deferred tuition program, and Governor Gilligan has recommended a similar plan for public universities in Ohio. Since repayment in the deferred tuition plans is based on the size of future income, students would not be penalized for choosing lower- rather than higher-paying occupations (i.e., entering teaching or social service as compared with business management or medicine). In addition, the wide choice of institutions that the deferred tuition plan would make available to students is expected to provide an incentive for colleges and universities to become more responsive to the importance of good teaching in order to attract more students.

An increase in college enrollments of close to 50 percent, from 7.8 million to nearly 12 million, could not be accomodated without an expansion in staff, facilities, and expenditures. If the average number of students per faculty member should remain at 18 to 1 (the pupil-teacher ratio in higher education at the end of the 1960's), growth in enrollment would create a requirement for 213,500 more college teachers during the 1970's. Capital outlays to provide the physical facilities for these larger enrollments are expected to involve a modest increase from the $3.1 billion spent in 1969 to $3.5 billion a year by 1980. This slow growth in construction outlays stems from the expectation that the bulk of the enrollment growth will be concentrated in community colleges or urban "commuter" colleges, institutions that do

[57] At this repayment level, it was estimated that the Bank could be self-sustaining. Panel on Educational Innovation, President's Science Advisory Committee, *Educational Opportunity Bank,* August 1967.

not require dormitory facilities and, correspondingly, from the less-rapid expansion projected in graduate programs (e.g., Ph.D. programs) requiring costly plant and facilities.

Larger enrollments translated into greater instructional costs and capital outlays, together with a revival of growth in support for the R & D performed by colleges and universities, provide the basis for a projected increase in expenditures for higher education from the $21.7 billion spent in 1969 to the $38.5 billion listed as the cost of attaining the education goal in 1980. By 1980, outlays for higher education, in 1969 dollars, would be $5 billion greater than the spending for all levels of education in 1960. The estimated expenditures in 1980 for the education goal and the actual outlays in 1969 are summarized in Table 6–5.

Table 6-5   Estimated Expenditures for the Education Goal, 1969 and Projected 1980 (in millions of 1969 dollars)

Item	Actual Spending in 1969[a]	Projected Spending for Education Goal in 1980
Prekindergarten programs	$400	$5,300
Elementary and secondary education	41,550	78,800
Current expenditures	35,435	62,000
Special equalization expenditures	—	9,000
Capital outlays	4,915	5,900
Interest expenditures	1,200	1,900
Higher education	21,700	38,500
Student aid	825	3,300
Organized research	2,740	5,700
Other current expenditures	15,035	26,000
Capital outlays	3,100	3,500
Local public libraries	700	1,200
Total, all education	64,350	123,800
Expenditures as percent of the GNP	6.9%	8.8%

[a] U.S. Office of Education, *Statistics of Local Public School Systems,* 1968–69, June, 1971, p. 12; *Statistics of Public Schools* (Fall, 1969), 1970, p. 27; *Projections of Educational Statistics,* 1969 ed., 1970, p. 87.

The outlays projected as the cost of attaining the education goal would raise spending for education from slightly under 7 percent of the GNP in 1969 to almost 9.0 percent of the far larger GNP in 1980. While this change in proportion would represent a massive increase in expenditures, the projections for the education goal, because of slow growth in enrollment in elementary and secondary schools, represent a lesser growth in outlays than the estimates for the related social goal areas of health and social welfare. However, the money outlays underestimate the true cost of education to society since they do not include the earnings foregone by full-time students who would be working, producing output, and earning income if they were not attending college or, less frequently, high school.

The rationale underlying the projections for the education goal assumes that exposure to education yields a return, often difficult to measure, in economic, social, and personal terms. This presupposition underlies the current discussions of greater Federal aid to education, or of measures for narrowing the differentials in expenditures per pupil within states or between states, or of the deferred tuition plans to enable more students from low-income backgrounds to attend college. The reasoning entering into the cost estimates assumes that a national commitment to education as a means for achieving both greater equality of opportunity and greater personal fulfillment will characterize the nation in 1980 as in 1970 and earlier.

Chapter Seven

GOALS IN HEALTH:
DOLLARS, ACCESS, AND
INSTITUTIONAL CHANGE

I

The nation's goal in health is to provide access to effective health care to the entire population, regardless of income, race, age, or place of residence. Attaining objectives in health in the next decade is estimated to involve more than a doubling of national health expenditures, an increase, in 1969 dollars, from the $64 billion spent in 1969 to an estimated $148 billion in 1980. However, attempts to pursue health goals by spending more dollars can readily be frustrated in the 1970's by continued shortages of health resources, especially manpower, and by built-in inefficiencies in their use.

Measured in terms of dollars, our society has assigned a higher priority to health in the 1960's than to most other goals. Spending for health increased by about 135 percent between 1960 and 1969, a growth from $27 billion in 1960 to $64 billion in 1969.[1] By comparison, in the same period Government purchases for national defense, even with the impact of the war in Vietnam, rose by slightly more than three-fourths, from $45 to $79 billion.[2] As a percentage of the GNP, national health expenditures grew from 5.4 percent in 1960 to 6.9 percent in 1969, and to over 7 percent by 1971.

Offsetting the dollar indicators of a greater willingness to commit resources to health care are the many signs of unequal access to medical services and of far-reaching gaps between the potentials of modern medical technology and the health care available to Americans. For example, in spite of a substantial overall improvement in the socioeconomic status of nonwhites in the past two decades, the life expectancy of Negroes and other nonwhites at birth in 1970 was 64.6 years, more than 7 years less than the 71.7-year life expectancy at the same age for whites.[3] Medical services are unevenly distributed by income group and by region. The distribution of physicians underscores the problem. In some areas of New York City, to

---

[1] U.S. Department of Health, Education, and Welfare, Social Security Administration, *National Health Expenditures, Fiscal Years 1929–70 and Calendar Years 1929–69, Research and Statistics Note No. 25,* 1970, Table 1.

[2] *Annual Report of the Council of Economic Advisers,* 1970, p. 177.

[3] U.S. Public Health Service, *Vital Statistics of the United States,* 1972.

cite a leading instance, there is one private doctor for every 200 persons. In the less-affluent sections of New York City, there is often one private doctor for as many as 12,000 persons.[4] In the middle 1960's, there were 170 M. D.'s per 100,000 population in New York and Pennsylvania, and about half that number, 89 per 100,000 population, in Alabama and Georgia. A comparable situation exists in the nursing profession and a roughly similar one in dentistry.

There have been dramatic improvements in health and in life expectancy for Americans in this century. These have been mainly the results of developments that have affected the health of the younger age groups. The incidence of infectious diseases such as diptheria, measles, polio, and whooping cough has declined significantly in the past 50 years. Medical research has been less successful in developing the knowledge needed to counteract the degenerative diseases of old age (e.g., heart disease, cancer, stroke, and arthritis). Accordingly, the life expectancy remaining at age 5 has increased by about 12 years since 1900, but the remaining life expectancy at age 65 has risen by less than 3 years.[5] For the very young, infant mortality rates in the United States, a significant indicator of the quality and availability of medical care, were higher at the end of the decade than in Sweden, Switzerland, Denmark, or France, all countries with lesser medical care expenditures per person than in the United States.[6]

Many elements, other than the availability of medical services, affect the span of life expectancy free of major disability or disease. Pollution, smoking, diet, the safety features built into automobiles, or the tensions present in modern urban life are examples. A full accounting of the outlays for health care includes aspects of the expenditures for the goals linked with all of the factors that influence good health. By concentrating on spending for medical services, facilities, and research, the health goal estimates focus on elements that are predominant in the treatment of ill health and less important in its prevention.

[4] *Health Message of the President,* 1971, p. 7.

[5] U.S. Department of Health, Education, and Welfare, *Toward a Social Report,* p. 1.

[6] While infant mortality rates in 1969 were considerably higher for nonwhites than for whites, 31.6 as compared to 18.4, the rates for both groups were greater than those in the nations listed. *Annual Report of the Council of Economic Advisers,* 1972, p. 137.

II

Four developments have influenced national expenditures for health care during the 1960's. One was the rapid growth in public spending intended to bring medical care within reach of low-income groups and the elderly. Another was the increase in the share of personal health expenditures, especially for hospital care, financed by private health insurance plans. A third was the slow growth in health manpower and facilities and in innovations in the delivery of medical services. An attendant development related to all of these was a chronic inflation in medical care costs during the past decade.

The steady movement in the health economy in the 1960's toward a system in which third parties (e.g., government and private insurers) have come to finance the bulk of personal health care expenditures is summarized in Table 7–1.

Table 7-1   **Personal Health Care Expenditures, by Source of Funds, 1960 and 1969[a] (in millions of 1969 dollars)**

Item	1960 Amount	1960 Percent of Total	1969 Amount	1969 Percent of Total
Total personal health care expenditures	$23,758	100.0%	$55,296	100.0%
Private expenditures	18,601	78.5	35,776	64.5
Direct payment	13,068	55.0	21,615	39.0
Insurance benefits	4,996	21.0	13,322	24.0
Philanthropy and other	537	2.5	839	1.5
Government expenditures	5,157	21.5	19,520	35.5
Government and insurance benefits	10,153	42.5	32,842	59.5

[a] U.S. Department of Health, Education, and Welfare, *National Health Expenditures, Fiscal Years 1929–30, and Calendar Years 1929–69, Research and Statistics Note No. 25,* 1970, Table 5.

In 1960, direct payment by the individuals concerned made up the largest single source of funds for personal health expenditures accounting for well over half of the total (55 percent). By 1969, third parties had taken over the primary responsibility for financing personal health expenditures, and they had become the source of funds for nearly three-fifths of these outlays. Government and private insurance companies, mainly government, financed almost three-fourths of the increase in personal health expenditures during the 1960's. With this shift, health care, in effect, had lost its status as a service to be purchased by individual buyers who bore the costs, attempted to minimize their outlays, and reaped the benefits of their expenditures.

The largest single factor in the greater spending for personal health care was the growth in expenditures intended to bring modern medical care within reach of such needy and high-risk groups as the elderly and the poor. Of the $15.4 billion increase in public spending for health care between 1965 and 1970, for example, $12 billion was composed of greater outlays for health insurance for the aged and for medical payments for low-income families under the Medicaid program.[7] The growth in government outlays was accompanied by lesser increases in spending for private health insurance, largely financed by employers, to provide health insurance protection to persons in the labor force and their families. By 1968, for example, three-fourths of the population was covered by private health insurance for hospital care.[8]

The social conscience and the political and economic pressures that prompted the enactment of Medicare and Medicaid and the expansion of the private health plans during the 1960's were unaccompanied by a comparable effort to increase the number of doctors, dentists, or medical technicians, or to embark on major new efforts to expand potentially more effective systems for providing health care. Accordingly, the 1960's witnessed a chronic inflation in medical care costs in which the prices for medical services rose by nearly double the increase in the overall price index, 43.5 percent for medical care in the 1960–1969 period as compared with 24 percent for all consumer goods and services. The component of health care with the most substantial escalation in price were the daily hospital charges. They increased by 127 percent in this period.[9]

Many factors contributed to the steep rise in the charges for medical care in the 1960's. Medical technology has become more complex and costly

[7] *National Health Expenditures, Fiscal Years 1929–70, op. cit.,* Table 2.

[8] Louis S. Reed, "Private Health Insurance, 1968: Enrollment, Coverage, and Financial Experience," *Social Security Bulletin,* December 1969, p. 30.

[9] *Annual Report of the Council of Economic Advisers,* 1972, p. 247; *Statistical Abstract, 1971,* p. 62.

(e.g., the artificial kidney). The wages of the persons employed in hospitals have increased, and the earnings of those in the more poorly paid occupations, such as hospital attendants, have begun to reach, and sometimes to exceed, the national minimum-wage levels. Physicians' fees went up by an average of more than two-fifths during the decade. In addition, health insurance plans or public health programs that very generally pay hospital or physicians' bills as they are presented to them supply only modest incentives to hospitals or physicians to keep costs down.

Allowing for these considerations, slow growth in manpower and facilities entered into the medical inflation of the 1960's, and it constituted an important part of the explanation for the escalation in charges. National health expenditures in this period, including personal health outlays, increased at more than double the percentage growth in the health industry work force. Table 7–2 shows the relationship between the growth in spending and the increase in personnel and hospital beds in the past decade.

Health expenditures in the 1960–1969 period increased by more than 100 percent. Employment in the health service industries, however, grew by slightly more than half, and the supply of hospital beds by approximately a fourth. The number of physicians increased least of all, by less than a fourth. With the supply of physicians growing at a far slower pace than spending for

Table 7-2   Selected Indicators, Health Expenditures, Health Personnel, and Hospital Beds, 1960 and 1969[a]
(dollars totals in billions of dollars)

Item	1960	1969	Percent Increase, 1960 to 1969
National health expenditures	$27.0	$63.8	136%
Expenditures for hospital care	9.1	24.2	166
Expenditures for physicians' services	5.7	12.4	118
Employment in health-service industries (in thousands)	2377	3618	52
Number of physicians (in thousands)	275	338	23
Number of short-term hospital beds (in thousands)	639	806	26

[a] *Research and Statistics Note No. 25, 1970, op. cit.; ibid.,* November 1, 1972; M. Y. Pennel, and D. B. Hoover, *Health Manpower Source* Book, Vol. 21; U.S. Public Health Service, *Health Resources Statistics, Health Manpower and Health Facilities, 1970, 1971.*

health care, less highly skilled workers—nurses, technicians, and aides—have come to provide the bulk of the medical care, especially in hospitals. In 1960 there were 8.5 workers in the health service industry for every physician. By 1969, the comparable ratio had grown to 10.5. Even with these shifts, the growth in the health industry work force was insufficient to prevent manpower bottlenecks from developing in health care during the decade.

The National Advisory Commission on Health Manpower describes the effects of the shortages of manpower and facilities for health care in terms of "long delays to see a physician for routine care, . . . hurried and sometimes impersonal attention, . . . reduction of hospital services because of a lack of nurses, . . . [and] uneven distribution of care, as indicated by the health statistics of the rural poor, urban ghetto dwellers, migrant workers . . . and other minority groups."[10]

In economic terms, the shortages of manpower and hospital beds in the 1960's point to an underlying imbalance between demand and supply in health. The most visible evidence of this imbalance has been rampant inflation in the prices charged for medical care. In human terms, the bottlenecks underline the unresponsiveness of health institutions to growing and changing needs and to new definitions of objectives. The unresponsiveness that has come to characterize the educational system, the judicial system, or the penal system, to cite instances, has also come to characterize manpower supply and the delivery of services in health care.

III

Goals in health care in the United States have focused on making medical care more readily available to persons for whom it was frequently unavailable in the past. Related elements include the provision of good quality medical care, and supplying health services with reasonable efficiency. To a considerable extent, these objectives have been inconsistent with one another. A high priority for the access objective in the recent past has made it more difficult to simultaneously achieve the quality and efficiency objectives. The

[10] *Report of the National Advisory Commission on Health Manpower,* 1967, p. 1.

changes proposed in the health system toward the end of the decade seek to reconcile the three elements by encouraging far-reaching departures in the organization of health services. The recent emphasis on health maintenance organizations is an illustration.

Payment by government and private health insurers—the "third-party" payment system—has "opened up" medical care to many for whom it would otherwise have been absent or obtained at a grave financial sacrifice. However, the assistance provided has sometimes been arbitrary when viewed from the perspective of the relationship between benefits and needs, the system often encourages inefficiency in the use of health facilities, and it subsidizes the treatment of illness rather than its prevention.

Private health insurance coverage, for example, is closely related to income. Fewer than three-eighths of the population under 65 with incomes of less than $3000 a year were covered by hospital insurance in 1968. The comparable proportion for families reporting incomes of $15,000 or more was 93 percent.[11] The private health plans are more heavily concentrated in some aspects of medical care than in others. Toward the end of the 1960's, about three-fourths of the population were covered by hospital insurance. Only slightly over two-fifths possessed insurance coverage for office and home visits by physicians.

The recent expansion of third-party payment system accompanied increases in the number of hospital admissions and in the average length of stay in hospitals, and these increases have probably contributed to the pressures on hospital facilities. Since Medicare began in 1967, for instance, hospital admissions per 1000 beneficiaries have risen by 17 percent. The average length of stay in hospitals, excluding mental and TB hospitals, increased from 9.3 days in 1960 to 9.8 in 1968.[12] Part of the growth in hospital utilization in the second half of the 1960's probably reflected the fact that persons who previously had needed but had not received hospital care were not receiving it. In addition, the more widespread insurance coverage for hospital treatment than for home or office visits has served as an inducement to physicians to treat some patients in hospitals who could have been treated at home. Aside from these consequences, by reducing the cost of medical care borne by patients without providing alternative incentives to minimize costs, the third-party system has also reduced incentives of hospitals, doctors, and patents to economize in incurring medical care costs.

[11] U.S. Public Health Service, *Hospital and Surgical Insurance Coverage—1968, Vital and Health Statistics Series 10, No. 661,* 1972, p. 5.

[12] U.S. Office of Management and Budget, *Special Analyses: The Budget of the United States Government, Fiscal Year 1973,* p. 166; *Statistical Abstract, 1971,* p. 70. The average length of stay, however, decreased to 9.5 days in 1970. *Ibid., 1972,* p. 74.

The combination of personnel shortages and rapid increases in demand for health services has often become translated into poor quality medical care. Emergency room medical care is an instance. From 1965 to 1970, hospital admissions across the country rose by about 10 percent. Emergency room visits in the same period grew by nearly 50 percent. "There are scores of hospitals operating emergency rooms that shouldn't be," according to Dr. Sam Seeler of the National Academy of Sciences' National Research Council.[13] Surveys show that more than half the emergency room patients are there because they have no place else to go for treatment. Lacking in staff and facilities and typically manned by the least experienced medical personnel, the emergency rooms have frequently been overwhelmed by a massive influx of patients who have received inadequate and superficial treatment often given after lengthy delays.

Prepaid group practice (e.g., health maintenance organizations) has received the support of the Nixon Administration and others as an approach to health care with built-in safeguards for discouraging overutilization of hospital facilities, for increasing efficiency, and for strengthening the emphasis on preventive medicine. The basic principle in the prepaid practice is the payment of a fixed fee to doctors and hospitals for the care of a given number of patients for a period of time, usually a year. The fixed fee, it is widely believed, provides incentives to keep costs down and to make use of preventive measures such as annual checkups to detect symptoms of ill health before they develop into serious illnesses requiring elaborate and extensive treatment. The incentive to minimize costs is present with this type of practice because, to quote President Nixon, the physicians' income "grows not with the number of days a patient is sick but with the number of days he is well."[14] Acting on this belief, President Nixon recommended Federal loan guarantees in 1971 to initially underwrite $300 million in privately sponsored loans to health maintenance organizations.

The belief that the health maintenance organizations are more efficient than the standard fee-for-service practice receives support in several recent studies. A study of health benefit programs for Federal employees in the late 1960's showed that the employees participating in health maintenance organizations were about half as likely to be hospitalized or to undergo surgery as those covered by the regular hospital or surgical insurance plans.[15] Reports of prepaid group health systems in California indicate that some of these organizations that provide high quality care utilize fewer physicians in

[13] *The Wall Street Journal,* October 5, 1971, p. 1.
[14] *Health Message of the President,* 1971, p. 5.
[15] *Special Analyses, Fiscal Year 1973, op. cit.,* p. 163.

relation to the number of patients served than in medical practice generally. The California organizations referred to reported 91 physicians per 100,000 population served by the group health systems. The average for the entire United States was 147 per 100,000 population.[16]

While there is considerable support for expanding the role of prepaid group practice, the extent to which this system can constitute an alternative to the present fee-for-service system is, as yet, unclear. The experience of the current health maintenance organizations may not be replicable in a greatly expanded national network serving a population different in significant respects from the population presently covered in age, socioeconomic status, or health prior to entry into the system. There are also fears that the pressures to minimize costs will make it difficult for the group practice organizations to practice high-quality medical care, and that the institutionalized checks such as peer review committees made up of physicians or consumer representation in policy making will prove inadequate for this purpose.

The experience in treating the mentally ill illustrates other alternatives in devising more effective systems for providing health care. The major change in the treatment of psychiatric illness in the past generation has been the large-scale use of drug therapy beginning in the 1950's. Largely as a result of the drug therapy, the number of days spent by patients in mental hospitals declined from 1659 per 1000 population in 1950 to 958 in 1969. Drug therapy aside, "the structure of the public treatment system [in mental hospitals] has remained essentially the same as it was in the 19th century,"[17] and innovations in practice have shifted to coping with mental illness outside of the hospital setting. Community mental health centers and other forms of ambulatory psychiatric treatment such as halfway houses have come to represent a new approach in treating the mentally ill before they require hospitalization and in serving as a follow-up treatment center for persons released from mental hospitals. In 1971 some 300 of these centers were in operation, and another 180 were in the design stage. The community mental health centers face many problems in defining their role. They also contain the potential for a breakthrough toward new modes of treatment for the mentally ill, including those from low-income groups for whom the traditional individual psychotherapy is typically too costly to be a viable alternative.

Community mental health centers and health maintenace organizations represent new departures offering the promise of improvements in the orga-

---

[16] Charles L. Schultze, et al., *Setting National Priorities, the 1972 Budget,* 1971, p. 217.

[17] "Community Mental Health Centers: Growing Movement Seeks Identity," *Science,* December 10, 1971, p. 111.

nization of health services in the decade ahead. The Comprehensive Health Manpower Act of 1971 illustrates options for increasing manpower supply and changing the makeup of the work force in the medical services industry. Implementing this legislation is expected to lead to Federal expenditures of more than half a billion dollars a year. These outlays will support grants based on enrollments to medical schools and other institutions training health professionals and other grants to encourage a rapid expansion of training in the allied health occupations such as medical technicians and to stimulate projects to create new occupational roles in health care (e.g., the physician's assistants). Because of the developments represented by the new health manpower legislation and related moves to shorten the period of medical training, U.S. Government sources anticipate that the total number of medical school graduates (M.D.'s and O.D.'s) will be more than 50 percent greater by 1979 than the 9450 graduated in school year 1970–1971. With increases of this magnitude, together with continued utilization of American and other graduates of foreign medical schools, the supply of physicians is expected to increase to approximately 435,000–440,000 by 1980. The importance of the physicians educated outside of the United States, frequently physicians from the less-developed nations, is indicated by the fact that in 1970 about one out of every five doctors in the United States was educated in a foreign medical school.[18]

The recent health manpower legislation, like the community mental health centers and the health maintenance organizations, is intended to expand the supply of medical resources in the 1970's. New initiatives receiving widespread consideration in the past few years would increase the demand for medical care, again, as in the 1960's, by enlarging the role of third parties as a source of payment for personal health care expenditures. The Administration's proposed National Health Insurance Partnership and the Kennedy-Griffiths bill, later set aside, make up the alternatives receiving general consideration in the early 1970's.

The Administration's plan would extend private health insurance coverage to the great majority of the work force and their families by requiring employers to provide health insurance benefits for their employees. The insurance coverage would include hospital care and physicians' and laboratory fees with especially extensive protection for catastrophic illness. Employers would pay 65 to 75 percent of insurance costs estimated to average $300 per employee, and employees would pay for the remainder. The proposal

---

[18] *Manpower Report of the President,* 1972, pp. 130–31. However, it is reasonable to anticipate that other nations, especially the less-developed nations, will take measures to minimize the loss of trained physicians who are in even shorter supply in their own societies.

also includes a Family Health Insurance Plan concerned with basic health insurance protection for low-income families, largely, but not entirely, financed by Federal Government sources. The Administration's program would rely on regulation of the private health insurance industry and growth in health maintenance organizations to stimulate efficiency and restrain cost increases.[19]

The Kennedy-Griffiths National Health Insurance Bill would transfer most of the financing of medical services from the private to the public sector. Full coverage would be provided without charge for virtually all medical expenditures other than dental care for adults, cosmetic surgery, most outpatient psychiatric therapy, and some drugs. The program would be financed through a Government trust fund for health supported by taxes on payrolls and from general revenues. Cost and efficiency controls would be maintained by compensating medical practitioners with a fixed annual payment per patient cared for and by allocating fixed budgets to hospitals each year.[20]

The Kennedy-Griffiths bill would have compensated about 70 percent of personal expenditures for health care in 1970. The net cost of the program to the Federal Government, if it had been in full operation in 1974, was estimated at about $60 billion. Of this total, $52 billion would represent substitutes for what had previously been privately financed expenditures. Under the Administration's program, only Medicare and Medicaid and the Family Health Insurance Plan charges would enter into the Federal Government's budget.[21] In addition, the Administration's plan, according to preliminary estimates, would increase spending by employers and employees for health insurance by about $6 to $7 billion a year by the middle 1970's.

"Health," according to John Veneman, then Undersecretary of HEW, "is going to be the major political issue in the next couple of years."[22] Health care may or may not outrank inflation, unemployment, or pollution as an issue in the 1970's. It is likely to figure as an important political issue in the sense that it is one of a number of competing priorities for substantially greater public and private support, support to be achieved primarily through

[19] For the Administration's presentation of the proposed National Health Insurance Partnership see *Health Message of the President,* 1971.

[20] For an analysis of the Kennedy-Griffiths bill see *Setting National Priorities: the 1972 Budget, op. cit.,* pp. 233 ff. Senator Kennedy in 1974 offered a new health bill placing primary reliance on expanding the coverage and benefits of the private health insurance plan.

[21] *Ibid.,* pp. 234–237; *The 1973 Budget,* p. 247.

[22] See Leonard A. Lecht, "Health Manpower: Adapting in the 1970's," National Health Forum, National Health Council, 1971.

new Federal legislation. Recent developments suggest that health care will constitute a public issue because new and important programs are under way or receiving consideration that could rapidly increase both the supply and the demand for health resources. The form many of these developments will take is at present often unknown. But many signs indicate that third-party payment and greater reliance on prepaid medical practice will loom more prominently in the next decade than in the past one.

IV

Goals in health care are questions of more or less rather than of an absolute standard. Many elements contribute to the goal of expanding access to effective medical care for all Americans in the next decade. The utilization of health facilities and expenditures for health care will increase markedly in the 1970's because of economic growth and social and demographic changes. New initiatives to increase the availability of medical care, to reduce the incidence of illness and its cost, and to enlarge the supply of health resources are also expected to enter into the pursuit of health goals in the next five or 10 years.

The effects of economic growth and social and demographic changes for the utilization of health services can be assessed in terms of the average number of visits to physicians each year. The national average in the second half of the 1960's, according to the U.S. Public Health Service, was 4.3 visits per person a year, and it rose to 4.6 visits by 1970.[23] Individuals with above average education, older persons, women, persons living in urban areas and especially in the larger metropolitan centers, and those in families earning $5000 or more (in 1967 prices) had a greater-than-average number of visits to physicians. These factors probably affect the frequency of visits to physicians because they are related to an awareness of needs for health care, greater requirements for physicians' services, the likelihood of insurance coverage, the income available for direct payment, or the proximity of health facilities. Rising educational and income levels, growth in the propor-

[23] U.S. Public Health Service, *Physician Visits, United States—July 1966–June 1967, Vital and Health Statistics, Series 10, No. 49,* 1968, pp. 3–21; *Statistical Abstract, 1972,* p. 69.

tion of older persons and women in the population, and greater urbanization are expected to raise the average number of visits to physicians to 4.9 by 1980. They are also estimated to raise the average visits to dentists from 1.5 to 1.7 a year. Allowing for population growth and for continued increases in the costs of physicians' and dentists' services, even after adjusting for inflation, these growth factors would increase outlays for physicians' and dentists' services from $16.5 billion in 1969 to $36.8 billion by 1980. Taking into account the impact of recent trends in hospital utilization, medical construction, and other health care activities, economic growth and social and demographic changes are projected to lead to an increase in national health expenditures amounting to more than $50 billion in the coming decade. The anticipated growth in national health expenditures is summarized in Table 7–3.

Table 7-3   Estimated National Health Expenditures,
1969 and Projected 1980, Growth Projection
(in millions of 1969 dollars)

Item	Expenditures in 1969[a]	Projected Expenditures in Growing Economy in 1980
Health services and supplies	$58,930	$113,004
Hospital care	23,897	44,877
Physicians' services	12,486	30,070
Dentists' services	4,031	6,718
Other health services and supplies	18,516	31,339[b]
Medical construction	3,056	3,100
Health R & D	1,841	2,920
Total, national health expenditures	63,827	119,024

[a] *Research and Statistics Note No. 25, 1970, op. cit.*, Table 3.
[b] U.S. Department of Health, Education, and Welfare, Social Security Administration, *Projections of National Health Expenditures, 1975 and 1980, Research and Statistics Note No. 18, 1970*, Table 1. The estimates in Table 7-3 have been deflated to 1969 prices.

In the absence of major new intiatives in health care, outlays for medical care could be expected to increase by over five-sixths between 1969 and 1980. This estimate assumes that spending for medical construction, in constant prices, remains close to the 1969 level in the next decade. This anticipation reflects the easing of the shortages of hospital beds in the early 1970's, an easing partially attributable to the then-prevalent recession but also partly because of efforts to reduce the average length of hospital stays by a greater emphasis on ambulatory treatment of patients outside of hospitals. Similarly, without major changes in national policy, spending for health R & D is expected to remain at the same percentage of the GNP in 1980 as in 1969.

The increase in spending for health care in the 1970's resulting from economic growth in a changing society would reflect greater demands for medical care because of the presence, for instance, of more older, or better-educated, or prosperous persons. It would also represent greater availability of medical services for many persons who would benefit from the expansion of insurance coverage or of the present types of public programs. Growth alone would do little to change health institutions, to restrain the inflation in medical care prices, or to expand access for many groups who currently face serious barriers in seeking to obtain adequate medical care, barriers illustrated by the regional maldistribution of physicians and health facilities or the distribution of private physicians within the large urban centers.

The increase in health expenditures and in the utilization of health services that would arise from providing all Americans with what is currently regarded as adequate medical care is represented by the differentials in outlays under recent health insurance plans, plans that contain markedly different degrees of coverage and benefits. The highly insured group typically possesses coverage for hospital and surgical costs, for x-ray and laboratory services, for visits to physicians, and for drugs and medicines. The groups with health insurance coverage listed as "moderate" usually receive benefits limited to reimbursement for hospital and surgical costs. Since the insurance benefits either reduce or eliminate the costs of additional medical treatments once the deductible has been met, the utilization of health service of many kinds rises along with the scope of the insurance coverage.

Several recent studies have reported on the differentials in health expenditures between the persons who are highly insured, those who are moderately insured, and the noninsured.[24] The studies suggest that it requires an increase in the health expenditures of the uninsured group of nearly three-fourths (72 percent) for the individuals in this group to command the same ability to purchase medical services as the highly insured. An increase of 21 percent would be necessary for the moderately insured group to increase

[24] See Anderson, Collette, and Feldman, *Changes in Medical Care Expenditures and Voluntary Health Insurance,* 1963; G. Wirick, and R. Barlow, "The Economic and Social Determinants of the Demand for Health Services," *The Economics of Health and Medical Care,* University of Michigan, 1964; A Scitovsky, and N. M. Snyder, "The Effects of Coinsurance on Use of Physicians Services," *Social Security Bulletin,* June 1972, pp. 3–19.

its demand for medical care to the level of the highly insured. Allowing for the expected changes in the proportion of the population with different types of insurance coverage in the 1970's, it would require an anticipated increase in personal health expenditures of 23 percent beyond the growth in outlays expected to arise from economic and social changes for all groups to enjoy the same access to medical care as the highly insured group by the end of the decade.

Making the equivalents of the benefits of the more adequate health insurance systems available to everyone would still leave major gaps requiring new initiatives in health care. Dental care is an instance. In the late 1960's, for example, less than 3 percent of the population were covered by health insurance for dental care.[25] Raising the low-income and rural groups with less than the average amount of dental care to the anticipated national average of 1.7 visits to dentists annually would add over 100 million dental visits to the national total. These additional visits imply an increase of $1.8 billion to the $6.7 billion outlay projected for dentists' services in 1980 in the absence of new programs for persons with inadequate dental care.

Upgrading the health care of the groups with inadequate access to medical services would increase spending for medical construction as well as for medical services. More hospital beds would be needed, especially in the central city slums and in rural areas with inadequate health facilities, as in the southeastern states. There would be large percentage increases in spending to construct more health maintenance organizations and community health centers as these more innovative health institutions came to supply a larger proportion of the nation's health services.

Similarly, new initiatives in health research would require greater-than-anticipated expenditures, outlays very largely financed by the Federal Government. Health research policy in the past few years has assigned a high priority to seeking causes and remedies for cancer, and spending for cancer research is estimated to reach over $400 million in 1973.[26] Health research in the coming decade is also expected to concentrate on seeking more effective treatments for the diseases of old age, such as heart disease, stroke, and arthritis. The potentials for significant breakthroughs are likely to lead to a considerably greater research effort in understanding the biological and social roots of mental illness and to large-scale development and demonstration projects to encourage far greater use of new technology in health care. The uses of computer technology as an aid in diagnosis or as the basis for automated medical laboratories are instances. With these new initiatives,

[25] *Private Health Insurance, 1968, op. cit.,* p. 30.
[26] *Special Analyses, Fiscal Year 1973, op. cit.,* p. 157.

spending for health R & D is estimated to reach $4.6 billion by 1980, two and a half times the 1969 level. This increase in research outlays would be sufficient to utilize the 77,000 professional health research workers that the National Institutes of Health reported will be needed in the 1970's.

The expenditures projected for the health goal in 1980, including the greater outlays to provide effective medical care to the groups bypassed by growth, are listed in Table 7–4.

Table 7-4   Estimated Expenditures for Health Goal, 1969 and Projected 1980 (in millions of 1969 dollars)

Item	Expenditures in 1969[a]	Projected Expenditures for Health Goal in 1980
Health services and supplies	$58,930	$134,770
Hospital care	23,897	55,154
Physicians' services	12,486	35,323
Dentists' services	4,031	8,536
Other professional services	1,388	2,694
Drugs and medicines	6,599	14,586
Nursing home care	2,639	6,343
Public health services and other health activities	7,890	12,134
Medical construction	3,056	6,000
Health R & D	1,841	4,600[b]
Total, national health expenditures	63,827	148,370
Per capita health expenditures	315	651
Health expenditures as percent of the GNP	6.9%	10.3%

[a] *Research and Statistics Note No. 25, 1970, op. cit.,* Table 3.
[b] Of this total, $4.2 billion is expected to be made up of Federal outlays.

All told, achieving goals in health as they are currently conceived in the next decade is projected to about double per capita health outlays and to raise the claim on the nation's resources represented by health care from slightly under 7 percent in 1969 to over 10 percent by 1980. Most of this increase in spending could be expected to occur because of economic growth and demographic and social changes without major new initiatives in health care but with continued expansion in third-party payment in financing personal health expenditures. The greater expenditures beyond those associated with growth would represent the costs of developing more effective and equitable systems for supplying health care.

The level of health care that will be achieved in the 1970's is partially a question of priorities, that is, of public and private decisions to allocate more resources to health services than to alternatives in personal consumption or in government programs such as mass transit, the space shuttle, or housing. The limits to a high priority for health would depend as much on the growth of health manpower and facilities as on the increase in spending for health care. The supply of physicians illustrates the problem. In 1969, there was one physician for every $168,000 of health expenditures, excluding outlays for medical construction and dentists' services. The Department of Labor estimates the supply of physicians in 1980 will increase to 436,000.[27] To support the level of expenditures implied by the health goal with this number of physicians would involve approximately $300,000 of comparable health outlays for each physician. A change of these dimensions would entail an acceleration in the substitution of other health personnel and of medical technology for physicians, along with widespread acceptance of new approaches to health care as in the health maintenance organizations.

A continuation of the experience of the past decade into the next one would indicate a high priority for objectives in health in the 1970's. But spending more dollars without changing health institutions would also continue the chronic inflation in medical care costs that has so substantially offset the efforts to increase the availability of medical care in the 1960's.

[27] *Manpower Report of the President,* 1972, p. 131.

Chapter Eight

GOALS IN TRANSPORTATION:
ALTERNATIVES IN
THE MOVEMENT OF
PEOPLE AND GOODS

I

The overriding objective in transportation is to provide safe, convenient, and economical ways of moving people and goods and moving them by means consistent with the pursuit of other national goals as in environmental pollution control, energy conservation, or urban development. This objective is frequently obscured because so much of the growth in transport facilities and services represents a response to the requirements of economic growth and population increase rather than an effort to plan a serviceable transport economy for contemporary America. Consideration of the potentials for more effectively implementing objectives in transportation is again often obscured by the predominance of the motor vehicle-highway complex in the transportation system.

The importance of the transportation sector in the economy is illustrated by the employment it generates. In the early 1970's the operating transportation companies—railroads, airlines, and trucking companies, for example —and their suppliers employed about 4.7 million workers. The auto industry and its suppliers and services and distribution network represented an additional 4.7 million workers while government agencies employed an additional 800,000 persons in transportation activities.[1] The more than 10 million persons employed in producing transportation facilities or supplying transportation services made up more than an eighth of the employed civilian labor force. In 1969, expenditures for the purchase of transportation facilities of all kinds and research and development in transportation amounted to over $61 billion. In addition, consumers were spending approximately $40 billion a year for transportation services and commodities ranging from purchases of automobile insurance, gasoline, and auto parts to fares for the use of public transportation.[2]

The transportation system, according to the Urban Coalition, "clearly illustrates, in its marvels and its horrors, both the stimulating effects of bold Federal programs and the chaos when government fails to consider the total

[1] The National Urban Coalition, *Counterbudget: A Blueprint for Changing National Priorities,* 1971, p. 156.

[2] C. K. Park, *Transportation: Goals, Activities, and Expenditures,* Working Paper prepared for the National Planning Association (unpublished), 1971, p. 82.

impact of its policies."[3] The Federal Government has been actively involved in financing the construction of transport facilities, in regulating rates
and service policies, and in enacting legislation requiring that the undesirable side effects of moving people and goods be taken into account by the
different transport modes. The Federal Government's activities have significantly expanded facilities for some types of transportation and restricted the
scope of others. For example, total Federal expenditures for transportation
facilities of all kinds amounted to nearly $9 billion in the 1972 fiscal year.
Close to three-fifths of this total—56 percent—was made up of spending for
highways.[4] The role of the Federal Government, accordingly, is critical both
in creating the problems in transportation that require solution and in providing the resources that could enable the nation to arrive at better solutions.

II

The forces making for change in the transportation economy show up strik-
ingly in the shifts in the distribution of traffic between the different modes in
the past two decades. Two elements predominate in these shifts. One is the
sharp decline in railway traffic, especially railway passenger traffic, and the
mushrooming of passenger travel by air. The other is the overwhelming predominance of the private automobile in intercity passenger traffic, other
than for long-distance trips. The dominance of the automobile is so marked
that close to 6 miles of auto travel took place in the late 1960's for every
mile of intercity travel by public carrier.

The changes in the distribution of intercity freight traffic between 1950
and 1969 are summarized in Table 8–1.

The decline in the railroads' share of the domestic freight is the most
striking development in the shifts described in Table 8–1. Much of the
long-haul freight formerly moved by rail is now moved by truck or oil pipeline. Pipeline traffic has increased more rapidly and continuously than truck
traffic, an increase attributable to the massive increases in the use of gasoline and other petroleum products. While air carriers have become consider-

---

[3] *Counterbudget, op. cit., p. 156.*
[4] C. L. Schultze, et al., *Setting National Priorities: The 1972 Budget,* 1971, p. 260.

Table 8-1   Distribution of Intercity Freight Traffic, by Type of Carrier,
                  1959, 1960, and 1969[a]

	1959	1960	1969
Total intercity freight (in billion ton-miles)	1094	1330	1895
Percent moved by			
Rail	57.4%	44.7%	40.9%
Truck	15.8	21.5	21.3
Inland waterways	14.9	16.6	16.0
Oil pipelines	11.8	17.2	21.7
Air freight	less than 1/ of 1%		

[a] *Statistical Abstract, 1971*, p. 525; *Statistical Abstract, 1972*, p. 536.

ably more active in the movement of freight, air cargo still accounts for only
a small fraction of 1 percent of the total intercity freight volume, and it is
largely confined to small bulk, high value, or highly seasonal commodities.

The changes in the distribution of passenger traffic have been more far-
reaching than those for freight traffic, and intercity travel by one mode—rail
—has virtually disappeared outside of a small number of densely populated
areas. The shifts in this traffic since 1950 are described in Table 8–2.

Table 8-2   Distribution of Intercity Passenger Traffic, by Type of Carrier,
                  1950, 1960, and 1969[a]

	1950	1960	1969
Billion passenger-miles by			
Private automobile	438	706	977
Public carrier	70	78	161
Percent of public carrier traffic moved by			
Rail	46.3%	27.8%	7.6%
Buses	37.6	24.9	15.5
Inland waterways	1.7	3.5	2.4
Airways	14.4	43.8	74.5

[a] *Statistical Abstract, 1971*, p. 525; *Statistical Abstract 1972*, p. 536.

Six-sevenths or more of all intercity passenger travel since 1950 has consisted of travel by automobile. Mushrooming growth in air travel has led to a

modest decline in the proportion of intercity travel accounted for by the private automobile, and to sizable declines in the percentages for rail and bus travel. Travel by air carriers within the United States in 1969 exceeded the combined total of all the other intercity public carriers—rail, buses, and inland waterways—by nearly a three-to-one margin. The availability of safe, speedy, and low-cost air travel has been a major factor in transforming international travel from a luxury of the rich to mass travel for pleasure, education, or business. By the end of the 1960's, for instance, over 95 percent of all American foreign travel was made up of travel by air.[5] Within the United States, for distances of over 300 to 400 miles, the speed of air travel, and frequently the total trip cost, confer an advantage outweighing the potentially greater comfort of travel by rail or the greater flexibility of travel by automobile.

The steep decline in railway passenger travel for trips of less than 300 to 400 miles in the more populated areas has stemmed from developments peculiar to the American transportation economy rather than from causes inherent in modern transportation costs or technology. Railroads in Great Britain, to cite another and only partially comparable instance, remain major carriers of passengers. Their traffic volume in 1970 was roughly triple the 284 billion passengers carried by all the railroads in the United States in that year.[6] Similarly, bus travel has become considerably less important in intercity passenger travel. Near universal automobile ownership in American families with incomes above the poverty level and the availability of air travel are responsible for this decline. Travel by bus remains important in areas where air or rail transportation is limited and as a low cost means of travel for shorter trips.

The Federal Government's outlays were partially responsible for the changes in the transportation economy in the past two decades, both as a cause of the shifts in traffic and as a response to them. The distribution of the Federal expenditures in 1972 are listed, by type of transportation facility, in Table 8–3.

The Government's outlays in Table 8–3 very largely represent investments in capital facilities. Nearly four-fifths of these expenditures represented support for highways or for airways development. The $1.6 billion listed for water transport includes subsidies both for ship construction and to offset the higher cost of ship operation with American crews. Railroads and urban mass transit accounted for less than 5 percent of the total. This pattern in the distribution of Federal support for transportation is maintained by built-in mechanisms such as the Highway Trust Fund, a fund whose $4.8

[5] *Statistical Abstract, 1971,* p. 205.

[6] *The Washington Post,* December 12, 1971, p. F–1.

Table 8-3   Federal Outlays for Transportation Programs, by Type of Carrier, in 1972[a]
(in millions of dollars)

Component	Amount	Percent of Total Outlays
Highways	$4923	56.0%
Airways	1870	21.3
Water transport	1611	18.3
Urban mass transit	327	3.6
Railroad	57	0.7
Other	3	—
Total	8791	100.0

[a] C. L. Schultze et al., *Setting National Priorities: The 1972 Budget,* 1971, p. 260. Estimates refer to fiscal year 1972.

billion surplus at the end of the 1972 fiscal year was largely derived from the sale of gasoline, oil, and tires. Each time a new expressway is built with Highway Trust Fund support, according to Ben Kelley, formerly Director of Public Affairs for the Federal Highway Commission, "It produces an increase in highway use which . . . adds a new increment to gasoline and tire sales which . . . generates an increase in money available to build more highways."[7]

III

The transportation system in the United States is essentially a dual economy. One segment is made up of automobiles, trucks, and highways, and the other consists of commercial carriers by air, rail, water, and pipeline. Accommodating the role of the automobile with the nation's objectives for other transport modes or in land use, public health, environmental protection, or urban development is likely to figure as the major challenge in transportation planning in the next decade.

[7] Quoted in *Business Week,* March 15, 1971, p. 74.

Many of the changes that shaped national policy in transportation in the past decade can be expected to influence objectives and developments in the next one. These include the steady increases in demand for transportation services resulting from economic growth, and the adoption of new transportation technology stemming from research and development, R & D often undertaken because of concern with the negative aspects of transportation activities as in pollution. Since the changes considered are partially unique to each type of carrier, they are summarized separately for the different transport modes.

Motor Vehicles and Highways

Congestion, pollution, high repair and operating costs, including sharply rising gasoline costs, and changes in life styles and social values have caused automobile ownership to lose much of its significance as a status symbol. Yet after allowing for these elements, the stock of automobiles is projected to grow by 35 million between the end of the 1960's and 1980, 85 million in 1969 as compared with 120 million in 1980.[8] The heavy reliance on automobiles, trucks, and highways creates a series of conditions that rule out some solutions to transportation problems, suggest other solutions, and create new problems as old ones are dealt with. As Wilfred Owen points out with reference to metropolitan development, automotive transportation "has created many of the conditions that people strive to escape, but it has procided the means of escaping them, and, therefore, the means of avoiding solutions."[9]

The solutions that have evolved on an *ad hoc* basis are costly in terms of land use. Enabling masses of automobiles to keep moving involves a heavy investment in supporting systems such as freeways, streets, and parking facilities, all systems that utilize space. Automobiles take up an average of 300 square feet of urban space whether moving or parked. In Los Angeles, the country's most motorized city, two-thirds of the downtown area is allocated to maintaining the flow of automobile and truck traffic—for moving, parking, or otherwise servicing motor vehicles.[10]

---

[8] This estimate is based on changes in the ratio of population 20 and over to the automobile stock, and it allows for increases in average family personal income and multiple car ownership. See C. K. Park, *op. cit.*, pp. 32–34.

[9] W. Owen, *The Metropolitan Transportation Problem*, 1966, p. 20. Urban mass transit facilities are dealt with in connection with the urban development goal. See Chapter Three.

[10] *Business Week*, February 28, 1970, p. 54.

Much of the recent Federal regulation of automobiles, trucks, and buses has been concerned with the consequences of their use for health and safety. While fatal accidents involving motor vehicles have declined with the introduction of seat belts and other safety features, at the end of the 1960's some 55,000 Americans were still being killed annually in motor vehicle accidents. This amounted to about half of the fatal accidents from all sources. More than 5 million persons were injured in these accidents in 1970.[11] In addition to the human suffering and the property and wage loss, medical expenses and insurance costs associated with those accidents amounted to more than $11 billion a year.[12]

Motor vehicles, to cite the U.S. Public Health Service, are responsible for about 60 percent of the air pollution in the large cities. The dimensions of the air pollution problem are illustrated by the carbon monoxide levels in Manhattan. During heavy daytime traffic these levels soar to 30 parts per million in the atmosphere, twice the "safe" level. This is about equivalent in its effects on the human lungs to smoking two packs of cigarettes a day.[13]

Highways, together with public welfare assistance, make up the two largest items in the Federal Government's grant-in-aid program to state and local governments, with each accounting for approximately $5 billion or more in the 1973 fiscal year.[14] Much of this support for highways has gone for the 42,500 mile Interstate Highway System, a system for which the Federal Government bears 90 percent of the construction costs. To a considerable extent, the Government's spending for highways has been determined by the amount of revenue paid into the Highway Trust Fund from the sale of gasoline, oil, and tires. As concern with the ecological, economic, and social consequences of highway construction has mounted in recent years, these considerations have come to play a part, although as yet frequently a minor one, in planning new highway projects. At the turn of the decade, for instance, some 60,000 persons a year were being displaced from their homes because of highway construction.[15] For reasons such as this, the Federal Highway Act of 1968 requires highway planners to take into account the environmental and social effects of highway construction in determining the location of new construction.

---

[11] *Statistical Abstract, 1971,* pp. 540, 541.

[12] National Safety Council, *Accident Facts,* 1969, 1970.

[13] *The Wall Street Journal,* May 26, 1970, p. 1. See also Chapter Ten dealing with environmental quality.

[14] U.S. Office of Management and Budget, *Special Analyses, The Budget of the United States Government, Fiscal Year, 1973,* 1972, pp. 252, 253.

[15] U.S. Federal Highway Administration, *Relocation Statistics,* December 28, 1970.

Alarm over the spread of air pollution has led to the enactment of legislation with stringent standards for reducing the volume of pollutants coming from automobiles. By the middle 1970's, according to the Clean Air Act, manufacturers of automobiles must have vehicles available whose carbon monoxide and hydrocarbon emissions are 90 percent less than was allowed at the beginning of the decade. While the Environmental Protection Agency has postponed the deadline for meeting the standards for one year and petroleum shortages in 1974 have been prompting further extensions, the stringency of the standard symbolizes the national concern that pollution is a deep-seated problem, and one unlikely to be resolved without far-reaching changes in automobile manufacture and use. Similarly, concern with automobile safety has been the motivating force in Federal legislation and regulations dealing with motor vehicle brakes, tires, lights, safety belts, and bumper strength. Many safety experts urge the need for a passive safety device requiring no initiative on the part of the passengers to come into use. This search is largely a response to the fact that only 20 to 30 percent of those who own auto safety belts are estimated to use them. According to the Director of the National Highway Safety Bureau, Douglas W. Toms, safety bags designed to inflate automatically in the event of a collision would reduce auto traffic fatalities by 50 percent in five to seven years.[16] The standards concerned with pollution control or safety are likely to be modified by or supplemented with other standards aimed at improving gasoline utilization arising out of higher costs for petroleum products and uncertainties about future supplies. Proposed standards include a "miles per gallon" target and a tax increasing with the horsepower or weight of automobiles.

The basic need in building safer automobiles or in reducing air pollution is the development of technology to make motor vehicles less accident prone or less likely to give off exhaust and crankcase fumes. Advances along these lines include modest changes to improve the performance of the present internal combustion engine such as improved afterburners to reduce exhaust fumes or the development of less costly lead-free gasoline. Also relevant are research and development to improve the alternatives to the internal combustion engine. Automobiles powered by steam, electricity, natural gas, or, within several decades, by fuel cells are among the candidates receiving consideration . The advantage of steam propulsion is that it produces 95 percent less carbon monoxide than the current engines while cars powered by electrical batteries produce virtually no pollution. Natural gas, to cite another alternative, is both more economical to operate and less prone to pollute the atmosphere. The options available in seeking a long-term solution to the pollution stemming from motor vehicles were summed up by President Nixon

[16] *The Wall Street Journal,* April 8, 1970, p. 1.

in his statement that "I hope the automobile industry's present determined effort to make the internal engine sufficiently pollution-free succeeds. But if it does not, then unless motor vehicles with an alternative, low-pollution power source are available, vehicle-caused pollution will once again begin an inexorable increase; therefore, prudence indicates that we move now to ensure that such a vehicle will be available if needed."[17]

One of the hurdles in devising more effective automobile safety and pollution controls is the likelihood that they will add significantly to the costs of purchasing and operating an automobile at a time when these costs, especially for gasoline, are already increasing. Effective catalytic devices to burn exhaust fumes are estimated to add amounts ranging from $200 to $300 to the price of an automobile. The lead-free gasoline that produces fewer pollutants increases the gasoline consumed by automobiles by an average of 10 percent or more, and the engines that use this fuel require more frequent and more expensive maintenance. The engine for the steam automobile costs $500 more than for an equivalent internal combustion engine.[18] The batteries for a compact electrically powered car cost about $2000 and this outlay would purchase an automobile viewed primarily as a "small secondary car for special urban uses."[19] Breakthroughs in automobile technology and production on a larger scale can be expected to reduce the cost and increase the efficiency of the alternatives to the present automobile engine. These considerations suggest that the internal combustion engine, with many improvements, will continue to figure as the primary, but far from exclusive, power source for motor vehicles in the decade ahead.

Railroads

The prospects for the American railroads in the 1970's and 1980's will depend largely on technological advances to stem the losses in the railroad's share of traffic, on capital expenditures to take advantage of these advances, and on changes in regulatory policies to encourage the railroads to expand traffic in the areas where they have an economic advantage. The potentials

[17] *Pollution Message to Congress,* 1970. However, several of the alternatives to the ternal combustion engine would add to other environmental problems. Automobiles powered by electrical batteries, for example, would increase the demand for electrical energy to recharge the batteries and, therefore, for low-sulfur coal to produce electricity without generating more pollution.

[18] A. Jamison, *The Steam-Powered Automobile,* 1970, p. 93.

[19] L. Lessing, "The Revolt Against the Internal Combustion Engine," *Fortune Magazine,* July, 1967.

for stopping, if not reversing, the dramatic declines in railway freight and passenger transportation are illustrated by the "piggy back" containers and by the Metroliner.

Containers make it possible to minimize the differences between the different transport modes by developing an integrated transportation system organized around a function rather than around a specific type of carrier (e.g., trucks or railroads). In this way, containers make it feasible to combine the advantages of transoceanic movement by ship, transcontinental shipment by rail, and pickup and delivery by truck. While the number of freight cars loaded with highway trailers and containers has been increasing more rapidly than the total volume of railway freight, the containerized shipments still make up only about 5 percent of the freight moved by the railroads.[20] Absence of standardized containers, and the difficulties inherent in integrating the operations of several types of carriers frequently regulated by different Federal agencies, have contributed to slowing down the growth of containerized transportation.

Much has been made, and with reason, of the near disappearance of railway passenger service in many parts of the United States. By 1946, for example, nearly half of the 20,000 passenger trains operating in 1929 had been discontinued. By late 1971 only 360 intercity passenger trains remained in service and over 100 of these were involved in discontinuance proceedings.[21] Yet it is far from evident that the present low level of railway traffic in densely populated areas reflects the potential advantages of railway travel as compared with its alternatives. For instance, railroads offer greater economies in land use than do highways. They are estimated to typically carry at least five times as many people per track-hour as a single lane of highway.[22] In addition, railroads are safer and less polluting than automobiles and generally less costly, for a given distance and class of service, than commercial air travel. The 40 percent increase in railroad travel between New York and Washington in 1969 following the introduction of the Metroliner indicates widespread consumer acceptance of travel by rail in attractive circumstances on trips of this length.[23]

The Metroliner experience suggests that the inherent advantages of railway passenger travel lie in the heavily populated areas such as the Boston-

---

[20] *Association of American Railroads, Yearbook of Railroad Facts,* 1969, pp. 31–33.

[21] C. L. Schultze, *op. cit.,* pp. 273–274.

[22] Quoted from "High-Speed Trains: New Hope for Travelers," *The Morgan Guaranty Survey,* June, 1969, p. 7.

[23] J. W. Diffenderfer, "Tangible Developments with Metroliners in the Northeast Corridor," in Carnegie-Mellon University, *High Speed Ground Transportation,* 1969, p. 7.

New York-Washington corridor or the urbanized area on the West Coast extending from San Diego to Los Angeles. The history of the Metroliner reveals some of the problems as well as the potentials. To cite one, the present cars were built to operate at speeds of up to 160 miles an hour. Yet in all the 226 miles of track between Washington and New York there are only 21 miles of track straight enough to permit speeds of this magnitude. The Metroliner, therefore, essentially remains a conventional train that seldom attains speeds greater than 110 miles an hour. Studies show that if the roadbed and track were upgraded sufficiently to maintain extended speeds of 150 miles an hour, patronage could expand by as much as 65 percent.[24]

Part of the railroads' traffic losses, especially in freight traffic, stems from Federal regulatory practices and from subsidies extended to other carriers. These could be changed without large-scale increases in expenditures. Only 13 percent of the water carriers and less than 40 percent of the motor carriers, to cite instances, are Federally regulated as compared with the close to 100 percent Federal regulation of railroads. The growth of motor and water carriers has been heavily subsidized by public investments in facilities such as highways and waterways. The Corps of Engineers subsidizes inland water transport by permitting "any boat or barge operation . . . [to] pass through enormously expensive lock systems free of user charges."[25] One authority, James C. Nelson, estimates that misallocation of freight among the major transport modes because of irrational pricing policies fostered by outmoded regulatory practices adds at least $5 billion a year to freight costs.[26]

Aviation

The history of the air transport industry has been one of remarkable progress in speed, comfort, and size of planes, with progress primarily identified with speed. The large piston engine aircraft doubled the speed of the earlier DC-3. The first generation of jet-powered planes in the early 1960's again doubled operating speeds. The Boeing 747, the first of the second-generation jets entering into the commercial market, has somewhat greater speeds than the earlier jets, while the proposed supersonic air transport plane, the SST,

[24] "The Rail Problem in Perspective," *The Conference Board Record,* September 1969.

[25] *Counterbudget, op. cit.,* p. 162.

[26] *The New York Times,* November 8, 1971, p. 16.

would double the speed of the Boeing 747. A redesigned SST equipped to cope more effectively with problems such as sonic boom may gain acceptance and Federal support before 1980, at least for transoceanic trips. Yet defeat of the proposed Federal appropriation of an additional $300 million for SST development in the early 1970's marks a significant departure from the identification of progress with speed attained through technological advances in air travel.

Reductions in air fares in the coming decade can be expected to generate more increases in air travel by attracting persons who would otherwise not travel, rather than by diverting passengers from other transport modes. The wide-bellied "air bus" type of aircraft—the Boeing 747, Douglas DC-10, and Lockheed L-1011—have considerably greater seating capacity than the standard jets, an advantage that should permit them to operate at lower costs when filled reasonably close to capacity. The Boeing 747, for instance, can carry between 300 and 400 passengers, about double the capacity of the earlier large jets. The anticipation of reductions in the cost of air travel in the 1970's is evident in the projection that by 1980 70 percent of all air travel passengers will represent flying on leisure-oriented trips rather than for business purposes.[27]

While air passenger travel has mushroomed in the past decade, air freight is still in its infancy. The introduction of jet freighters with greater payload capacity than the present all-freight planes, such as the Boeing 747F, the freighter version of the 747 passenger aircraft, is expected to increase the volume of air freight by reducing rates. As with the railroads, growth of containerization would increase the attractiveness of air freight by linking it more closely with other freight carriers. Even with these advances, the higher cost of air freight can be expected to stress its role as transportation for high value, low-bulk commodities with a premium on quick delivery.

General aviation, travel in smaller planes owned by business firms or by private individuals, generates more than a fourth of all traffic at many of the nation's large airports. Civilian planes in the general aviation fleet increased from 76,500 in 1960 to 131,000 by 1969, and they are projected to grow to 225,000 by 1980.[28] The typically smaller and less well-equipped general aviation aircraft add more than proportionately to airport traffic congestion since they are slower and require more time to take off and land than the larger and more sophisticated craft.

---

[27] L. F. Huck, "The Airlines—Expanding Our Travel Sphere," in *Land: Recreation and Leisure,* 1970, p. 43. According to the Air Transport Association, 50 percent of all air travel is currently leisure-oriented.

[28] U.S. Federal Aviation Agency, *Aviation Forecasts: Fiscal Years 1970–1981,* 1970, p. 33.

Since the giant jets carry many more persons per plane than the smaller craft, they reduce the traffic control problems in the air. Correspondingly, the air buses add to congestion on the ground. Most airports are still far from well-equipped to handle the 300 or more passengers and the 500 or more pieces of luggage that are discharged from a single 747, and many airports are located at distances that require time-consuming and costly trips, often by slow buses, to and from the terminals. Much of the speed advantage of the new jets is offset by congestion and delays at airports or in arriving at and departing from them.

To cope with these problems, the Airport and Airways Development Act of 1970 authorizes Federal aid of $2.5 billion over a 10-year period for a long-range program to improve airport ground and traffic control facilities. The program is to be financed by revenues derived from user charges for airport facilities to be paid into a trust fund similar to the Highway Trust Fund. An important departure in this legislation, a departure reflecting current environmental concerns, is the emphasis in airways planning on taking into account the effects of air travel and airport location on the surrounding environment. So, according to the 1970 Act, no airport project application can be approved unless the governor of the state submitting the application certifies that the project complies with existing air and water quality standards.

Water Transport and Pipelines

In the next decade the United States will be faced with the choice of abandoning its historic role as a major merchant marine power or undertaking to develop and subsidize the utilization of the technology for asserting this role. To illustrate the problem, as recently as 1950 almost 40 percent of the U.S. seaborne cargo tonnage was carried in ships of American registry. By the end of the 1960's this proportion had declined to 5 percent.[29] Roughly three-fourths of the American merchant ships are now more than 20 years old, and most of this fleet will become obsolete in the next few years. The Administration's ten-year program for modernizing the merchant fleet is intended to maintain a role for an American merchant marine by subsidizing the cost of building 300 ships in the next decade, ships that will make use of modern technology to enable them to become more nearly competitive on the high seas.

Standardized designs are widely believed to hold the key to the construc-

---

[29] *Statistical Abstract, 1971*, p. 561.

tion of ships that can carry combinations of standard, "roll on" freight, and containerized cargo. These ships would make use of heavily automated systems, such as the LASH gantry crane to pick up preloaded barges or lighters, stack them in cells throughout the ship, and unload them back in the water on arrival at their destination. As in the case of the railroads and air freight, containerization offers much of the potential for growth of the American merchant marine. With containerization, even such a hard-to-handle commodity as natural gas can become "intermodal cargo" by utilizing newly developed techniques to cool and liquify natural gas and transport it in special containers by ship, rail, or even truck. However, much of the case for maintaining a large American-built, registered and operated fleet, according to the advocates of this policy, rests on its significance in the event of a national defense emergency. On this basis, the American merchant marine has been assisted both by a Federal construction subsidy and by a subsidy to offset much of the differential between operating costs on American and other ships.

The prospective requirements for oil pipeline construction reflect the growth in consumption of petroleum products. Substitution of other sources of power for the internal combustion engine, such as steam or electric automobile, could slow down this growth. Greater demand for natural gas as a clean, nonpolluting fuel that can be shipped by pipeline, rail, or in special ships could also contribute to expansion in pipeline traffic and facility needs in the 1970's.

In spite of the national concern with safety, pollution, and congestion, few of the more radical departures in transportation technology since World War II, other than the jet aircraft engine, have come into everyday use during the past decade. The innovations that have tended to gain acceptance are those that fit in with the existing technologies, the existing investments in facilities, and the existing service and distribution systems. The Wankel engine—lighter, smoother, and leaving more room under the hood for pollution control devices—or the catalytic afterburners for pollution control are instances. Where developments that are technically and economically feasible have major limitations in fitting in with the prevailing systems, as in the case of the Metroliner, potentials have only been partially realized. The more far-reaching departures such as hydrofoils, hovercraft, and similar innovations, so far, have had little more than a marginal effect on transportation within the United States. Similarly, the short-takeoff (STOL) and vertical-takeoff (VTOL) planes are just beginning to arrive at the cost levels and carrying capacity required to make them important candidates for short-haul traffic within densely populated urban corridors.

The problems that can be expected to provide the incentive for new departures in transportation technology are summed up by the efforts early in 1973 to implement plans for meeting the 1977 deadlines for complying with the standards for the abatement of air pollution, largely the abatement of hydrocarbons given off by motor vehicles, in the Clean Air Act of 1970. Complying with these standards in Los Angeles with the present motor vehicle technology, to cite a strong case, was estimated to involve cutbacks in automobile use ranging as high as 80 percent, cutbacks sufficiently severe to require gasoline rationing and the conversion of some commercial vehicles to other fuels such as natural gas.[30] Cities such as New York, Chicago, or Washington would face similar, if less drastic, prospects in attempting to meet the Federal requirements. For these reasons, the large cities were given a two-year extension in their implementation deadlines. Cutbacks in automobile use of these magnitudes could mean a virtual paralysis of economic and social life in metropolitan regions that have grown and flourished on the basis of unrestricted access to automobiles. These prospects reflect the high cost of continuing past choices in minimizing the alternatives to the internal combustion engine.

IV

National goals in transportation are made up of a range of public and private proposals for adapting to the changes that have affected the movement of people and goods. At one end of the spectrum is the frequently expressed interest in assigning a larger role to the alternatives to the private automobile, a concern summed up in President Nixon's statement that "until we make public transportation an attractive alternative to private car use, we will never be able to build highways fast enough to avoid congestion."[31] National objectives are also reflected in the recent legislation requiring highway and airport planners to take into account the ecological and economic consequences of their planned developments. At yet another end of the spectrum shaping goals in transportation are the millions of consumers

---

[30] *The New York Times,* Sunday, January 14, 1973, Section I, p. 1.
[31] *The Wall Street Journal,* December 24, 1971, p. 16.

choosing among the presently available alternatives in their dollar spending to continue, but with more qualifications than in the past, the automobile's sovereignty in passenger transportation.

The diverse objectives included in the transportation goal are grouped into four broad categories:

1. Economic efficiency in speed and convenience of movement for a given cost.
2. Optimal use of environmental resources as reflected in land use, air pollution, and noise levels.
3. Improvements in safety to minimize the loss of human life and property.
4. Support of other national objectives as in environmental protection, urban development, or national defense.

The extent to which these objectives will be implemented can be expected to show up in the distribution of freight and passenger traffic in the coming decade. Table 8–4 presents a projected distribution of traffic by mode which illustrates the kinds of changes implied by the objectives for the transportation goal.

Table 8-4   Estimated Distribution of Intercity Traffic, by Type of Carrier, 1969 and Projected 1980

Component	1969	Projected 1980
Total intercity freight (in billion ton-miles)	1895	2772
Percent moved by		
Rail	40.9%	40.0%
Truck	21.3	22.1
Inland waterways	16.0	14.8
Oil pipelines	21.7	22.7
Air freight	0.2	0.5
Billion passenger miles by		
Private automobile	977	1340
Public carrier	161	383
Percent of public carrier traffic moved by		
Rail	7.6%	9.0%
Buses	15.5	10.2
Inland waterways	2.4	1.5
Airways	74.5	79.3

The major shifts implied by the projected traffic distribution for 1980 are the ending in the decline in the role of the railroads, both passenger and freight, and a marked increase in the proportion of intercity passenger traffic moved by public carriers rather than by private automobiles. In effect, the volume of traffic accounted for by the railroads would increase substantially as the sharp reductions in their share of the traffic characterizing the post-World War II period came to an end. The estimates take it for granted that consumers' preference for their automobiles will remain as a major force to be dealt with in transportation planning in the next decade. However, intercity travel by private automobile in the projections is estimated to increase by half as compared with a growth of over 100 percent for the public carriers. Similarly, while the volume of air passenger travel is expected to increase, the spectacular rise in the share of the passenger traffic moved by air is projected to slow down as Metroliner-type trains come to move a sizable proportion of the passenger traffic in the larger urbanized megalopolitan concentrations ranging up to approximately 300 to 400 miles.

According to a report recently released by the U.S. Department of Transportation, upgrading the present Washington-New York-Boston main line sufficiently to allow trains to cruise at 150 miles per hour on the present right-of-way would involve an investment of $1.6 billion. An alternative plan utilizing an entirely new right-of-way designed to permit speeds of up to 200 miles an hour is estimated to cost $2.6 billion for the Washington-Boston route and $20 billion over a 10-year period for similar facilities in the 10 other high density corridors in which the potential ridership is considered sufficiently high to support this mode of mass travel.[32] These systems would push at the present limits of the conventional wheel-rail technology. Potential systems which depart from this technology include a tracked air cushion vehicle running on a thin cushion of air in a guideway designed for speeds of 300 miles an hour, and a more speculative gravity vacuum transit system utilizing a cylindrical vehicle travelling on rails in a downward sloping tube to enable gravity to accelerate the vehicles' speed. Utilizing the present technology to automate freight yards and to control freight movements, and to modernize as well as enlarge the supply of freight cars to take advantage of the possibilities of greater speeds, larger cars and containerization is estimated to involve capital outlays reaching over $2.5 billion a year by 1980. Halting the railroads' loss of freight traffic would also entail changes such as those in the proposed Transportation Regulatory Modernization Act of 1971 to allow domestic freight carriers greater flexibility in pricing their services.

[32] U.S. Department of Transportation, *Cost Analyses for NECTP*, Vol. I., *High Speed Ground Modes*, 1969.

The other major option in slowing down the growth of intercity automobile traffic is expanded air travel. By 1980 it is anticipated that the jumbo jet and air bus will come into general use on the major domestic routes, and that the short-takeoff (STOL) and vertical-takeoff (VTOL) aircraft will be in everyday use as short-haul planes. In the next 5 years the Pan American Airline, for instance, plans to inaugurate "Metroflight" service in the Boston–Washington route. The Metroflight would be competitive with the high-speed passenger trains as well as other types of planes. It would make use of advances in helicopter technology, advances initially developed by the military, such as a civilian version of the Sikorsky S65.[33] The STOL and VTOL craft would make use of existing airports. They would also create a need for more downtown heliports, and for new systems of air-traffic control and guidance adapted to the larger capacity of the new helicopters, aircraft capable of seating more than 40 to 50 passengers. Small downtown "metroports" would relieve congestion at the larger airports, solve the airport access problem, and significantly shorten door-to-door trip time.[34] Proposals to stretch out present ground facilities to accommodate more conventional planes and luggage as well as the STOL and VTOL craft include "moving sidewalks" that reduce the strain of walking long distances in airports dominated by the sprawl pattern of construction and underground trains connecting a series of terminals, as in the new Houston airport. More far-reaching departures include a plan to conserve space and reduce noise and pollution in surrounding urbanized areas by constructing airports in floating tables of steel and concrete removed from densely populated areas. The capital costs for aircraft allowing both for traffic growth and technological advances are estimated at $3.6 billion a year by 1980, nearly double the annual level at the end of the 1960's. Cost for airport and airways construction, following the Federal Aviation Agency's forecast, together with innovations in air navigation and traffic control such as a fog disposal system are estimated at $1.4 billion a year over the next decade.

Legislation such as the Clean Air Act of 1970 can be expected to accelerate research and development in alternatives to the internal combustion engine for automobiles, trucks, and buses. By 1980 this R & D is expected to have become sufficiently translated into technically and economically feasible products so that one-third of the purchases of new automobiles, and one-fifth of those for trucks and buses, will be equipped with new power sources such as steam engines, electric batteries, and gas or, in the case of trucks and buses, with the gas turbine engine. The remaining automobiles would typically be lighter and smaller vehicles utilizing lead-free gasoline

[33] *The Washington Post,* June 3, 1970, June 10, 1970

[34] T. Alexander, "Wheels-Up Time for STOL," *Fortune Magazine,* November, 1968.

and they would frequently be powered by Wankel engines. The higher costs of automobiles because of these improvements in pollution control together with widespread adoption of automobile user charges to cover more of the costs of making use of streets and off-street parking space in cities, often in the form of auto commuter taxes, are likely to substantially restrict auto use in the large central cities in the next decade.

**Table 8-5   Estimated Expenditures for the Transportation Goal,
1969 and Projected 1980
(in millions of 1969 dollars)**

Mode	Estimated Expenditures in 1969[a]	Projected Expenditures in 1980
Motor vehicles	$53,800	$87,400
Automobiles	33,900	53,400
Trucks, buses, and trailers	7,500	12,400
Highways	12,400	21,600
Railroads	1,500	5,100
High-speed passenger systems	—	2,200
Other facilities and improvements	1,500	2,900
Air transportation	2,600	5,000
Aircraft	1,900	3,600
Airport and navigation facilities	700	1,400
Oil pipelines	200	500
Water transportation	1,400	2,500
Transportation research and development	1,900	3,800
Total	61,400	104,300
Expenditures as percent of the GNP	6.6%	7.5%

[a] *Survey of Current Business,* July, 1970, p. 540; *Motor Truck Facts and Figures,* 1970, pp. 3, 17; Interstate Commerce Commission, *Transportation Economics,* April, 1971, p. 6; *Aerospace Facts and Figures,* 1970; *Appendix, The Budget of the United States Government, Fiscal Year 1971,* 1970, pp. 346, 738; National Science Foundation, *Research and Development in Industry, 1969,* pp. 44, 54; *Statistical Abstract, 1971,* pp. 536, 550.

Expenditures for the transportation goal in 1980 are listed in Table 8–5. The estimates refer to public and private outlays for transportation facilities for plant, equipment, and right-of-way, and also for the R & D that would outmode much of the present transportation technology.

Spending for transportation facilities would increase markedly in the next decade even if the present traffic patterns and technology were to remain as they were in the early 1970's. More trucks, freight cars, pipelines, and air-craft are required because of growth in output and in economic activity. Rising levels of personal income together with growth in the population of young adults would assure a steady expansion in air travel and in the num-ber of automobiles in use. In 1969, spending for transportation facilities and R & D amounted to 6.6 percent of the GNP. If this spending amounted to the same proportion of the close to $1.4 trillion dollar GNP expected in 1980, the comparable outlays for transportation would rise to $92 billion, about $12 billion less than the costs projected for the transportation goal.

What the projections provide are benchmarks for illustrating changes in prospective transportation outlays that would follow from present efforts to shift priorities to obtain a transportation system assigning a greater weight than at present to the social costs of different types of transportation serv-ices as well as to their private costs. A shrinking proportion, but still more than half of the outlays, are accounted for by automobiles, 51 percent in the projections as compared with 55 percent in 1969. However, the large per-centage increases are listed for the alternatives to the present motor vehi-cles-highway complex. Railroads, air transport including STOL and VTOL craft and R & D to develop new transport modes and improvements in the existing types of automobiles are instances. In the water-transportation esti-mates the projections allow for the Maritime Administration's program for building 300 merchant ships in the next 10 years—a development expected to raise the share of waterborne American export-import commerce hauled in ships of United States registry to 30 percent of the total by the end of the decade. These outlays would involve continuation of present subsidies for ship construction.

The funds for financing the construction of a better balanced transporta-tion system could be made available by transforming the present Highway Trust Fund and Airport Development Trust Fund into a Transportation Trust Fund to be used for all domestic public transportation facilities in-cluding urban mass transit. One state—Maryland—has already taken steps to establish a statewide comprehensive transportation trust fund to be sup-ported by revenues from highway user taxes, aviation charges, and motor vehicle fees, for example. The fund will be used to finance the development

of highways, ports, airports, and mass-transit facilities.[35] The establishment
of a Transportation Trust Fund in connection with the Administration's proposed special revenue sharing program in transportation would provide state
and local governments with options in making use of their transportation tax
receipts that extended beyond the choices of building more highways and
airport facilities. Transforming the present separate trust funds into a Transportation Trust Fund could substantially increase the likelihood that spending more dollars for transportation would facilitate, rather than retard, the
pursuit of national goals.

[35] *The Wall Street Journal,* August 18, 1971, p. 15. Legislation enacted in 1973 provides for the limited use of Highway Trust Fund revenues to finance urban mass
transit facilities during the next three years. See *The New York Times,* August 14,
1973, p. 17.

Chapter Nine

GOALS IN RESEARCH
AND DEVELOPMENT:
NATIONAL SECURITY
OBJECTIVES AND
CIVILIAN SOCIETY R & D

I

Our long-term goals in research and development are to improve men's lives, to add to knowledge, to meet increasing domestic and international economic needs, and to protect the nation's security. Changes in national priorities have transformed the research revolution of the early 1960's into the research depression of the past few years. A greater role for social, economic, and environmental priorities in research and development can play an important role in reversing this decline in the 1970's.

R & D contributes to national economic growth and to the growth patterns of individual regions and industries. Support for research and development is tied in with the nation's choice of goals in many different ways. R & D makes it possible to adopt new goals that previously would have been regarded as unattainable. The decision to undertake the manned lunar landings in the 1960's is probably the classic case. Many of the nation's goals are concerned with remedying the unintended and undesirable by-products of technological advance. Control of pollution in its many guises is an instance. Moreover, the country's priority choices influence the volume of R & D since research figures more prominently in the pursuit of some goals (e.g., space or health) than in others such as urban development. To some, national goals affect the utilization of research resources to such an extent that they "can provide a frame of reference to establish priorities to which science policy can respond in the allocation of resources, and program selection and emphasis."[1]

Changes in public attitudes toward the priorities implied in R & D programs is a major reason why the R & D prosperity in the first half of the 1960's was followed by the R & D depression in the last part of the decade. The "technological renunciation" involved in the defeat of the proposed Federal appropriation of an additional $300 million for development of the supersonic air transport plane in 1970 illustrates the changes in public attitudes toward research and development. The potential contribution of the SST to technological and economic advance was insufficient to outweigh the

---

[1] Science Policy Research Division, Congressional Research Service, Library of Congress, *Science Policy: A Working Glossary,* prepared for the Committee on Science and Astronautics, U.S. House of Representatives, 1972, p. 17.

anticipated enviromental side effects such as noise and atmospheric pollution.

There has been widespread debate, in and out of the scientific community, over what is regarded as a probable or desirable reordering of priorities in the next 10 years. The physical and social decay of the cities, the chaos of our mass transit systems, the prevalence of enviromental pollution, and the inadequacies of our health and educational systems have been the subjects for general discussion and concern. It appears to many scientists and others that the thrust that was given to research and development in the early 1960's by the pursuit of defense and space goals can find an equivalent in the 1970's in a far-reaching expansion of R & D that is applied to seeking more adequate solutions to these pressing social, economic, and environmental problems. One by-product of this emphasis, it is widely believed, would be to generate job opportunities in new fields for scientists and engineers including new graduates trained to enter these fields.

Continued erosion of support for R & D could impede progress in the efforts to devise new technology for recycling waste products into economically useful materials, to uncover the causes of schizophrenia or sickle cell anemia, and it could facilitate chronic imbalances in the balance of payments as other nations forge ahead in the high-technology industries. A reversal of the R & D recession characterizing the early 1970's implies a change in emphasis in the nation's research and development effort. These potentials are illustrated by the scenario for the R & D goal that assumes a continuation of defense, space, and atomic energy research while allowing for rapid increases in research devoted to civilian-sector needs and basic research. The changes included in the standard for the R &D goal are estimated to involve an increase in spending for R & D from $27 billion to $49 billion in 1980 (in 1969 dollars).

II

The growth and decline in the nation's R & D effort in the 1960's was dominated by two elements. One was the reversal in the priorities assigned to space and, to a lesser extent, to national-defense R & D. The other was the continued expansion of nonfederally funded, largely industry-financed, research and development. The mushrooming of spending for R & D in the first part of the decade primarily reflects the impact of the space program coupled with rapid growth in industry-financed R & D. The slowdown in R & D outlays after 1966 stems from large decreases in space and later in defense research and development unaccompanied by offsetting increases in Federal support for other research and development objectives. As a result, total R & D expenditures in the United States, public and private, fell from 3 percent of the GNP in 1964 to slightly more than 2.6 percent of the far larger GNP in 1971.[2]

The predominance of defense and space objectives in the expansion and contraction of the research and development effort in the past decade is summarized in Table 9–1.

Table 9-1   Changes in R & D Expenditures, 1960 to 1970[a]
(in millions of dollars)

Type of R & D	Changes in Outlays Between		
	1960 and 1966	1966 and 1969	1969 and 1971
Total R & D	$8536	$3913	$ 671
Federally funded R & D	5240	921	143
Defense R & D	40	1671	−1091
Space R & D	4495	−2015	210
Nonfederally funded R & D	3296	2992	814

[a] National Science Foundation, *National Patterns of R & D Resources, Funds and Manpower in the United States, 1953–1972*, NSF 72–300, 1971, Tables B-5, B-9, pp. 32, 34.

Over five-sixths of the increase in Federal R & D outlays between 1960 and 1966, 86 percent, was accounted for by one program, the space program. The research cutbacks after 1966 were set in motion by a $2 billion dollar decrease in Federal spending for the space program between 1966 and 1969 followed by a decline of about half that amount in defense-related R & D between 1969 and 1971. The decline in spending for the space program in the late 1960's was sufficiently large, about $650 million a year, that if it had continued, the space program would have been terminated by the middle 1970's. Because of these cutbacks, Federally financed R & D spending, after adjusting for inflation, declined at an annual rate of 4 per-

[2] National Science Foundation, *National Patterns of R & D Resources, Funds and Manpower in the United States, 1953–1972*, NSF 72–300, December, 1971, p. 1.

cent between its 1967 peak and 1971.[3] The severity of the decline in Federal outlays for space and national defense research and development was mitigated by large increases in nonfederally financed R & D in the last years of the decade and by modest absolute but large percentage increases in Federal R & D spending for civilian sector needs. Health and pollution control research are instances.

Three closely related sets of forces contributed to the R & D depression at the end of the decade. One was the growing skepticism about the "Science —the Endless Frontier" approach to research and development—the belief that it was self-evident that the new knowledge or technology gained by a greater expenditure for R & D would benefit mankind.[4] A second stemmed from the rapid upsurge of interest in technology assessment, in techniques for anticipating and appraising the indirect and often-unintended consequences of technological advance. By underscoring the negative as well as the positive contributions of research and development, technology assessment served to restrain enthusiasm for projects such as the SST which would have received greater public support if only their technological potential had been taken into account. For another consideration, as disenchantment with the prolonged and unpopular war in Vietnam became common, the disenchantment came to encompass R & D as part of what had come to be known as the "military-industrial complex."

The end result of these changes in outlook in a period of rising government budgets and inflation is reflected in a decline in R & D expenditures from 12 percent of total Federal budget outlays in 1965 to 9 percent in 1969 and to 7 percent in 1972.[5] By mid-1971, unemployment and underemployment had become a serious problem for many scientists and engineers for the first time in well over a decade although their unemployment rate, about 3 percent, still lagged considerably behind the comparable rates of close to 5 percent or more for blue collar workers. The Department of Labor reported in 1971, for example, that some 50,000 to 65,000 scientists and engineers were unemployed.[6] The highest unemployment rates were listed for engineers who had previously been employed in connection with space program activities. To some, to quote Dr. Philip Handler, then President of the National Academy of Sciences, it appeared at the time that the "national apparatus for the conduct of research is not yet dismantled, but is is falling in-

[3] *Annual Report of the Council of Economic Advisors,* 1972, p. 127.

[4] Vannevar Bush, *Science: The Endless Frontier,* National Science Foundation, NSF 60–40, 1960.

[5] Derived from National Science Foundation, *An Analysis of Federal R & D Funding by Budget Function,* NSF 71–25, 1971, Tables C–1, C–2, pp. 81 ff.

[6] *Manpower Report of the President,* 1972, p. 121.

to shambles."[7] To others, the problem was that "science today is perceived as defense-oriented, university-oriented, and industry-oriented. This is not good enough."[8]

III

The recent concern with cutbacks and priorities in research and development grows out of developments affecting R & D within the United States. Lesser attention has been given to the international aspects of R & D in fostering cooperation between nations and as a factor influencing the economy's balance of payments problems.

Differences in definition, in the scope of inflation, and shifts in exchange rates mean that comparisons of R & D expenditures in different countries involve a considerable degree of imprecision. However, to illustrate the magnitudes involved, Table 9–2 lists the percentage of the GNP made up of R & D outlays in selected leading industrial nations in the late 1960's.

Table 9-2   Estimated Expenditures for Research and Development as a Percentage of the GNP, Selected Nations, 1971[a]

Country	R & D Expenditures as Percent of the GNP
Union of Soviet Socialist Republics	3.0%
United States	2.6
United Kingdom	2.1
Germany, Federal Republic	2.0
Japan	1.8

[a] National Science Board, *Science Indicators 1972*, 1973, p. 102.

[7] Testimony, Dr. Philip Handler, in *Toward a Science Policy for the United States,* Report of the Subcommittee on Science, Research, and Development, Committee on Science and Astronautics, U.S. House of Representatives, 1970, p. 29.

[8] Testimony, Mr. William D. Carey, *ibid.,* p. 26.

Judging from these data, two advanced industrial nations spend roughly equivalent proportions of widely diverging gross national products for research and development. They are the United States and the USSR. The United Kingdom and West Germany spend a somewhat lower percentage. The country that experienced the relatively greatest advance in the manufacture of technology-intensive products in the 1960's—Japan—spent only two-thirds the percentage of its far smaller GNP for R & D in 1971 than was the case for the United States. The defense-space-nuclear trilogy comprised over 80 percent of the government outlay for R & D in the United States in the late 1960's as compared with 33 percent for the United Kingdom and 17 percent in West Germany.[9] The comparable proportions in the Soviet Union and in Japan are unknown.

The benefits of research and development extend beyond the borders of the performing nation. Basic research findings are generally available for all nations to use and this has been increasingly true of applied research other than in national security areas. R & D facilitates international cooperation in projects such as the International Geophysical Year and through the international communities of scientists attached to a common discipline.

Aside from these contributions to knowledge and to national security, R & D also fosters competition in the export of high-technology products and in the export of advanced technology as well. When R & D spending in the United States was at its peak, about 1967, it was contended that a research and development gap was emerging between the United States and other industrialized nations. It was argued that advances in technology in the United States (e.g., in computer technology), had so far outdistanced other nations as to encourage a far-reaching penetration of their economies by American corporations through control of markets in these high technology fields or the establishment of subsidiaries or branch plants abroad. In recent years, as the pace of the R & D effort has slackened and balance of payments difficulties have come to constitute a recurring problem, it has come to be widely believed that other nations have caught up and reversed the American lead in technology in world markets. Our previously favorable balance of trade in technology-intensive products with Western Europe and Japan, according to testimony before the House Committee on Science and Astronautics, declined from $2 billion in 1962 to $700 million by the end of the decade.[10]

---

[9] U.S. Office of Management and Budget, *Special Analyses, The Budget of the United States Government, Fiscal Year 1971*, 1970, p. 266; Communities Europeenes, *Comite de Politique Economique a Moyen Terme, Le Financement Publique la Recherche et du Development dans les Pays de la Communitie, 1967–1970*, Brussels, May 1970.

[10] Testimony, Mr. Patrick E. Haggerty, in *Toward A Science Policy for the United States, op. cit.*, p. 32.

IV

The critical element in revitalizing the nation's R & D effort, to many observers, involves creating new demands for engineers and scientists and markets for the firms that employ them in seeking better solutions to civilian sector problems. R & D applied to these problems could make a significant contribution to national well-being. The effects of such a shift for R & D expenditures and employment in the 1970's will depend on the scale of the increases and on the importance attached to the development component in the research and development related to environmental, health, social, and urban problems.

The Federal Government's support for research and development has been a strategic factor in generating requirements for scientific manpower. Federal funding was responsible for the employment of over half—55 percent—of all scientists and engineers primarily engaged in R & D at the peak of the research and development effort about 1966 or 1967. In keeping with the allocation of the Federal Government's support, programs in pursuit of national defense and space objectives employed about 80 percent of the scientists and engineers, excluding those employed within the Federal Government itself, who were at work in Federally supported programs.[11]

Much of the growth in the Federal Government's spending for research and development, and the manpower requirements generated by these expenditures, has been because of the development part of R & D. Recently, the Federal support for development has exceeded that for basic and applied research by more than a three-to-two margin. The Federal support for development is more heavily concentrated than the spending for research. In 1972, for instance, the national defense, space, and atomic energy programs are estimated to account for more than nine-tenths—93 percent—of all Federal outlays for development.[12]

---

[11] Robert L. Aronson, *Federal Spending for Scientist and Engineer Employment,* U.S. Department of Labor, Bureau of Labor Statistics, Bulletin No. 1663, 1970, p. 2.

[12] U.S. Office of Management and Budget, *Special Analyses, The Budget of the United States Government, Fiscal Year 1972,* pp. 275, 276.

The massive development projects associated with the introduction of new weapons systems, nuclear reactors, space craft or launch vehicles have few counterparts, if any, in coping with urban blight, environmental pollution and deterioration, or the inadequacies of the nation's mass-transit systems. For example, there has been a wave of interest in new technology for the mass production of low-cost housing and housing components. The experience with Operation Breakthrough has symbolized the translation of this interest into a development program. The Department of Housing and Urban Development, the sponsor of Operation Breakthrough, is estimated to have spent $56 million for R & D in the 1972 fiscal year, including $34 million for development. This $34 million outlay amounted to slightly more than one-third of 1 percent of the $9.6 billion total which the Federal Government expected to spend for development in 1972. The relatively minor role for substantial development projects in civilian sector R & D helps to explain why only about one-fifth of the Federal Government's R & D budget in fiscal year 1972—21 percent—was allocated to areas other than defense, space, or atomic energy.[13]

Research and development is only one of several activities that can make an important contribution toward achieving civilian sector goals in the next decade. In housing, to cite a leading instance, long-standing obstacles such as the building codes, restrictive practices, and the organization of the industry into a few large and many small firms have often posed barriers to the utilization of the technological advances that have been available. In environmental pollution control, the adoption of more effective measures for assessing the costs of pollution as a charge to be borne by those who generate it is probably as significant as R & D for the effective pursuit of environmental goals enjoying general support. Institutional resistances make it unlikely that technology can be put to use in rebuilding cities, for instance, in the same way it has been used in sending men to the moon. It is also true that, other than in health R & D, our society is just beginning to overcome a reluctance to seek to solve problems through large-scale R & D projects for civilian sector goals. For this reason, large percentage increases in Federal research and development spending for social, economic, and environmental goals in the next few years are consistent with modest increases in dollar spending and in requirements for scientists and engineers.

[13] *Ibid.,* pp. 273, 276.

V

Several recent developments underscore the options that are likely to enter into goals for research and development in the decade ahead. One is the Administration's proposal to spend $6.5 billion over the next 6 years to develop a reusable space shuttle. A second is the proposal in a recent Presidential Message to Congress to spend $700 million in the next year for applied research and development to improve everyday living. A third is suggested by the rapid growth in nongovernmental, largely industry-financed R & D.

The reusable space shuttle is the current version of the large development projects that have been associated with national defense or the space program in the past decade. The shuttle as currently conceived could remain in orbit for up to 30 days, and carry a four-man crew and more than a dozen passengers. The cost per pound of putting a payload in space would be reduced, according to official sources, from a range of $600 to $700 per pound to about $100. The military and scientific advantages of a space vehicle that, in principle, would be reusable in the same sense that an airplane is reusable provides the major rationale for the space shuttle. Another consideration, to quote President Nixon, is that "robust activity in the aerospace industry is healthy for everyone . . . not just in jobs and income but in the expansion of our capabilities in every direction."[14] One of the anticipated consequences of the expansion of activities attributable to the space shuttle program would be the creation of some 50,000 new jobs, about half of them on the West Coast, the region most adversely affected by the recession in the early 1970's in the aerospace industry.[15]

A second line of development for R & D in the 1970's could follow the recommendations in the President's 1972 *Message on Science and Technology* for an increase in research and development spending "to enrich the quality of our lives." The Administration's proposal would have added $700 million for R & D projects to be concentrated in areas where a modest extra effort is "most likely to produce a breakthrough and the breakthrough is most likely to make a difference in our lives."[16] More specifically, the Ad-

[14] *The New York Times,* January 6, 1972, p. 1.

[15] *Ibid.*

[16] White House *Message on Science and Technology; Fact Sheet in Message on Science and Technology,* March 16, 1972.

ministration's plan would have provided additional resources for developing new and more economical clean energy sources, for advances in pollution control technology, for improving emergency health care services, and for similar applied projects. A more current instance of this type of program is suggested by the recent plans for the Federal Government to spend $2 billion a year for R & D to develop new energy resources and to conserve existing ones. The objective of this applied research program would be to make use of R & D to deal with a wide range of civilian needs and also to utilize research and development to lead to the creation of new markets, to offset losses of employment, and to improve the country's trade position.

A third option in utilizing R & D to further the pursuit of national goals could take the form of a more rapid growth in research and development financed by nongovernmental sources, especially private industry. In 1972, industry provided about two-fifths of all the support for research and development in the United States, and universities and nonprofit research organizations supplied about 6 percent of the total.[17] More than in the Federally funded R & D, the industry-financed outlays are concentrated on development, specifically on product development. Like the Federally supported effort, the industry-financed R & D is concentrated in a few areas: in aircraft and missiles, electrical machinery and communications, automobiles and transportation equipment, and chemicals and allied products. These industries, other than automobiles and transportation equipment, also account for the bulk of the Federally funded R & D performed by industry.

The industry-financed effort, like publicly supported R & D, can contribute to social needs such as improving transportation and communications services or increasing standards of living. The diffusion of this R & D effort to include a greater allocation of resources to the technologically less-sophisticated industries such as textiles or construction could increase the contribution of the company-funded R & D in serving national needs. There have been many expectations in the past, in industry and in government, that the company-supported R & D might be used to transfer technology developed in the defense and space programs to civilian uses as in health or mass transit. Examples of this type of activity include a company known for its development of bombsights and navigational aids that has been engaged in developing and seeking to market a computerized multiphasic health screening system for use in hospitals. Another organization, known for its production of military aircraft and space vehicles, has been involved in utilizing its R & D and systems capability to design a new type of hospital from planning the building to detailing the flow of personal and material traffic once the

[17] Derived from *National Patterns of R & D Resources, 1953–1972, op. cit.,* Table B–5, p. 32.

hospital is in operation. The scope for this type of conversion of R & D capabilities depends, to a large extent, on the changes in priorities and, therefore, in public and private spending patterns that would generate substantial markets in fields such as health, pollution control, or mass transit for the firms that converted their R & D capabilities for use in these areas.

VI

Current goals in research and development imply an emphasis on continuing and accelerating applied research to improve everyday living while also allowing for growth in R & D to expand our knowledge and to protect the nation's security. Achieving these objectives is estimated to involve an increase in R & D outlays, public and private, rising to $49 billion by 1980 (in 1969 dollars). As a claim on resources, measured in terms of GNP, this would represent an increase from 2.9 percent of the GNP in 1969 and 2.6 percent in 1971 to 3.5 percent of the nearly $1.4 trillion GNP anticipated in 1980.

The largest single dollar increase in the projections for the R & D goal is made up of outlays for defense-related R & D. If developments such as the SALT talks were to succeed in leading to a substantial degree of disarmament in the 1970's, a large volume of defense-related research would continue, in part as a kind of insurance as expenditures for conventional forces and the procurement of new weapons systems were declining. This research would include strengthening the technology base essential to the development of new military systems in such fields as electronics or materials research. It would also allow for the development of more specifically military technology including the B-1 aircraft, improved antiballistic missiles systems, underwater surveillance systems, and similar advances. Greater resort to prototype development can be anticipated, that is, a resort to a system in which a number of working test models are made of different weapons systems before a commitment is made to mass produce them. Allowing for these developments, defense-related R & D is projected to increase from $7.5 billion in 1969 to approximately $11 billion by 1980.

The objectives for the space research and technology in the R & D goal follow the recommendations of the space panel of the National Academy of Sciences for a program concentrating on the scientific aspects of space exploration and on practical applications rather than a single massive project such as a manned landing on Mars.[18] This would entail unmanned probes of other planets, especially Venus and Mars, extensive lunar exploration, and research in the use of satellites to improve weather forecasting and tele-communications. Space R & D in the next decade is also likely to include extensive development of an earth orbiting space station ("skylab"), the reusable space shuttle, and work on a small nuclear engine for unmanned probes of other planets and similar applications. With this program, spending for the conduct of space R & D would decline from $4.3 billion in 1969 to $3.3 billion by 1980.

The top priority in nuclear research in the 1970's is expected to be given to a program to develop a liquid-metal fuel-breeder reactor that would stretch the nation's supply of uranium by producing more fuel than it consumed while churning out electricity. The Atomic Energy Commission anticipates expenditures reaching as high as $4 billion to develop the "fast breeder" reactor to the stage of initial everyday use in power plants by the middle 1980's.[19] Toward the end of the 1970's it is expected that research will probably be stepped up to develop the use of the more efficient nuclear "fusion" process for power generation in the place of the present fission systems. The fast breeder reactor and other nuclear energy projects are estimated to increase annual outlays for atomic energy R & D, civilian as well as military, from $1.1 billion in 1969 to $1.6 billion by 1980.

The rapid increases in outlays for the R & D goal are projected to take place in civilian sector areas such as health care, environment and natural resources, transportation, or urban development. Health research in the next decade, as in the past, can be expected to concentrate on seeking the causes and cures of specific diseases such as cancer, heart disease, sickle cell anemia, or venereal disease. More than in the past, health research in the future will be directed at the prevention of illness through environmental health measures, and by improvements in well-being brought about by such measures as improved nutrition and family planning. So far, health R & D has been very largely research. Development projects can be expected to loom larger in health R & D in the future. These could include a chain of community health center development and demonstration projects, including mental health centers, and a number of projects to adapt and encourage the use of modern technology such as the use of computers as an aid in laboratory testing, diagnosis, record keeping and in hospital administration. As one by-product of this interest in development, the use of engineers in the

[18] *The New York Times,* October 1, 1968.
[19] *Science,* April 28, 1972, p. 391.

health field is projected to increase several times over in the coming decade, especially industrial engineers and those specialized in biomedical engineering.

Other candidates in an expansion of R & D to serve civilian sector needs include projects to develop an alternative to the present internal combustion engine, probably one powered by steam, electricity, or fuel cells, and research in oceanography to exploit the potentials from "mining" and "farming" the oceans. The thrust for expansion in R & D related to urban development and intercity ground transportation will frequently follow the lines of large-scale development and demonstration projects. Some of these projects could develop the potentials of high-speed intercity ground transportation reaching speeds of 200 miles an hour or more in the crowded urban corridors such as the Northeastern corridor extending from Boston to Washington. The projections for the R & D goal also allow for the construction of several "new towns" along the lines of the "green belt" towns in the 1930's to demonstrate new techniques in planning, land use, construction, design, and neighborhood organization integrating families from varied social and economic groups in the same community. This type of R & D would expand on the work undertaken by private developers in the 1960's, as in Columbia, Maryland, to experiment with communities of different sizes, locality, and proximity to metropolitan centers. In this way, R & D in the civilian sector would lessen its heavy concern with research alone and come to encompass research, development, testing, evaluation, and dissemination.

The current emphasis on applied research tends to play down the contribution of basic research in adding to knowledge, in seeking solutions for specific problems, and in the education and training of scientists and engineers. The search for more-effective cures for cancer or schizophrenia, or for radically new energy sources, is very likely to involve a substantial effort in basic research. The Federal Government finances about five-eighths of the nation's basic research. After allowing for inflation, there has been an overall 8 percent decrease in Federal support for basic research in the 1968–1972 period.[20] All told, the Federal Government spent $2.6 billion for basic research in 1972. The projections include a 50 percent, or $1.3 billion, increase beyond the 1972 level for the Federal Government's contribution to basic research by 1980, an increase approximately similar to the estimated growth in outlays financed by universities and nonprofit research organizations.

Federally supported research and development frequently leads to new technologies and new knowledge which could be applied in ways that go

[20] *National Patterns of R & D Resources, 1953–1972, op. cit.,* p. 16.

well beyond the immediate mission of the agency sponsoring the R & D. The applications of space R & D in telecommunications are an instance. To encourage the transfer of Federally funded R & D to a wider area outside of government, the National Technical Information Service was set up in the Department of Commerce and the Science Information Exchange at the Smithsonian Institution. Public expenditures to assist in the dissemination and utilization of scientific information amounted to under $200 million in 1969.[21] Assuming these efforts should double by 1980, as the materials to be disseminated increased, they would amount to $400 million. Similarly, the projections include an allowance of $200 million in 1980 for technology assessment research to appraise the indirect and often unanticipated and unintended effects of scientific and technical advance. An assessment of this type would be undertaken regularly in advance of all major Federally financed R & D projects and the assessment would be made public and considered in decisions to undertake, to modify, or not to undertake specific research projects.

The projections of Federal expenditures to achieve the R & D goal by 1980, together with the actual expenditures in these areas in 1969, are listed in Table 9–3. The estimates list public outlays for the conduct of R & D, R & D plant, and for related activities to disseminate scientific information and to assess the consequences of technological advances before they are introduced into everyday use.

The projections for the R & D goal imply a shift in emphasis within the Federally funded R & D effort. Total Federal outlays would increase by $12.3 billion with $11.4 billion of the growth representing greater spending for the conduct of R & D. About $8.5 billion would be made up by a growth in spending for research and development in areas other than defense, space, and atomic energy. Added to the peaceful uses of atomic energy as in the fast breeder reactors or the space satellites utilized in weather forecasting research, by 1980 most of the publicly supported R & D effort would be oriented primarily toward civilian purposes.

The estimates for the R & D goal assume that the privately financed R & D increases by over three-fourths, about the same rate as the Federally supported program. The large percentage increases in industry-financed R & D would take place in industries that currently engage in very little R & D, as in construction or textiles, or in converting R & D capabilities de-

---

[21] This estimate refers to outlays for documentation, reference, and information services, and for symposia and technical meetings. National Science Foundation, *Federal Funds for Research, Development, and Other Scientific Activities, Fiscal Years 1969, 1970, and 1971,* NSF 70–38, 1970, p. 75.

Table 9-3   Estimated Federal Expenditures for Research and Development Goal, 1969 and Projected 1980 (in millions of 1969 dollars)

Expenditures	Actual Expenditures in 1969[a]	Projected Expenditures for R & D Goal in 1980
1. Defense	$ 7,561	$11,000
2. Space	4,279	3,300
3. Atomic energy	1,149	1,550
4. Total 1–3	12,989	15,850
5. Health	1,158	4,200
6. Transportation	154	1,575
7. Agriculture	206	480
8. Environment, natural resources[b]	180	1,350
9. Increase in basic research	—	1,300
10. Other R & D	446	1,795
11. Total, conduct of R & D	15,133	26,550
12. R & D plant	696	1,150
13. R & D information and dissemination	182	400
14. Technology assessment	2	200
15. Total, Federal programs	16,013	28,300

[a] National Science Foundation, *Federal Funds for Research, Development, and Other Scientific Activities, Fiscal Years, 1969, 1970, and 1971,* NSF 70–38, 1970; *An Analysis of Federal R & D Funding by Budget Function,* NSF 7–25, 1971; *Special Analyses, The Budget of the United States Government, Fiscal Year 1970; ibid., 1971.*

[b] Excludes atomic energy research in nuclear energy sources.

veloped initially for defense or space research to civilian sector uses, as in health, pollution control, or mass transit. It is unreasonable to expect the major sources of basic research—the universities and nonprofit research organizations—to finance a large share of their R & D outlays from institutional funds. The erosion of endowments through inflation and the greater demands on these organizations from a variety of sources are likely to pose formidable obstacles. R & D expenditures financed by these organizations are listed as increasing to $2.7 billion by 1980, about two-thirds accounted for by universities. If universities and nonprofit organizations were to spend $2 from Federal sources for every dollar of institutional funds in R & D, they would be spending over $8 billion for research and development by 1980, nearly double their effort in 1972. Table 9–4 lists the sources of funds from all sources for the R & D goal in 1980.

**Table 9-4   Estimated Public and Private Expenditures for R & D Goal,
by Source of Funds, 1969 and Projected 1980
(in millions of 1969 dollars)**

Source of Funds	Expenditures in 1969	Projected Expenditures for R & D Goal in 1980
1. Federal Government	$16,013	$28,300
2. Industry	10,012	17,750
3. Universities and nonprofit research organizations	1,254	2,700
4. Total expenditures	27,279	48,750
5. R & D expenditures as percent of the GNP	2.9%	3.5%

The projections indicate that the outlays required to achieve the R & D goal would involve an expenditure level by 1980 nearly four-fifths greater than in 1969. The non-Federally financed R & D would account for about two-fifths of the total in both years.

An increase in R & D spending of this magnitude would have important implications for the utilization of scientific manpower. In 1969 some 559,000 scientists and engineers (full-time equivalents) accounted for the expenditure of $26.4 billion in public and private funds for the conduct of research and development. This amounted to an average R & D outlay of $47,200 for each scientist and engineer.[22] By 1980, the average R & D out-lay per scientist and engineer is projected to increase to approximately $60,000 (in 1969 dollars) to allow for higher real incomes and for shifts in the fields in which scientists and engineers are employed. On this basis, and deducting the items in the projections for the R & D goal that do not pertain to the performance of research and development, the number of scientists and engineers employed in R & D would increase to over 750,000 by 1980. This would represent nearly a 225,000 increase over the number employed

[22] Derived from *National Patterns of R & D Resources, 1953–1972,* Tables B–5, B–10, pp. 32, 34.

in 1969, and 265,000 more than those employed in 1971. Accordingly, the anticipations of chronic surpluses of scientific manpower in the 1970's must be qualified by taking into account the potential demands that could be generated for scientists and engineers if a high priority were accorded to the pursuit of research and development goals in the decade ahead.

The significant change in the projections for the R & D goal is not so much the estimated growth in dollar outlays as the shift from a concentration on defense and space research to a concentration on the environmental, health, industrial, and social needs of a highly urbanized society. This shift in emphasis, it is anticipated, could make the barriers to continued economic growth arising from pollution and energy shortages loom less large in the next decade than has appeared to be the prospect for the future implied by developments in the recent past.

Chapter Ten

PROTECTION OF
ENVIRONMENTAL QUALITY:
ENERGY SHORTAGES,
POLLUTION ABATEMENT,
AND THE REDEFINITION
OF NATIONAL GOALS

I

Priorities for natural resources in the past decade have come to be dominated more and more by considerations of energy shortages and of environmental quality. Sharply rising costs for petroleum products and periodic power blackouts and brownouts in the urban areas symbolize the emerging energy supply problems. Concern with the environment is evident in such measures as the designation of a separate "Earth Day" in 1970, and in the mass of recent legislation, enacted or proposed, to expand the scope of environmentally oriented legislation or to raise standards for the abatement of air and water pollution. The anticipated impact of these concerns in the next decade is highlighted by the estimate that attaining the objectives included in the environmental quality goal, objectives largely reflecting current legislation, would involve expenditures amounting to $55 billion a year by 1980.

Proposals for coping with environmental deterioration and misuse range from specific abatement measures—devices to control the exhaust emissions from automobiles—to recommendations that economic growth be slowed down to protect the environment or to forestall an emerging crisis threatening to halt the economy's growth in the next century. So, according to Barry Commoner, the changes in technology that have spurred the economy's growth in the past few decades have introduced new products and processes inducing environmental deterioration on a larger scale than was true of the technical advances a generation earlier. The use of detergents in the place of soap is an instance. Similarly, a recent report, the *Limits to Growth,* contends that "if the present growth trends in world population, industrialization, pollution, food production and resource depletion continue unchanged, the limits to growth on this planet will be reached sometime within the next 100 years."[1] To others, the underlying problem is not so much economic growth as the fact that the damages to health, materials, and aesthetics arising from environmental deterioration are seldom taken into account in decisions regarding the use of resources because they do not figure in the costs

[1] D. H. Meadows, et al., *The Limits to Growth,* 1972, p. 23.

and prices of the activities that produce the deterioration. So, to quote a recent Brookings Institution study, "the environment becomes degraded when it is treated as a free resource and when the economic system provides no incentives to use it sparingly."[2]

The environmental quality goal provides a framework for integrating two major components that are closely related to one another. One is made up of programs and objectives in pollution abatement. The other consists of natural resource considerations involving the supplies of energy from fossil fuels and other sources, land use and land conservation, protection of wildlife, and measures to increase the availability of water for irrigation, human consumption, and other purposes. The two components are closely related because developments in each affect the other. Part of the current involvement with the "energy crisis," for instance, arises from the shift from coal to the less abundant but more pollution-free natural gas, and also from the reduction in the miles-per-gallon output obtained from automobile engines because of "add-on" pollution devices installed by the manufacturers. The expenditures in 1969 for the different components that enter into the environmental quality goal are summarized in Table 10–1.

Solid waste disposal was the largest single environmental program at the end of the last decade. However, the substantial increases over the next 5 or 10 years are projected for air and water pollution measures, frequently for programs that were just beginning to emerge in the late 1960's. Concern with providing an adequate supply of energy for industrial and commercial needs as well as home heating and recreational uses over the coming years will also figure prominently in the environmental quality goal. The consequences of implementing the environmental measures can be expected to ramify throughout the economy. As governments move to reduce air and water pollution the actions taken are likely to influence energy use, the location of industrial and commercial establishments, patterns of urban and suburban growth, employment in a number of industries, and the prices of many products both to domestic consumers and in international trade. Since air currents, rivers, and ocean spills traverse international boundaries, the preservation of environmental quality will increase the urgency of cooperation between nations in the coming decade.

[2] R. H. Haveman and I. Gutmanis, "Environmental Quality," in C. L. Schultze, *Setting National Priorities: The 1972 Budget,* 1971, p. 239.

Table 10-1   Estimated Expenditures for the Environmental
Quality Goal in 1969[a]
(in millions of 1969 dollars)

Component	Expenditures in 1969
Pollution abatement	$12,000
Air pollution control	2,170
Motor vehicles	240
Stationary sources	1,730
Other[b]	200
Water pollution treatment	2,990
Municipal	1,740
Industrial	1,250
Solid waste disposal	5,600
Research and development	940
Monitoring and surveillance	300
Natural resources conservation and development	4,085
Land conservation	1,000
Water storage[c]	310
Timber protection and management	600
Outdoor recreation, land acquisition and improvement	900
Fish and wildlife propagation and management	150
Materials stockpile	300
Research and development	825
Energy R & D	525
Other	300
Total	$16,085

[a] U.S. Council on Environmental Quality, *Environmental Quality, Annual Report,* 1970, 1971, 1972; McGraw-Hill Economics Department, *Survey of Business plans for New Plant and Equipment,* 1970; *and Survey of Pollution Control Expenditures,* 1971, 1972; U.S. Office of Management and Budget, *The Budget of the United States Government, Fiscal Year 1971; Special Analyses, The Budget of the United States Government, Fiscal Year 1974;* 1973; *Message to Congress on the Energy Crisis,* April 18, 1973.

[b] Refers to government costs not included in the other items.

[c] Refers to Federal outlays for dams to maintain water flows.

II

Pollution abatement, as it has emerged as a major national problem in the past decade, has come to include a variety of considerations involving degradation of the environment extending from the emission of toxic materials into rivers by industrial plants to a buildup of junked vehicles estimated to have reached a recent peak of between 20 and 40 million vehicles.[3] These considerations are linked with the uses made of the economy's natural resources. They are also closely related to the social and economic problems involved in urban development, since most types of pollution in the United States occur with greater frequency in the urban areas, and especially in the central cities, than elsewhere.

Summing up the national concerns with the environment as shown in legislation and government programs, Table 10–2 indicates the individual elements that have come to figure as the primary sources of pollution requiring public and private controls.

Table 10-2   Major Elements in Pollution in the United States[a]

Air Environment	Water Environment	Earth Environment
Particulates (smoke)	organic wastes including sewage	solid wastes— refuse and garbage, clutter and litter
Sulfur dioxide		
Hydrocarbons	nutrients—nitrogen and phosphorus	
Carbon monoxide	toxic heavy metals	pesticides
		radioactive wastes
Oxides of nitrogen	waste heat from electric power production	noise
Oxidants		

[a] R. U. Ayres, *National Goals as Related to Environmental Quality,* National Planning Association (unpublished), 1971, p. 5.

[3] R. U. Ayres, *National Goals as Related to Environmental Quality,* National Planning Association (unpublished), 1971, p. 33.

The conventional breakdown of the pollution media along lines of the air, water, and earth environments facilitates comparison, but it tends to gloss over important relationships between different types of pollutants. To cite an instance, the wet scrubbers used to remove effluents from stack gases decrease the volume of pollutants in the air, but they do so by diverting the wastes into bodies of water, and they, therefore, increase water pollution. In addition, while the air environment is basically a physical system (i.e., the atmosphere) the water and earth environments are inseparable from the biological organisms that inhabit them. These organisms provide many vital services in protecting the environment including decomposition of dead organisms, recycling of waste materials, flood control, pest control, and recreation and aesthetics.

Air pollution generally results from combustion or other energy conversion processes originating in stationary sources or from the vehicles used to transport people and goods. Stationary sources range from home-heating operations to smelting and refinery installations and large electric power plants. The stationary sources are the primary producers of sulfur dioxide, carbon dioxide, particulates, and the nitrogen oxides. The use of coal and crude oil with a high sulfur content is the largest single source of the air pollution generated from stationary sources. Motor vehicles, or more specifically, the internal combustion engine, have been responsible, in the late 1960's, for about three-fifths of the carbon monoxide emissions, nearly half of the hydrocarbons, and two-fifths of the nitrogen oxides. Motor vehicles also produce over nine-tenths of the lead emissions.[4] Automotive pollutants, and especially unburned hydrocarbons and nitrogen oxides, have been identified as the chief causes of the photochemical "smog" that causes smarting eyes. More significantly, smog has been implicated in cardiovascular and bronchial ailments, including heart disease, lung cancer, emphysema, chronic bronchitis, asthma and other diseases.

Public interest in water pollution has historically focused on sewage treatment, and the primary purpose in treating sewage in the past was the prevention of disease rather than pollution abatement. Ecologists have recently begun to emphasize that treated sewage is a form of fertilizer containing all the elements essential for plant growth, particularly nitrogen and phosphorus. Sewage in the United States has become highly enriched with phosphorus, mainly from detergents. Economic growth and urbanization have brought about a sharp alteration in the natural balances enabling streams to accept additional fertilization, especially phosphates. Urban population concentrations produce wastes in quantities that are too large to be returned to the soil, and they are therefore, usually pumped into the nearest body of

---

[4] *Ibid.*, pp. 14–15. See Chapter Eight.

water. The effects of overfertilization, or "eutrophication," in using up the dissolved oxygen in lakes and slow-moving streams are seen in the conversion of these bodies of water into swamps and bogs. The disappearance of fish from Lake Erie, for example, has been attributed to this process rather than to the discharge of industrial wastes.[5]

Water pollution from industrial sources is generally more toxic than the municipal sewage. Heavy metals such as mercury or arsenic are discharged into waterways largely from industrial sources. Manufacturing establishments in the middle 1960's, to cite the most recent information available, were said to discharge water wastes with a biological oxygen demand, that is, the oxygen needed to decompose the organic wastes, four to five times larger than the demand generated by the entire population in the United States.[6] More recent information suggests that point sources of water pollution, such as municipal and industrial discharges, may frequently be overshadowed in importance by runoff sources such as farms, feedlots, and possibly urban runoff. A survey of water pollution from all of these sources in 1970 reported that approximately three-tenths of the stream miles within the continental United States were polluted. This proportion exceeded two-fifths in the highly industrialized Northeast.[7] The estimate does not include the marine pollution in the ocean from sewer discharges, the dumping of other wastes at sea, or ocean spills from breakups of tankers.

Solid waste disposal illustrates the close connection between pollution and urbanization. An estimated 5.7 pounds of solid wastes per person of the types handled by sanitation departments are reported to be generated daily in urban areas as compared to 3.9 pounds in rural areas. By 1980, the overall per capita figure is expected to increase to a daily average of 8 pounds. In many urban areas, the disposal of solid wastes creates environmental as well as aesthetic hazards since only 100 of the 300 municipal incinerators now in use have adequate air pollution controls.[8] Recycling of solid wastes is regarded as most appropriate for bulky items such as junked cars or old tires. Changes in materials requirements in the steel industry have contributed to a buildup of junked vehicles. Considerations of transport costs and the initial capital outlays pose barriers to extensive recycling of junked vehicles and other heavy materials. For example, giant hammer mills can be used to reduce the steel hulks of junked automobiles to fragments that can be separated magnetically. The large capital outlays involved suggest that it may be

[5] *Ibid.*, pp. 23, 25.

[6] Council on Environmental Quality, *Environmental Quality, Second Annual Report,* 1971, p. 79.

[7] Ayres, *op. cit.*, p. 27.

[8] *Ibid.*, p. 31.

necessary for a single installation to handle all the junked cars in several states. In many cases the costs of transporting the hulks to the mill would probably exceed their scrap value.

Strip and surface mining, largely coal mining, makes up another activity conducted on a large scale that degrades the earth environment. A recent Bureau of Mines study reported that 3.2 million acres of land had been disturbed by strip and surface mining by 1965, with the heaviest concentrations in the Appalachian coal-producing states. Between 1965 and 1970, the number of acres disturbed by stripping doubled, rising from 50,000 to 100,000 acres a year.[9] The increase was largely the result of a greater demand for coal to generate electricity.

The evidence from many sources including the information on solid waste disposal and the pollution of rivers and streams indicates that pollution is as much a problem of urban development as it is a question of natural resources. Air pollution, the Council on Enviromental Quality reports, "hangs more heavily over the inner city than the rest of the urban area."[10] Studies of pollution in 22 metropolitan areas show that the emission densities for carbon monoxide, sulfur dioxide, and particulates are highest in the core city and diminish with distance outward.[11] Similarly, concentrations of pollutants such as particulates in nonurban areas are reported to reach a level half or less than the average in the urban areas. For lead emissions in the air, the largest American cities have a concentration 20 times greater than those in the air over more thinly populated areas.[12]

III

The recent "energy crisis" has underscored the importance of environmental quality considerations along with growth in demand and greater dependence on foreign sources of supply in redefining objectives for developing the nation's natural resources in the decade ahead. Concern with pollution has

[9] See Council on Environmental Quality, *Environmental Quality, Third Annual Report*, 1972, pp. 24–25, 48–49.

[10] *Environmental Quality*, 1971, *op. cit.*, p. 191.

[11] *Ibid.*, p. 194.

[12] *Science*, November 5, 1971, pp. 574–575.

stimulated a search for new and "cleaner" sources of fuel since most of the growth in air pollution in the past two decades has been due to the burning of fossil fuels such as coal or petroleum in homes, motor vehicles, factories, and plants for generating electricity.

An upsurge in energy demand in the United States took place after the middle 1960's. Historically, the increase in energy use has lagged behind the growth in the GNP. From 1930 to 1965, for example, the GNP, in constant dollars, increased at an annual average rate of 3.5 percent. Energy consumption grew by an annual average of 2.6 percent. The price of energy during this period rose less sharply than the overall price level (as measured by the GNP deflator) so that energy became cheaper as compared with most other commodities. Between 1965 and 1970, these relationships became reversed as the economy's output grew by slightly more than 3 percent a year while energy consumption rose at an annual rate of about 5 percent.[13]

Many factors have contributed to the concern with energy shortages that emerged in 1972 and 1973. These include underestimates of future requirements in official and unofficial sources. Some government officials have expressed doubts as to the scope of shortages—petroleum is an instance—and they have tended to believe that the prospective shortages may be overstated by the producing industries as a basis for raising prices or improving their market control. However, the higher priority assigned to pollution abatement has meant that the acceptable domestic supplies of fossil fuels have become more scarce in the face of growing demands for energy. Environmental quality considerations largely explain the recent spurt in demand for natural gas. These same considerations have encouraged a shift to low-sulfur oil from the Middle East, a shift involving greater dependence on sources of supply which can be manipulated, as in 1973 and 1974, for political purposes arising out of the Arab-Israeli conflict. In the same vein, one of the barriers to the construction of the Alaska pipeline has been the expectation that hot oil running through the underground portions of the line would melt the permafrost beneath the tundra. Apprehension over thermal pollution and radioactive wastes are among the causes delaying construction of new plants for generating electricity, especially nuclear power plants. In addition, measures for controlling pollution frequently add to energy requirements. The air-pollution control devices added to the 1973 automobiles, to cite a leading instance, are estimated to increase fuel consumption per automobile by 10 percent.[14] While these short-term effects of the greater weight given to environmental considerations add to the energy crisis, over longer time pe-

---

[13] Council of Economic Advisors, *Annual Report,* 1972, pp. 118–119.
[14] *The New York Times,* April 19, 1973, p. 53.

riods the nation's concern with the growth of pollution may prove to be a major element in developing new energy sources (e.g., solar energy) or new techniques for more economically producing clean energy (e.g., the fast-breeding nuclear reactor).

Over 90 percent of the energy consumed in the United States comes from three sources: coal, natural gas, and petroleum. Coal is the fossil fuel in greatest abundance with American reserves sufficiently large, according to recent Administration estimates, to provide for the nation's energy needs for over a century.[15] However, to quote David Freeman, head of the Ford Foundation's energy studies, "there are two things wrong with coal today. We can't mine it, and we can't burn it."[16] Eighty percent of the coal supply is high in sulfur content. Half of the coal that is mined makes use of surface mining techniques that, if uncontrolled, contribute to environmental degradation and add to water pollution.

Natural gas is the least pollution-prone of the fossil fuels, but reserves of natural gas are considerably less plentiful than coal. Since 1966, for example, natural gas consumption has increased by more than a third while the proven and available reserves have decreased by a fifth.[17] Natural gas, therefore, is the fossil fuel most clearly in short supply in 1972 and 1973, a shortage which the Administration believes has been induced or accelerated by "ill-considered regulation" that has kept prices below their market levels thereby stimulating the demand for natural gas while discouraging the development of new sources of supply.

The shift to low-sulfur petroleum and the greater consumption of oil and gasoline have been responsible for an increase in oil imports, to a large extent from the Middle East, from 19 percent of American petroleum requirements in 1966 to 29 percent by 1972.[18] More immediately, in 1973, in recognition of the greater requirements for petroleum from abroad, the Federal Government suspended all tariffs on imports of petroleum.

In the early 1970's nuclear energy was still only a minor part of the total energy supply. It supplied an estimated 4 percent of the nation's electricity and 1 percent of all energy. The more far-ranging prospects for future growth are summarized by the fact that 70 percent of the new capacity for producing electrical power contracted for in 1972 consisted of capacity for generating nuclear power.[19]

---

[15] *Message to Congress on the Energy Crisis,* April 18 ,1973.

[16] *The New York Times,* April 17, 1973, p. 26.

[17] *Message to Congress on the Energy Crisis, op. cit.*

[18] *Statement,* Darrell M. Trent, Acting Director, Office of Emergency Preparedness, *OEP Release,* April 11, 1973.

[19] *Message to Congress on the Energy Crisis, op. cit.*

The premium placed on speed, inefficiencies in construction and production, and, above all, a way of life stressing the utilization of many energy-using consumer durables contribute to the mushrooming demands for energy in the United States. A reduction in the average speed of automobiles on turnpikes by 20 miles an hour would save from 15 to 20 percent per car in gasoline use.[20] Smaller automobiles with less optional equipment such as air conditioning would lead to a similar result. A greater role from mass transit, especially in the large metropolitan centers, could significantly diminish gasoline use. Improved home insulation and the production of more efficient heating and air conditioning equipment would conserve on the use of electricity, natural gas and oil for heating. The annual energy consumption from all sources in the United States in the late 1960's amounted to almost 4000 BTU's per person.[21] This was about double the consumption level in the nation with the next highest per capita income—Sweden— and approximately four times the per capita consumption in France or Japan. The typical American, to quote *The New York Times,* "floods his home with light . . . He heats rooms until they are hot as ovens. He drives a gas-devouring car for a pack of cigarettes rather than walk a block. There are electric brushes, combs, tie racks, and hair driers . . . . It is this way of life, together with the greater concern with environmental quality, that is the basic source of the energy crisis in the United States."[22]

IV

Progress in pursuing national goals in many areas has depended on the availability of an abundant supply of natural resources. Natural resource considerations in the past have loomed large when crises abroad such as wars or revolutions have posed threats to cut off supplies of raw materials, especially imported minerals. More recently, and with increasing importance, the needs of a growing and highly urbanized society for conserving

---

[20] *Statement,* Darrel M. Trent, *Office of Emergency Preparedness Release,* March 26, 1973. This consideration was on the basis of the 55 mile an hour speed limit introduced in 1973 to save gasoline.
[21] *The New York Times,* April 17, 1973, p. 26.
[22] *Ibid.*

land, storing and distributing water, and providing space and facilities for outdoor recreation have come to define the natural resource requirements which are critical for national well-being.

Allowing for these considerations, it remains true that the American economy depends on imports for many important raw materials. In 1970, for example, the United States imported all of its primary requirements for tin, and more than 90 percent of its aluminum, antimony, cobalt, manganese, and platinum. All told, the United States produced about 24 percent of the world's production of the minerals it used in the late 1960's while it consumed 28 percent.[23] Looking ahead, the National Commission on Materials Policy points out that "it is clearly evident . . . that in the case of a majority of our basic materials, the gap between our [U.S.] requirements and the remaining easily accessible world supplies is widening."[24] Offsetting this dependence on materials from other countries, in the aggregate, raw materials of the types that enter heavily into American imports, other than petroleum products, are probably declining in relative importance in the American and other highly industrialized societies. With technological advance and economic growth, the ratio of raw materials requirements to total output diminishes. For instance, the value of resources output (minerals, timber, and agricultural output) fell from 36 percent of gross product in the United States in 1870 to 21 percent in 1920 and to 12 percent in 1945.[25] While this decline is partially due to the greater availability of substitutes for raw materials, and to increases in the efficiency with which they are used, it is also related to the greater importance of the services component in the economy's output, a component with a low ratio of materials requirements to output. These considerations account for the widespread optimism concerning materials requirements through the early 1970's, an optimism reflected by Wilfred Malenbaum, of the University of Pennsylvania's Wharton School, in his report to the National Commission on Materials Policy that economic growth "is not governed by supply limitations of any specific input materials."[26]

The Administration's proposed reduction in the size of the national strategic stockpile is another indicator of the lesser role assigned to materials requirements in national policy in the past decade. Originally set up to assure

[23] National Commission on Materials Policy, *Toward A National Materials Policy, Basic Data and Issues*, April 1972, p. 4.

[24] *Ibid.*, p. 3.

[25] W. Malenbaum, *Materials Requirements in the United States and Abroad in the Year 2000, Report Prepared for the National Commission in Materials Policy*, 1973, p. 9.

[26] *Ibid.*, p. 2.

an adequate reserve of metals, minerals, rubber, industrial diamonds and other vital materials in the event of war, by 1973 the stockpile's value had grown to $6.7 billion. Contending that "our capability to find substitutes for scarce materials is far greater today than in the past," and as an anti-inflation measure, President Nixon has proposed selling as much as $6 billion worth of materials from the stockpile over the next few years.[27]

Water shortages in many parts of the United States pose more immediate problems than shortages of imported materials, again other than petroleum. In part, water shortages stem from the absence of incentives to encourage economies in the use of water since the charge to users seldom covers the full costs of storing and treating water. The shortages also grow out of jurisdictional entanglements and lack of planning. For instance, 17 western states suffer from chronic shortages of water. Yet, to quote a recent report, "the Southwest has plenty of water," and the shortages would largely have disappeared "if there were appropriate planning to eliminate wasteful habits and undertake appropriate multistate planning for its distribution."[28]

Much of the problem in planning for an adequate supply of water grows out of competing requirements for water for agricultural, residential, industrial, and recreational uses. These multiple uses of water imply that downstream users will frequently be offered water already withdrawn by upstream users for other purposes and then returned to the stream, frequently more polluted because of the withdrawal and use. The different uses and users of water are often in conflict with one another. To cite an illustration, the pollution brought about by discharges of DDT and heavy toxic metals such as lead or mercury into streams and rivers has deleterious effects on the efforts to increase the recreational uses of water for fishing or as bird preserves.

Land, like water, is often used for multiple and competing purposes. These include agriculture, forestry, wilderness areas, and parks, as well as urban open space and sites for roads, homes, factories and shopping centers. Far and away the largest use for land is as farmland and forests. About 1.7 billion acres of land were devoted to these two uses in the late 1960's as compared to about 62 million in cities and highways.[29] The measures taken to conserve land are undertaken primarily by farmers and secondarily by the Federal Government. Nearly a billion acres of land were in need of soil conservation, according to the 1967 Soil and Water Conservation Inventory,

---

[27] *Message to Congress Proposing Stockpile Disposal Legislation,* April 16, 1973.

[28] *The New York Times,* January 17, 1972, p. 17.

[29] U.S. Department of Agriculture, *National Inventory of Soil and Water Conservation Needs, Statistical Bulletin No. 461,* 1971, p. 4.

almost 100 million more than was reported in the previous survey in 1958.[30]

The Federally owned public lands comprise approximately one-third of the nation's land area. This land is used for national parks and wilderness areas, for grazing and timber, for wildlife preserves, and it frequently contains valuable minerals. The public lands contain 35 percent of the country's standing commercial timber. The largest single block of public land is in Alaska, and this land contains the oil-rich North Slope.

Lumber shortages have contributed to the rapidly escalating costs of home construction in the past decade. The higher prices for lumber are partially the result of the increase in demand stemming from residential construction, and they also reflect the slow growth in lumber production in the United States. Production in 1970, some 34 billion board feet, was only about 5 percent more than in 1960.[31] While the lumber industry has been urging that the "allowable" cut of timber in multiple-purpose national forests be increased to ease bottlenecks in the nation's wood supply, conservation-oriented groups have contended that the national forests are "over-logged" with the result that recreational and wilderness needs are downgraded.

The issue of priorities in the use of the public lands has become more pressing because since World War II the land devoted to public recreational facilities including national and state forests and parks has lagged behind the growth in visitors. Between 1950 and 1968, for instance, visits to the national park system rose from an annual average of 1.7 to 5.2 visits per acre.[32] Many of the highly popular national parks such as Yellowstone and Yosemite have become less attractive as they have become more overcrowded. Crowds at the Mesa Verde National Park, to cite an illustration, have been barred from going inside the cliff dwellings, their major attraction, because the masses of visitors have become so large as to threaten damage to the structures. At the Great Smokies National Park, chronic automobile traffic jams have brought on the first traffic-light system within a national park.[33]

Concern with the uses of land and water is apparent in the expansion of the Federal Government's list of endangered species to over 100 including the national symbol, the bald eagle. The importance of pollution for the

---

[30] *Ibid.*, p. 2; *National Inventory of Soil and Water Conservation Needs, Statistical Bulletin No. 317*, 1962, Tables 28–32.

[31] *Statistical Abstract, 1972*, p. 630.

[32] *Statistical Abstract, 1971*, p. 195.

[33] *Environmental Quality*, 1971, *op. cit.*, p. 326.

country's fish-and-game heritage is highlighted by the report that nearly 74 million fish were killed by water pollution in 1971.[34] The continued interest in wildlife as game is shown by the increase in hunting and fishing licenses from 42 million in 1960 to 53 million in 1970.

As the land used for highways, factories, shopping centers, housing and other aspects of urban development increases, the land remaining close to the cities and readily available for recreational and parkland uses decreases. Studies indicate a loss of more than 22,000 acres of urban parkland in the six years before 1972, much of it close to the central cities. Of the 491 million acres of public recreation land in the United States, less than 3 percent lies within 40 miles, the equivalent of a one-hour drive, from the center of the metropolitan areas with a population of more than half a million.[35] Yet 90 percent of the nation's population lives in these areas. The land-use planning for recreational and other purposes, which is an important aspect of natural resources and urban growth policies in many European nations, has, as yet, received substantially less consideration in the United States.

V

Pollution control has emerged as the central environmental issue in the early 1970's. Developments in the closely related energy crisis suggest that public apprehension over prospective energy shortages, an apprehension heightened by fears of gasoline rationing and power blackouts or brownouts, has come to occupy an equivalent place in the middle 1970's. Nationally, there has been considerably less sense of urgency about the nonpollution and nonenergy aspects of environmental quality such as land conservation or measures to achieve a more rational use of water resources.

Programs and objectives in pollution control are illustrated by the experience with air and water pollution. National policies to abate air pollution are currently governed by the Clean Air Act, especially the 1970 amendments to this legislation. The amendments set a national standard for control of each pollutant, and the individual states are required to draw up implemen-

---

[34] *Statistical Abstract, 1972*, p. 643.
[35] *Environmental Quality, 1971, op. cit.,* p. 200.

tation plans to attain the national standard. Air quality standards were announced in 1971 for the six most important pollutants—sulfur dioxide, particulate matter (smoke), photochemical oxidants, hydrocarbons, carbon monoxide, and the nitrogen oxides. Automobile manufacturers, for example, were initially required to produce automobiles by 1975 whose carbon monoxide and hydrocarbon emissions would be 90 percent lower than the allowable standards in the early 1970's, automobiles warranted to continue meeting the new standards for five years or 50,000 miles. A similar 90 percent reduction was originally imposed for nitrogen oxides, but with a 1976 implementation date.[36] These deadlines have recently been postponed for one year by the Environmental Protection Agency because of the automobile industry's claim that the catalytic converters on which they were relying to reduce emissions were insufficiently developed to meet the new standards, and further postponements have been recommended by the Administration in 1974 because of the gasoline shortages. Similarly, 38 large cities, including New York City, were given a two-year extension on their 1975 air pollution implementation deadline with the understanding that they would make use of the extension to introduce special measures to reduce motor vehicle-generated oxidants and carbon monoxide.[37]

The costs of air pollution abatement are largely imposed on the private sector, largely on individuals purchasing automobiles. The primary costs of reducing water pollution are imposed on industry and on municipalities aided by Federal grants. Current national programs to control water pollution stem from the water quality legislation of the middle 1960's and the expansion of programs and objectives contained in the 1972 amendments to the Water Quality Act. The 1972 amendments set forth the most ambitious measures that have as yet been adopted in national legislation to control pollution. In summary, the amendments require all industries discharging wastes into American waterways to apply the "best practical" treatment technology by the middle of 1977. By the middle of 1983, they will be required to install the "best available" technology. The ultimate goal of these provisions is the elimination of all the water pollution discharges from industrial sources. Municipalities are made subject to the less-severe provision that they install "secondary" sewage treatment facilities by 1977 that could reduce water pollution from sewage by as much as 90 percent.

The 1972 amendments illustrate two of the problems involved in adopt-

---

[36] In the middle of 1973 the Environmental Protection Agency and others came to question the 90 percent reduction standard for nitrogen oxides because of limitations in the data on which it was based.

[37] *The New York Times,* April 25, 1973. See also *The President's Energy Message to Congress,* January 23, 1974.

ing standards for pollution control. One centers on the fact that the incremental costs of pollution abatement rise, and sometimes sharply, as the stringency of the standards is increased. To underscore the magnitudes involved, the Environmental Protection Agency has estimated that it would cost $60 billion in the next decade to remove 85 to 90 percent of the water pollution stemming from municipal and industrial sources. To remove another 10 percent is expected to come close to doubling the costs, or to add nearly another $60 billion. At some level of abatement, as the Council of Economic Advisers points out in its 1972 *Report*, the incremental costs become so enormous "as to raise serious questions about the appropriateness of carrying removal this far."[38] For another consideration, a single standard for a particular type of pollutant overlooks the considerable differences in the costs of abatement or the social importance of the abatement in different contexts. Where recreational uses of water are important, say for swimming, the benefits of approaching a zero level of pollution are substantially greater than in a shipping channel. For these reasons, an "effluent charge" on industry-originated pollution has received extensive consideration as an alternative to the present type of regulation that would be applicable in instances where serious threats to human health were not involved. While the effluent charges have been questioned as providing a "license to pollute," they have received support as a means for providing firms with incentives to reduce pollution to socially more-desirable levels at lesser costs than those likely to be involved in the present regulations.

In effect, a new body of legislation, administrative law, and regulations has come into being in connection with the national interest in pollution control. For example, in 1972 the Department of Housing and Urban Development issued noise abatement regulations specifying maximum noise levels for HUD-financed dwelling units. To encourage the recycling of waste paper, the Federal Government's General Services Administration now requires that papers containing reclaimed fibers be used in specifications representing more than two-fifths of the annual paper sales to Federal agencies under GSA regulations.[39] The Environmental Impact Statements required by the National Environmental Policy Act (NEPA) illustrate measures arising from environmental considerations that can affect many different kinds of national programs. The Environmental Policy Act requires Federal agencies to have these statements prepared for all "major actions significantly affecting the quality of the human environment."[40] The intent of the require-

[38] Council of Economic Advisers, *Annual Report*, 1972, p. 123.

[39] *Environmental Quality*, 1972, *op. cit.*, pp. 131, 133.

[40] 42 United States Code, 4332(2)(C).

ment is to make government agencies more environmentally oriented so that environmental impacts will be taken into account in constructing highways and dams, in building airports, in granting permits to dredge or fill in navigable waters, and in activities that, on the surface, often appear remote from environmental quality concerns, as in decisions approving changes in railroad freight rates.

The increases in spending by government and industry for pollution control provide one indication of the changes in the scope of the national commitment to pollution abatement. The Federal Government's outlays, according to the Office of Management and Budget, are expected to rise from the $685 million spent in fiscal 1969 to an anticipated $3.1 billion in fiscal 1974.[41] Over half of the Federal spending in 1974 is estimated to be made up of grants-in-aid to state and local governments, mainly grants for the construction of water treatment plants. Capital outlays by industry for pollution abatement facilities, as reported by the McGraw-Hill Economics Department, grew from $1.7 billion in 1969 to $3.3 billion in 1971, and the investment planned in 1972 amounted to $4.9 billion. In addition, industry expected to spend more than $800 million in 1972 for research and development associated with control of pollution.[42]

In the absence of countervailing tendencies growing out of national policy, population increase, GNP growth, greater urbanization, and changes in the stock of motor vehicles would add significantly to pollution, to the demands for energy, and to pressures on natural resources in the 1970's and beyond. As one illustration, before the Arab oil embargo went into effect in 1973, the United States Bureau of Mines estimated that by 1985 one-third or more of the American petroleum and natural gas consumption would be supplied from imports. If this anticipation were to materialize, the American oil import bill could rise from around $4 billion in 1971 to $25 billion by 1985 (in 1971 prices).[43] Projections made since the Arab embargo and oil price increases have raised these estimates by several magnitudes. A study of American materials requirements in the year 2000, prepared for the National Commission on Materials Policy, estimates that by the end of the century the consumption of liquid fuels will exceed 1966-1969 levels by two and a half

---

[41] U.S. Office of Management and Budget, *Special Analyses, The Budget of the United States Government, Fiscal Year 1973,* 1972, p. 296; *ibid., Fiscal Year 1974,* p. 270.

[42] McGraw-Hill Publications, Economics Department, *Annual McGraw-Hill Survey of Pollution Control Expenditures,* 1971, 1972.

[43] U.S. Office of Emergency Preparedness, *The Potential for Energy Conservation: Substitution for Scarce Fuels,* 1973, p. 1.

times while the use of crude steel and natural gas will double.[44] In the case of natural resources whose supplies are unaffected by imports comparable increases in requirements are apparent. To cite the use of land for outdoor recreation as an example, keeping the annual number of visits per acre in national parks from rising beyond the levels at the end of the 1960's would involve adding 1.8 million acres a year to the national park system between 1975 and 1980.[45] In the case of timber, according to an earlier but authoritative study, *Resources in America's Future,* consumption is expected to nearly triple between 1960 and the year 2000.[46]

Measures to deal with these expected increases in demand span a range of programs and objectives. They include changes in international economic policy such as the removal in 1973 of the tariff restrictions on the import of petroleum. They also include domestic measures such as adding recreational land to parks, especially those near urban areas, banning pesticides such as DDT, or constructing dams to store water. To an increasing extent, research and development has come to figure as the strategic long-term ingredient in seeking better solutions to a host of environmental problems. The Federal Government's response to the mushrooming growth in demand for "clean" energy offers a case in point. Even before the Arab oil embargo, the Government's spending for energy-related R & D was expected to increase from $320 million in 1969 to an estimated $999 million by fiscal 1974.[47] Senator Henry Jackson, Chairman of the Senate Interior Committee, has more recently proposed a program on the scale of the manned lunar landing in the 1960's, a 10-year $20 billion effort, to make the United States self-sufficient in energy by 1983.[48] The Administration has proposed a five-year $10 billion research and development program including a major emphasis on the liquid-metal fast-breeder nuclear reactor as the "best hope" after 1985 for meeting the demand for both economical and clean energy. A $700 million fast-breeder demonstration plant is expected to enter into operation before the middle 1980's. Other high priority energy research programs include projects to

[44] *Materials Requirements in the United States . . . in the Year 2000, op. cit.,* pp. 34–35.

[45] N. Potter, *Land Conservation, Water Supply, Outdoor Recreation,* National Planning Association (unpublished), 1972.

[46] Landsberg, Fischman, and Fisher, *Resources in America's Future,* 1963, p. 815.

[47] White House Release, *The President's Energy Message—Fact Sheet,* April 18, 1973; *ibid.,* January 23, 1974.

[48] "Energy Research and Development," Report No. 93–589, U.S. Senate, 93d Congress, December 1, 1973. The Atomic Energy Commission projects expenditures reaching as high as $4 billion to develop the fast-breeder nuclear reactor to the stage of initial commercial use by the middle 1980's. See Chapter Nine.

remove the sulfur content from coal and oil and to convert coal into a low-sulfur gas or liquid that could be transported by pipeline. This technology is currently in the pilot-plant stage. More long-term efforts include research to develop the potentials of nuclear fusion or of solar energy already in use in Israel and Japan and to utilize geothermal energy—the hot water and steam in the interior of the earth. Research is under way to make it feasible to convert shale rock to commercially competitive oil and to dispose of the 80 percent of the shale that remains as waste after the oil is extracted. As far as these programs succeed, the nation would become less dependent on fossil fuels, and the fossil fuels that were in use would have a substantially reduced capacity to pollute.

VI

An assessment of the costs of protecting environmental quality in the decade ahead involves the consideration of three types of costs. One are the damage costs, the economic and social costs generated by environmental deterioration. The estimated $6 billion annual cost for the medical care and income loss in the early 1970's because of the illness caused by pollution is an example.[49] Second are the treatment costs, the public and private outlays to implement national programs for abating pollution, to add land to national parks and forests or for expanding research and development to devise inexpensive and nonpolluting energy sources. A third type of costs are the program impact costs. These are the costs to the nation of the consequences of pursuing environmental quality programs, for example, the higher prices that may result, the loss of jobs, or the potentials for diminishing the exports that contribute to international economic balance. The impact costs also include the indirect costs of programs to conserve energy such as the anticipated losses of income and employment in resort areas in 1973 and 1974 resulting from reduced allocations of petroleum to gasoline production, higher gasoline prices, or the 55-mile an hour speed limit for highway travel. The cost estimates for the environmental quality goal refer to the treatment costs in the public and private sectors.

The three groups of cost are interrelated in the sense that changes in one will typically bring about changes in the others. More effective pollution

[49] *Environmental Quality*, 1971, *op. cit.*, p. 106.

control measures, for instance, would substantially reduce the $16 billion loss a year estimated as the cost of the damages attributable to air pollution by the Environmental Protection Agency.[50] Undertaking extensive programs to reduce air pollution could increase the cost of manufacturing automobiles by as much as 10 percent, with the likelihood of some losses in employment, perhaps as many as 18,000 jobs in the industry over a four-year period.[51] The scope of the adverse impacts, such as loss of employment, can be expected to influence the stringency of the standards in the pollution control or energy conservation programs that will be adopted by the nation.

The damage costs arising from air pollution include the costs of medical care and the work loss due to illness, the erosion and other damages to vegetation and materials, and the reduction in property values in areas characterized by an especially heavy incidence of pollution. The Environmental Protection Agency reported in 1971 that the annual toll of air pollution for health, vegetation, materials, and property amounted to over $80 per person, or a total of $16 billion.[52] Damages to health make up the largest item in this total. The estimates of damage costs refer only to damages for which a ready dollar measure is available. They are incomplete because being deprived of "a clear view, of sunshine, of clean air, of a natural biological environment (birds, trees, etc.), of a beautiful landscape or a recreational opportunity is no less a loss for the fact that the amenity in question is not exchanged" and, therefore, a dollar yardstick is unavailable.[53]

The relevant treatment costs for pollution abatement include the capital outlays by business and government for equipment to control pollution, for example, waste water treatment facilities, the costs of operating the equipment once it has been installed, and the costs of manufacturing and maintaining the pollution control devices installed in motor vehicles. The Council on Environmental Quality has prepared estimates of the cost of abating pollution in the next decade on the assumption that the standards to be implemented reflect the legislation in effect early in 1972. The cost projections, to quote the Council, "represent a measure of national resources which must be used to meet environmental goals and are therefore unavailable for other uses."[54] The Council's projections have been translated into annual average capital and operating outlays over the 1971–1980 period. They are listed in Table 10–3.

[50] *Ibid.*

[51] *Environmental Quality,* 1972, *op. cit.,* p. 290.

[52] *Environmental Quality,* 1971, *op. cit.,* p. 107.

[53] R. U. Ayres, *op. cit.,* p. 42.

[54] *Environmental Quality,* 1972, *op. cit.,* p. 275.

Table 10-3 Estimated Annual Average Pollution Control
Expenditures, 1971 to 1980[a]
(in millions of 1969 dollars)

Component	Projected Annual Average Outlays, 1971 to 1980
Air pollution control	$ 9,600
Public outlays	700
Private outlays	8,900
Water pollution control	12,200
Public outlays	8,600
Private outlays	3,600
Solid waste disposal	7,800
Nuclear radiation control	200
Aircraft noise control	300
Surface mining damage reclamation	500
Total	$30,600

[a] Derived from Council on Environmental Quality, *Environmental Quality,*
1972, pp. 276–277. The estimates in this report have been translated
into 1969 dollars. They include entries for combined sewers and jet aircraft
noise control which are listed in the report but not included in their total.

The most costly of the pollution control treatments in the table are those
listed for water pollution control. The largest single increase beyond the
1969 expenditures are the private outlays for abatement of air pollution,
costs largely borne by automobile owners. The $30.6 billion listed as the av-
erage annual cost of implementing in the 1970's the standards in effect in
early 1972 would be the equivalent of 2.5 times the $12 billion spent for
pollution control facilities in 1969 (see Table 10–1).

The estimates derived from the Council on Environmental Quality's
projections, or from similar projections, need to allow for several considerations. For one, they do not take into account the changes in standards incorporated in the 1972 Water Quality Act Amendments. For another, the scenario implied in the estimates primarily relates to "end-of-the-line" treatment
to eliminate pollution, that is, treatment that eliminates the pollution in the
last stages of the production process or, as in the case of automobiles, once
the product comes into everyday use. There are few techniques for anticipating the extent of the technological changes that would result in departures from "end-of-the-line" treatment in another decade. As this technology is introduced, it would frequently initially increase capital outlays but,

over time, the new technology would often serve to reduce the costs of pollution abatement below present levels because of reduced operating costs.

To assess the magnitudes involved, the projections of treatment outlays should also consider the impacts costs anticipated from the program efforts represented by the expenditures. In a recent study of 12,000 plants in 11 industries likely to be affected by pollution-control programs, for example, it was estimated that 200 to 300 plants would be forced to close down because of pollution-abatement requirements.[55] The direct job loss resulting from the environmental regulations in these industries was estimated to range between 50,000 and 125,000 jobs over a four-year period, or from 1 to 4 percent of their employment level. Prices for their products were projected to go up from 0 to 10 percent over the period with the largest increases expected in the automobile industry. As one measure of international effects, the higher prices for automobiles were estimated to reduce net exports from the United States by as much as $700 million a year by 1980. Implementing the pollution control standards in effect in the early 1970's was regarded as having little more than a minor influence on the GNP growth rate, an effect sufficient to reduce the rate of GNP increase from the 5.2 percent assumed in the initial economic framework to 4.9 percent a year for the years providing the focus for the study, 1972 to 1976.[56] More impressionistic accounts of the expected impacts of pollution abatement programs include the fears expressed in the home-building industry that the "new zeal for water pollution control" would lead to a moratorium on further sewer construction, a development that could severely limit suburban expansion in many metropolitan areas.[57] In Bucks County, Pennsylvania, for instance, a 3000-unit project was cut back to 1000 units because of limitations on new construction of sewage facilities.

The cost projections for the environmental quality goal in 1980 take into account the estimated outlays for implementing the standards providing the basis for the Council on Environmental Quality forecasts. They also attempt to allow for the more stringent, and more costly, water quality standards in the 1972 Water Act Amendments, and for the beginnings of pollution control in some areas in which few initiatives have as yet been undertaken. The projections for the goal refer both to pollution control and to the conservation and development of natural resources. The estimates for natural resource outlays reflect changes in recent programs such as the rapid growth in energy-related research and development, in the greater recognition of specific bottlenecks (e.g., land for national parks), and they draw on esti-

---

[55] *Ibid.,* pp. 287–288.

[56] *Ibid.,* p. 302.

[57] *Business Week,* October 2, 1971, p. 54.

Table 10-4 Estimated Expenditures for the Environmental Quality Goal, 1969 and Projected 1980 (in million of 1969 dollars)

Component	Estimated Outlays in 1969[a]	Projected Outlays in 1980
Pollution abatement	$12,000	$45,700
Air pollution control	2,170	11,600
Motor vehicles	240	7,500
Stationary sources	1,730	3,400
Other[b]	200	700
Water pollution control	2,990	20,700
Municipal treatment	1,740	10,800
Industrial treatment	1,250	8,800
Other[c]	—[e]	1,100
Solid waste disposal	5,600	8,800
Nuclear radiation control	—[e]	300
Aircraft noise control	—[e]	300
Surface mining damage reclamation	—[e]	600
Acid mine drainage control	—[e]	1,000
Research and development	940	1,800
Monitoring surveillance, technical assistance	300	600
Natural resources conservation and development	4,085	9,650
Land conservation	1,000	2,500
Water storage[d]	310	700
Timber protection and management	600	1,200
Outdoor recreation—land acquisition and improvement	900	1,800
Fish and wildlife propagation and management	150	450
Materials stockpile	300	400
Research and development	825	2,600
Energy R & D[f]	525	2,000
Other	300	600
Employment adjustment assistance	—	550
Total, environmental quality goal	$16,085	$55,900
Expenditures for environmental-quality goal as percent of GNP	1.7%	4.0%

[a] See Table 10-1.
[b] Refers to government costs for air pollution control not included in the other items.
[c] Refers to expenditures for separate storm and sanitary sewers.
[d] Refers to Federal outlays for dams to maintain water flows.
[e] Unavailable.
[f] The $2.0 billion for energy R & D in 1969 dollars is the equivalent of $2.7 billion in outlays in 1974 dollars. The estimate takes into account recent proposals to spend about $2 billion in Federal funds annually for energy R & D.

mates of needs in other studies such as the Department of Agriculture's *National Inventory of Soil and Water Conservation Needs*. The projections are summarized in Table 10–4.

Nearly $34 billion of the projected $40 billion growth in expenditures to attain the environmental quality goal represents the additional cost of pollution abatement in the private and public sectors. Since the estimate for water pollution control seeks to allow for the impact of the 1972 Water Quality Act Amendments, it is $8.5 billion larger than the Council on Environmental Quality's anticipated annual average outlays for water pollution abatement during the 1970's. In total, outlays for water pollution control in 1980 are projected to reach seven times their 1969 level. The other major departure from recent experience are the increases listed for air pollution control, increases largely due to efforts to manufacture and maintain the equipment required to reduce the pollution generated by motor vehicles. The projections also allow for modest growth in pollution control fields in which the national effort in 1969 was insufficient to be reflected in the expenditures. These include programs intended to reduce noise pollution from aircraft, especially near airports, and to reclaim current and past damages to land because of surface mining. The major increases listed for natural resources conservation and development are for research, mainly energy R & D, and for programs to conserve the fertility of farm land and to increase the availability of land for outdoor recreational uses. In addition, the projections for 1980 include an allowance of $550 million, approximately 1 percent of the total, for employee readjustment allowances extending for up to two years and embracing the necessary retraining and relocation allowances for workers who had been displaced from their jobs because of pollution control measures. The allowances would be similar to but of lesser duration than those provided railway workers when railroad mergers take place.

An increase in expenditures for environmental quality objectives of the dimensions considered, approximately $40 billion, would serve as a powerful incentive to develop new technology or to accelerate the introduction of existing technology that was more efficient or more economical in abating pollution. Interest in controlling pollution, for instance, is expected to speed up the utilization of the Wankel engine in automobiles and to encourage the development of alternatives to the internal combustion engine based on steam, electricity or, perhaps, fuel cells.[58] In solid waste disposal, to cite another example, the problems of large seaboard cities such as Bos-

---

[58] The projections in Table 10–4 for outlays in 1980 for air pollution control for motor vehicles assume that by 1980 one-third of all new cars purchased are powered by sources other than internal combustion engines. See Chapter Eight.

ton may be eased in the next decade by the introduction of incinerator ships that will transport their wastes out to sea and dump the residues after incinerating them. In the production of iron and steel, the pelletizing process used in producing iron ore and the continuous casting process for producing steel are expected to come into everyday use by 1980, with their advent hastened because of their lesser propensity to add to air and water pollution. In petroleum refining, environmental considerations are likely to encourage a shift to hydrogen refining because this process gives off almost no carbon monoxide, nitrogen oxides, or particulates.[59] The new technology that is more effective in controlling pollution will often represent, or be incorporated in, the up-to-date technology that is superior on other grounds as well. As an offset of the impact costs of the environmental quality measures, the technological changes they hasten or induce can often yield impact benefits in the form of greater productivity for many purposes.

The increase in outlays listed for the environmental quality goal, from $16 to $56 billion, would represent a growth from 1.7 percent of the GNP in 1969 to 4 percent of the far larger Gross National Product anticipated in 1980. Part of the increase in the economy's output, depending on the priority given to environmental quality in comparison with other goals, would in effect be set aside as a cost of growth to provide the resources for abating pollution and conserving and developing energy-related and other natural resources. So, while economic growth increases the pressures on resources and the volume of pollutants, it also supplies the means for protecting environmental quality.

[59] I. Gutmanis, *The Generation and Costs of Controlling Air, Water, and Solid Waste Pollution, 1970–2000,* National Planning Association (unpublished), 1973.

Chapter Eleven

GOALS IN AGRICULTURAL
SUPPORT POLICY:
THE PUBLIC AND PRIVATE COSTS OF
PURSUING NATIONAL GOALS

I

Rapidly increasing productivity in agriculture together with slow growth in per capita consumption of farm products have been responsible for a history of chronic surpluses of human resources and output in the farm economy. Crop surpluses have only recently become converted to shortages, at least temporarily, for the first time in peacetime in this generation. National goals in agriculture have been concerned both with producing sufficient food and raw materials and also with assuring that the farm population participates more adequately in the American standard of living. In 1969, the Federal Government spent nearly $8 billion for programs contributing to agricultural support objectives. By 1980, the costs to government for attaining goals in agriculture are estimated to range between $6 and $11 billion depending on the program options selected. However, for most choices, the bulk of the costs to society represent costs to users of farm products because of the lesser availability and higher prices for food and agricultural raw materials.

Output per man-hour in the farm sector has grown at an annual rate of nearly 5.5 percent since World War II, a rate considerably above the 3.2 percent increase in the overall private economy.[1] The consumption of farm products has grown slowly, and it has declined as a proportion of total consumer outlays. In 1959, for instance, consumers spent 22 percent of their disposable income for food. By the early 1970's this proportion had declined to 16 percent.[2] In spite of the high productivity, income per person for the farm population was about a fourth lower at the end of the 1960's than for the nonfarm population, a differential considerably greater than the difference in the cost of living between rural and urban areas. One consequence of the lower incomes and declining employment opportunities in agriculture has been a continuous migration from the rural areas to the cities. The farm population, accordingly, declined from 23 million in 1950 to less than 16 million in 1960 and to less than 10 million by 1970.[3]

The Federal Government has sought to raise farmers' incomes through

[1] National Planning Association, *Economic Projection Series, Revised National Economic Projections to 1980, Report No. 71–N–2,* 1971, p. S–8.

[2] U.S. Department of Agriculture, *The Yearbook of Agriculture, 1971,* 1972, p. 278.

[3] U.S. Department of Agriculture, *Farm Population Estimates,* 1972.

measures aimed at reducing the supply of farm products and thereby raising their prices. Price supports and payments to farms for acreage diversion programs have been the leading instances. In 1969 the supply adjustment payments by the Federal Government accounted for nearly a fourth of the personal income from farming. The Government also adds to farmers' income by increasing the consumption of American farm output in the less-developed nations (e.g., the Food for Peace program) and by low-income groups at home (e.g., the school lunch and Food Stamp programs). These programs also contribute to national objectives in international aid and social welfare. Less support has been available to improve education, health, manpower training, or social welfare services in the rural areas. Recently, beginning in 1973, sharply rising food prices and threats of shortages have prompted legislation setting aside price supports and introducing income supplement payments to farmers if the market prices for wheat, feed grains, and cotton fall below target levels.

By 1980 employment in agriculture is expected to decline to 3 million or slightly less, a drop from 4.6 million in 1969.[4] National policy in agriculture in the next decade, therefore, must assure both an adequate income to the persons who remain in agriculture, and the education, training, and relocation assistance to prepare those who will seek employment outside of agriculture for alternative job opportunities in the cities and in the rural non-farm economy.

The long-standing problem of surplus human resources in the rural economy traces back to the continuing technological revolution in agriculture. To summarize the effects of this revolution, in 1950, one farm worker supplied about 16 persons with agricultural products, in 1960 about 26, and by the end of the 1960's the comparable figure had increased to 45.[5]

The technological transformation in agriculture has encompassed three major changes. One are the mechanical changes such as the shift from harvesting tomatoes by hand to harvesting them by a machine designed specifically for that purpose. A second are the scientific advances—the use of chemical pesticides developed in laboratories or the new strains of wheat or corn devised to provide high yields per acre. The widespread use of modern business management techniques to minimize costs and increase profits in commercial farms makes up the third element in this transformation. The changes brought about in the agricultural economy by these developments since World War II are described in Table 11–1.

[4] A. C. Eghert and J. D. Ahalt, "Agricultural Goals for the 1970's, Alternative Programs and Their Costs," National Planning Association (unpublished), 1971.

[5] U.S. Department of Agriculture, *Changes in Farm Production and Efficiency, A Summary Report,* 1971, p. 29.

Table 11-1   Selected Indicators of Change in Agriculture,
1950, 1960, and 1969[a]

Item	1950	1960	1969
Employment in agriculture (in thousands)	9926	7057	4596
Number of farms (in thousands)	5648	3962	2971
Average size of farm (in acres)	213	297	378
Crop production per acre (1950 = 100)	100	130	154
Total farm output (1950 = 100)	100	124	141
Disposable personal income per person, farm population (in dollars)	$ 841	$1100	$2418[b]
Disposable personal income per person, nonfarm population (in dollars)	$1458	$2017	$3175[b]
Average farm personal income as percent of nonfarm personal income	57.7%	54.5%	76.2%[c]

[a] *Annual Report, Council of Economic Advisers,* pp. 289–294; *Statistical Abstract, 1971,* p. 573; A. C. Egbert, and J. D. Ahalt, "Agricultural Goals for the 1970's, Alternative Programs and their Costs," National Planning Association (unpublished), 1971.
[b] Estimate.
[c] The ratio for 1968 was 74.5 percent.

Farm output increased by more than two-fifths between 1950 and 1969. This larger output, however, was produced on 2.6 million fewer farms and by a farm work force that had declined by more than half. The average size of farms, on the other hand, had increased by over three-fourths. The differential between farm and nonfarm incomes narrowed during this period so that disposable farm income per person rose from about 55 percent of the nonfarm equivalent in 1950 and 1960 to about 75 percent in 1969.

While the technological changes have primarily affected the larger commercial farms, both large and small farms continue to exist within agriculture. Commercial farms with annual sales of $20,000 or more in the late 1960's made up less than a fifth of the total number of farms. Yet, they received more than 70 percent of the total cash receipts from farming.[6] These larger farms earn the bulk of their income (two-thirds or more) from farming including government payments and nonmoney income from farm food and housing. At the other extreme are over a million farmers with cash sales of $10,000 or less in 1969. Many of these farms, and especially those with sales of $2500 or less, are more appropriately termed "farm residences" than "farms" since their occupants typically combine some farm work with more work outside of agriculture. More than half of the income of the farmers in this group is derived from nonfarm sources, and in the farms with the smallest volume of sales, those with $2500 or less, nonfarm income exceeded farm income in 1970 by a seven-to-one margin.[7]

Although farms have been getting larger and this tendency is expected to continue in the next decade, corporate farming, the "factories in the field," is largely confined to particular segments of agriculture, such as livestock grazing or fruit and vegetable farms in California. Elsewhere the requirements for operating a "family farm" have been radically changing. Most of the 3 million farms now in existence meet the definition of a "family farm" on the standard basis of employing less than 1.5 man-years of hired labor annually. But these farms had an average net worth of approximately $80,000 in the late 1960's.[8] Thus, it has become difficult for a family to choose farming as a sole occupation unless the family members inherit a large commercial farm or acquire substantial wealth outside of agriculture.

The farm work force included 1.2 million hired farm laborers in the early 1970's, approximately half the number employed in 1950.[9] Farm laborers with at least a minimum occupational attachment to agriculture are among the most poorly paid of all American workers. Their earnings from farm and nonfarm work combined averaged slightly less than $1900 in 1969. While the unemployment rate for the entire economy was only 3.5 percent in that year, wage and salary workers in agriculture listed a 6 percent rate, an unemployment rate considerably higher than that reported for any other industry. Men in the 25-to-44 age bracket were the only group among the hired farm laborers in the late 1960's with sufficient work and earnings to

[6] Egbert and Ahalt, *op. cit.*, p. 26.

[7] *Statistical Abstract, 1972*, p. 587.

[8] Egbert and Ahalt, *op. cit.*, p. 29.

[9] *Annual Report, Council of Economic Advisers, 1972*, p. 291.

sustain a family of four above the poverty line.[10] Aside from low earnings, farm workers and private household workers are frequently excluded from the national labor standards and social insurance protections.

Continued outmigration from agriculture has been a primary response by the farm population to diminishing manpower requirements within it. The average annual net migration from the farms has been tapering off steadily since the middle 1950's, but this decline has been mainly the result of the decline in the number of persons remaining in the farm population.[11] Since the migrants consist of a greater-than-proportionate number of young adults, the population left behind is made up of older and less well-educated groups than in the nonfarm economy. In 1970, for instance, nearly half—45 percent—of the farm residents 25 and over had finished eight years of school or less. The comparable figure for the rural nonfarm population was one-third, and in the metropolitan areas it was one-fourth. Blacks moving out of the rural South have made up a substantial element in this migration. Between 1960 and 1970, for example, the percentage of Negroes and other nonwhites in the farm population fell from about a sixth to less than a tenth of the total.[12]

Economic, political, social, and technological changes in the past two decades have blurred the distinction between "farm" and "nonfarm" and between "rural" and "urban." The outmigration from agriculture has been so massive that by 1970 an estimated three-fourths of the farm-reared adults no longer lived on farms.[13] For those remaining in agriculture, nearly half of their personal incomes was derived from sources other than farming.[14] Communications media, and especially TV, are eroding the distinction in ways of life between "city folk" and "country folk." The once-potent farm bloc no longer exists as a separate politically powerful entity in Congress.

As the distinction between "farm" and "nonfarm" becomes blurred, the problems of the farm population increasingly come to resemble those of the larger society, but with a special emphasis because of the rural context in which they take place. Poverty and an archaic public welfare assistance system constitute a severe problem in the rural areas as well as in the large cities. In 1969, for example, about 350,000 families of farmers and farm managers, about 1 in 5, were classified as poor. Two out of every 5 families

---

[10] *Manpower Report of the President,* 1971, p. 122.

[11] For the period 1965–1969, the rate of net migration from farms, 5.2 percent of the farm population, was not much different from the rate in the first half of the decade, 5.7 percent. *Ibid.,* p. 114.

[12] *Ibid.,* pp. 115–116.

[13] *Ibid.,* p. 115.

[14] *Council of Economic Advisers, 1972, op. cit., p.* 289.

headed by hired farm workers were reported to be poor in that year.[15] Health, education, social welfare, and manpower services are considerably less available in the rural areas than in the cities. In the late 1960's, visits to doctors in metropolitan areas amounted to an annual average of 4.5 per person. The average for farm residents was only 3.3 visits.[16] Although relatively few young people in the rural areas are likely to remain in agriculture, the primary vocational programs in many rural high schools are in agriculture. About 70 percent of the enrollment in these programs is in basic farming, the "agricultural production" courses. In fiscal 1970, skill training programs sponsored by the Department of Labor enrolled about 42,000 persons in rural areas, or less than a tenth of the annual net migration out of agriculture in the second half of the 1960's.[17] So, only a small proportion of the migrants from the rural areas receive the education or training needed to enter the more skilled and better paid jobs in the cities. Those who remain earn lower incomes and have less adequate health services and public services available to them than to the nation generally.

II

Agricultural support policy in the United States has been mainly concerned with narrowing the differentials between income levels in the farm and the nonfarm sectors of the economy. Until recently this objective has been pursued primarily by measures such as price supports aimed at limiting the supply of farm products on the market. Government programs have also added to farmers' incomes by expanding the consumption of farm products by low-income families and in the less-developed nations. Other Federal programs include research and technical assistance, farm marketing services, and the farm credit measures.

The Federal Government's programs in agricultural support policy are very largely conducted through the Department of Agriculture. The expenditures for these programs in 1969 are summarized in Table 11–2.

[15] *Manpower Report,* 1971, *op. cit.,* pp. 121–122.

[16] *Yearbook of Agriculture, 1971, op. cit.,* p. 151.

[17] *Manpower Report,* 1971, *op. cit.,* pp. 131, 133. Refers to institutional and on-the-job training conducted under the Manpower Development and Training Act.

Table 11-2   Federal Expenditures for Agricultural Support Objectives in 1969[a]
(in millions of 1969 dollars)

Activity	Outlays in 1969
To limit market supply	$4325
Price-support payments	3868
Acreage diversion and other production-adjustment payments	457
To encourage consumption	1778
Food Stamp and other domestic programs	650
Food for Peace and other foreign-assistance programs	1128
Research, technical assistance, marketing services	669
Farm credit and insurance	777
Job training and mobility allowances[b]	77
Other[c]	125
Total	$7751

[a] Derived from U.S. Office of Management and Budget, *Special Analyses, The Budget of the United States Govenment,* Fiscal Years 1970, 1971, 1972, and various other budget documents. Estimates, unless otherwise noted, refer to calendar year 1969.

[b] Refers to expenditures for the Department of Labor's Operation Mainstream program and the Department of Agriculture's Youth Development and Family Living Program in fiscal 1969.

[c] Refers to expenditures for administration and related purposes.

All told, Federal expenditures in support of agriculture amounted to nearly $8 billion in 1969, or slightly less than 5 percent of the total Federal budget outlays. Over half—55 percent—of these expenditures represented payments to limit market supply through price supports, acreage diversion payments, and similar measures. In some instances the programs supported by the Federal Government serve purposes which are inconsistent with one another. For example, in 1969 the Federal Government spent close to $700 million for research and technical assistance in agriculture. This research was devoted to developing improved crop strains, to innovations in fertilizer use, and to the eradication of plant and animal diseases. The long-term effects of the research in agriculture supported by the Federal Government and its dissemination through agencies such as the Agricultural Extension Service has been to increase productivity in agriculture and, therefore, to add to the supply of farm output that other government programs have sought to diminish.

The farm programs preceding the 1973 income support legislation trace back to the 1950's, when many persons came to realize that agricultural surpluses were a long-term rather than a temporary phenomenon. The programs that followed came to include three major elements. One consists of voluntary acreage diversion payments, "rental" payments to farmers for retiring land from production in crops for which there is a surplus. A second are the price support loans and related government food storage measures to support farm prices. In these programs the Government advances producers a sum equal to the loan price of the commodity taking as collateral the produce covered by the loan. If the market price fails to rise enough to prompt the farmer to redeem his loan, he can forfeit the collateral and keep the loan. In addition, farmers receive direct payments for some crops that are based on the difference between the loan price and the support price the Government wishes to maintain. More than three-fourths of all the Federal Government's outlays for price supports are devoted to three major crops, wheat, feed grains, and cotton.[18]

Aside from the supply adjustment measures, the Federal Government is involved in a variety of programs to expand the consumption of farm products at home and abroad. The Food for Peace program, Public Law 480, has been an important form of economic aid to developing nations. Outlays amounted to more than a billion dollars in 1969 and they increased to an estimated $1.3 billion in fiscal 1972. Barring natural disasters such as large-scale drought, growth in food production in a number of the recipient countries is likely to limit the need for massive commodity aid from the United States. Other arrangements, however, can be anticipated that will increase markets for American farm products abroad. A recent example has been the negotiation of an agreement between the United States and the USSR in 1972 by which the Soviet Union has agreed to buy $750 million in grains over a three-year period.[19]

The Federal Government also contributes to increasing the consumption of farm products at home by programs that make agricultural commodities available to low-income families at no cost or at a reduced cost. The Food Stamp and school lunch programs are among the major instances. Some 14.5 million persons received assistance from the Federal family food programs in 1972, double the number in 1969.[20] The total cost of the food

[18] C. L. Schultze, et al., *Setting National Priorities, The 1972 Budget*, p. 297.

[19] *White House Release*, July 8, 1972.

[20] U.S. Office of Management and Budget, *Special Analyses, The Budget of the United States Government, Fiscal Year 1973*, p. 183.

distributed by the Federal Government in the Food Stamp program rose from $229 million in 1969 to an estimated $2.2 billion in 1973. Welfare reform legislation such as the proposed Family Assistance Plan (H.R.1) and similar measures typically propose to continue the distribution of food to low-income families outside of regular market channels as part of the income supplement programs to be underwritten by the Federal Government.

The Government's programs in agriculture in the 1960's were largely, although far from exclusively, concerned with the problem of surplus output. The programs to limit market supply, and especially the price support program, mainly benefited the large commercial farmers. So, the wealthiest 10 percent of all farmers were estimated to have received more than 50 percent of the price support payments.[21] In addition to the measures specifically concerned with farm prices and output, the Administration proposed a $1.1 billion special revenue sharing rural development program in 1972 to create job opportunities for persons in rural areas outside of agriculture.[22] Much of this outlay would initially substitute for current spending in area or regional redevelopment programs, as in Appalachia. However, substantially improving transportation, power, school, health, and similar facilities in the rural areas would involve significant increases in spending beyond current levels, and these outlays could create many jobs for farmers and farm workers who were no longer required in agriculture. For instance, if one job were directly created for every $25,000 of outlays in the rural development programs, an expenditure of $1.1 billion a year could be expected to generate some 44,000 jobs in the rural areas.

III

Long-term goals in agriculture as defined by successive administrations in the past decade have continued to emphasize income parity as the primary objective of policy. As stated by President Johnson, the basic policy objective in the rural economy is to develop an "opportunity for the efficient fam-

---

[21] National Urban Coalition, *Counterbudget: A Blueprint for Changing National Priorities, 1971–1976,* 1971, p. 194.

[22] *State of the Union Message,* January 20, 1972, pp. 31–32.

ily farmer to earn parity of income from farming operations."[23] Similarly, President Nixon in his 1972 *State of the Union Message* comments that "American farmers deserve a fair share in the fruits of our prosperity. . . . In 1950 the income of the average farmer was only 58 percent of that of his nonfarmer counterpart. Today that figure stands at 74 percent—not nearly high enough but moving in the right direction."[24] Thus, income goals in agriculture have continued to receive national support, although without significant increases in supporting public outlays, through changes in the party in power, the waxing and waning of the Great Society programs, the escalation and deescalation of the war in Vietnam, and similar developments.

Income parity goals in any of several versions can be expected to continue to receive a high priority in agriculture so long as the farm economy is dominated by the problem of low incomes and surplus human resources. Productivity gains in agriculture in the 1970's are projected to average slightly less than the 5.5 percent annual rate characterizing the 1960's. With a continuation of the recent price support and related programs, farm output is estimated to increase by 20 percent in the next decade. However, this larger output could be produced with an anticipated employment level of 3 million or less by 1980. This is 1.6 million less than at the end of the 1960's.

By 1980, disposable personal income per person in the nonfarm sector is expected to reach an average, in 1969 dollars, of $4500.[25] If the parity objective can be defined as an average level of disposable income per person in the farm economy equal to 90 percent of the comparable nonfarm income, partity would imply an average farm disposable income of $4100 per person by 1980. A $4100 income level would represent an increase in per capita purchasing power in agriculture of close to 70 percent beyond the comparable figure in 1969.

To facilitate the movement from farm to nonfarm employment, the standard for the agriculture goal also includes a job training and mobility assistance program estimated to cost an average of $3300 per trainee. This sum is expected to cover the anticipated cost of the training, job interview and moving expenses, and to provide a subsidy to help defray minimum living expenses for as long as three months for farm migrants with job skills who were seeking employment elsewhere. Outlays for programs to expand domestic food consumption by the low-income population as in the Food

[23] *Budget Message to Congress on Agriculture,* August 5, 1965.

[24] *State of the Union Message,* January 20, 1972, p. 31.

[25] The comparable figure in 1968 dollars is $4290. See Egbert and Ahalt, *op. cit.,* p. 71.

Stamp Plan are projected to amount to $2.5 billion a year. Spending to encourage consumption of American farm products in the developing nations, such as the Food for Peace program, is expected to remain at current levels as are the expenditures for research, technical assistance, and farm credit.

Three routes are available to attain the 90 percent income parity goal by 1980. One is by a continuation of the recent types of supply adjustment programs emphasizing price supports and acreage diversion payments. A second is the route of restricting farm production until the prices of agricultural commodities rose sufficiently to yield the target income of $4100 per person. An alternative to this cartel-like arrangement similar to the 1973 farm legislation would be to allow unconstrained production and sale of farm products at prices determined solely by market forces. The Federal Government would then provide income supplements sufficient to raise the per capita disposable income of the farm population to an average of $4100. Each of these alternatives would have its particular impact on farm output, farm prices, and farm employment. The anticipated effects of each are summarized in Table 11–3, and they are discussed briefly below.

Table 11-3   Estimated Farm Output, Prices, Employment, and Income, Selected Program Alternatives, 1980

| | | Projected 1980 Level | | |
Item	Actual Level in 1969	With Supply Adjustment Programs	With Output Control	With Unconstrained Production
Farm output (1969 = 100)	100	121	106	127
Farm prices (1969 = 100)	100	100	143	84
Number of farms (in thousands)	2971	2000	2000	1800
Farm employment (in thousands)	4596	3000	2800	2800
Farm income support payments (in millions of 1969 dollars)	$4325	5400	—	2600
Disposable personal income per person, farm population (in 1969 dollars)	$2418	4167	4113	4100

Supply Adjustment Programs

If programs similar to the recent price supports and acreage diversion measures were continued for another decade, an output level one-fifth greater than in 1969 could be attained with 1 million fewer farms. Government supply adjustment payments to farmers amounting to $5.4 billion would be required for per capita farm purchasing power to reach $4100. Since farm employment, including hired and family farmworkers, would be 1.6 million less than in 1969, the costs projected for this goal include an annual outlay of $500 million to encourage the movement of 150,000 persons a year out of the farm work force through retraining and mobility allowances. Total costs to the Government including other program costs such as research and technical assistance are estimated to amount to $11 billion a year by 1980.

Direct Output Control

Income goals in agriculture could be achieved with a minimum of costs to the Federal Government by direct control of farm production to reduce supply and substantially increase farm prices. The demand for farm products is relatively insensitive to changes in the prices of food or of most agricultural raw materials. Prices, therefore, could be increased significantly by modest reductions in supply achieved through government programs. A reduction in supply of 15 percentage points below the level projected for 1980 in the supply adjustment alternative, for example, is estimated to increase prices by more than two-fifths. If this reduction in supply could be attained through market control measures, the price increases alone would be sufficient to raise farm purchasing power per person to the $4100 level by 1980. While the total number of farms is expected to remain the same under this approach as in the supply adjustment alternative, farm employment would be about 200,000 less, largely because fewer hired farm workers would be needed to produce the lower volume of output. Since the Federal Government would no longer be making production adjustment payments to farmers, costs to the Government in this alternative would be at a minimum. However, thorough and continuing control of production would be required for the market control programs to be successful. This would probably involve the issuance of vouchers to farmers authorizing them to plant a predetermined amount of a specific crop to minimize the incentives for individual farmers to expand their production and to discourage persons from entering farming.

Unconstrained Production

Unconstrained production supplemented by direct income payments to farmers offers a third alternative for attaining income goals in agriculture. With the removal of all government imposed limits on production, declining farm prices would check the tendency to significantly expand farm output so that the production of farm products in 1980 is projected to be only six percentage points greater than in the supply adjustment alternative. However, farm prices would be a sixth less. The number of farms would decline to an estimated 1.8 million as the average size of farms became larger in order to survive in a period of declining and frequently fluctuating market-determined prices. However, more farm laborers would be hired on the remaining farms because of the greater volume of production. With unconstrained production along these lines, the average disposable income of the farm population would rise to nearly $3650 per person by 1980, about $450 less than the target level. The estimated supplemental income payment to raise disposable personal income to the $4100 level would involve a cost to the Federal Government of $2.6 billion. With unconstrained production, an anticipated $800 million in training and mobility funds could assist the movement of 250,000 farmers annually out of agriculture into other fields.

Aside from considerations of the costs to the Government, unconstrained production raises a number of problems. Government costs would be minimal if, as in 1973, farm prices were to remain at high levels. Payments based on the volume of production, as in the 1973 legislation up to an annual limit of $20,000 per farmer, would concentrate most of the Government's support among the larger and wealthier commercial farmers. Concentrating payments among lower-income farmers runs the risks of encouraging more persons to stay in agriculture than are required to produce the anticipated output, more than are represented by the 1.8 million farms projected for 1980. Encouraging more farmers to remain in agriculture could lead to a greater than anticipated volume of farm output, lower farm prices, and income supplements that could be substantially in excess of the $2.6 billion included in the projections.

All of the options considered would leave large numbers of farmers, especially the smaller farmers, earning incomes that amounted to considerably less than $4100 per family member. Many of those farmers, and many farm laborers with low incomes, would be eligible for minimum income benefits included in the cost estimates for the social welfare goal. By 1980 these benefits are projected to include a Federally supported minimum income for a family of four amounting to about $4300 a year.

The cost estimates in the three alternatives refer to government costs based on estimates of farm output, prices, and productivity changes, the utilization of farm output from different sources, and the income earned by the farm population from farm and nonfarm sources. For instance, the income estimates are based on the anticipation that the nonfarm income of the farm population will exceed their farm income, including government sup-

Table 11-4   Estimated Government Costs for Alternative Programs
to Achieve Agricultural Support Goals, 1969 and 1980
(in millions of 1969 dollars)

| | | Projected 1980 Level | | |
Item	Actual Level in 1969	With Supply Adjustment Programs	With Output Control	With Unconstrained Production
To limit farm supply	$4,325	$5,400	$500	$300
Price supports	3,868	4,900	—	—
Acreage diversion and other production adjustments	457	500	500	300
Direct suplements to farm income	—	—	—	2,600
To encourage consumption	1,778	3,500	3,500	3,500
Food Stamp and other domestic programs	650	2,500	2,500	2,500
Food for Peace and other foreign assistance programs	1,128	1,000	1,000	1,000
Research, technical assistance, marketing services	669	700	700	700
Farm credit and insurance	777	775	775	775
Skill training and mobility allowances	77	500	800	800
Other	125	125	125	125
Total	7,751	11,000	6,400	8,800
Expenditures as percent of the GNP	0.8%	0.8%	0.5%	0.6%

ports, by 1980. The direct payment estimate for acreage diversion programs allows for an increase in the number of acres withdrawn to about 65 million by 1980, an increase expected to be required to maintain farm prices at their 1969 level. On the basis of past experience, the estimates presuppose that the diversion program would be only 80 percent effective because of increases in the intensity of production and larger yields from the acres which remained in production. Accordingly, payments would be required to remove five acres to reduce production by the equivalent of four acres' output. The costs to the Government for each of the three alternatives are listed in Table 11–4.

The three alternatives listed represent markedly different claims on the Federal Government's budget. Continuing the price support and acreage diversion programs of the 1960's, as in the supply adjustment projections, is the alternative with the largest government cost. The program option with the least government cost, output control, would involve a thoroughgoing cartelization of American agriculture. For all of the alternatives considered, the government outlays in support of agricultural goals would represent a diminishing claim on the nation's resources. Government outlays for the agricultural support goal in 1980, for all three alternatives, would remain, as in 1969, at less than 1 percent of the GNP.

IV

Government outlays make up only one element in the costs to society of the agricultural support programs. The additional costs to the users of farm products, largely consumers, are also part of the costs of these programs. The costs to the users include two elements. One is made up of the consumption of farm products that is foregone because of the higher prices brought about by the programs. The other consists of the reduction in the income available to consumers to buy other goods and services because of the higher prices of food and agricultural raw materials. For two of the alternatives considered, the market control and supply adjustment program approaches, the costs to the users of farm products exceed the costs to the Federal Government.

The user and government costs of the alternative routes for achieving the agricultural support goal are summarized in Table 11–5.

Table 11-5   Estimated User and Government Costs of Alternative Programs to Achieve Agricultural Support Goals in 1980 (in billions of 1969 dollars)

	Program Alternative		
	Supply Adjustment Programs	Output Control	Unconstrained Production
User costs[a]			
Reduction of purchasing power	$ 5.0	$10.0	$ 0.0
Consumption of food foregone	8.0	23.0	0.0
Total user costs	13.0	33.0	0.0
Government program costs	11.0	6.4	8.8
Total costs to society	24.0	39.4	8.8
Total costs as percent of the GNP	1.7%	2.8%	0.6%

[a] Egbert and Ahalt, *op. cit.*, pp. 39, 50. The price and output levels in the unconstrained production alternative provide the standard for deriving the user costs in the two other alternatives.

Government costs are inadequate indicators of the costs to society of the alternatives for attaining income goals in agriculture. The program alternative with the least government costs—output control—involves the greatest cost to the users of farm products and, therefore, to society. These high user costs follow from the substantial increase in farm prices, 43 percent beyond the 1969 level, which makes it possible to achieve income parity with minimum costs to government. The alternative involving the least cost to society is unconstrained production supplemented by income payments to farmers.[26] Continuing the recent supply adjustment types of farm programs would involve a maximum of government costs along with substantial costs to the users of food and agricultural raw materials.

Looking ahead to 1980, there is some likelihood, as the National Planning Association's Agricultural Committee points out in a statement issued in 1973, that "domestic and foreign demand will prove so strong that the excess capacity which has long plagued agriculture will not appear again."[27] However, it is at present unknown whether the sharp increases in farm prices in 1973 reflect a long-term surge in world demand for agricultural commodities, or whether the high prices stem from nonrecurring developments such as the large-scale recent wheat sales to the USSR. Accordingly, the NPA Committee expresses the judgment that farm policy in the United States must still reckon with a future in which "the excess capacity of U.S. agriculture may not have disappeared." In either event, the problems of low incomes for much of the farm population and of surplus human resources in agriculture are likely to remain as issues in the next decade. Continued mechanization, as in the new harvesting machines introduced in the past decade, will reduce requirements for hired farm labor in the 1970's. What is known stresses the importance of flexibility in income parity policy, and it also emphasizes the need to increase the attractiveness of the alternatives to full- or part-time farming for the smaller farmers or farm laborers. More and better educational and training programs, for example, can diminish the prospects that migration from the rural areas will add to the public welfare assistance rolls in the large cities. New approaches to agricultural policy in the next decade taking account of these potentials can reverse the tendency for rising productivity in agriculture to become translated into low incomes and lack of opportunity for the farm population.

[26] The greater risks of farming because of the greater fluctuations of farm prices accompanying unconstrained production could be considered as introducing an additional cost element beyond those included in the projections. However, the magnitude of the differences in the estimated costs to society between this program and the alternatives would outweigh very substantial risk charges.

[27] National Planning Association, "NPA Agriculture Committee Statement on Food and Farm Policy," July 1973.

APPENDIX A

RELATING THE EXPENDITURES FOR THE GOALS TO THE NATIONAL INCOME AND PRODUCT ACCOUNTS

RICHARD J. ROSEN

The goals analysis can provide a basis for classifying the nation's use of resources according to the economic, political, and social purposes for which the resources are used. To utilize the goals framework, it has been necessary to translate the expenditure projections for the individual goals into the national income accounts, into internally consistent and comprehensive categories that possess economic significance.[1]

Use of the national income accounting framework makes it possible to obtain net estimates of the costs of attaining the entire system of goals that can be related to a number of policy and analytic considerations. The net estimates are important because the gross expenditures listed for the individual goals in 1980 overstate their cost since they include substantial elements of double counting and transfers of assets. The double counting has been retained in the estimates for the individual goals to maintain consistency with the mode in which the goals are regarded in everyday discussion and debate. Policy makers traditionally look at one budget at a time (e.g., the defense budget), overlooking the fact that this budget includes outlays for retirement benefits that figure in the social welfare goal area or funds for research and development that make up the largest single item in the national budget for research and development. Similarly, in assessing private expenditures for the purchase of motor vehicles in the transportation goal area, it is necessary to recognize that this spending also increases outlays for air pollution abatement equipment included in the environmental quality goal.

[1] See, for example, U.S. Department of Commerce, *Survey of Current Business,* July 1972.

Double counting and transfer items that do not represent claims on the GNP are present in the expenditures for the individual goals for the following reasons:

1. Parts of the costs of some goals are included in the costs of other goals;
2. The expenditures for some goals largely represent transfer payments that add to the outlays for other goals;
3. Parts of the expenditures for some goals consist of expenditures for intermediate products that are included in the value of the end products; and
4. The expenditures for some goals (e.g., for the purchase of land) constitute transfers of assets rather than outlays for the purchase of current output.

Integrating the expenditures for the individual goals into a national income accounting framework eliminates the double counting. When this is done, the net cost of the 14 goals, a hypothetical GNP corresponding to the resources required to achieve all 14 goals (Goals GNP), can be compared with the resources expected to be available in 1980 (Growth GNP). Projections prepared by the National Planning Association provide a comprehensive and consistent series of estimates of the GNP and its components based on historical relationships, demographic shifts, anticipated productivity changes and other variables.[2] These projections serve as a basis for relating the expenditures for the goals to the national income accounts.

A number of steps are involved in translating the estimates of expenditures for the goals into the categories of the national income accounts. First, the items that do not represent claims on current output entering into the GNP are eliminated. Land purchases for national parks are an instance. Similarly, company-financed R & D spending or company outlays for operating pollution abatement facilities are netted out since these outlays are also reckoned in the costs of the final products. Next, the duplicating items of expenditure are eliminated by removing the overlapping items from all goals other than the one that is closely identified with a sector of the national income accounts. The personal consumption expenditures for health, for instance, are eliminated from the health goal and retained in the household consumption goal. The private capital outlays for high-speed passenger trains are removed from the transportation goal and retained in the private plant and equipment goal. And, third, the transfer payments and related private cash benefit payments to individuals, payments primarily in the social

[2]See National Planning Association, *U.S. Economic and Demographic Projections: 1972-81, Report No. 72-N-2,* January, 1973.

welfare goal, are translated into the claims for consumer goods and services these additions to the incomes of their recipients are expected to generate. After eliminating the double counting and transfers, the 14 goals lose their separate identities and become parts of the four sectors of the national income accounts: personal consumption expenditures, gross private domestic investment, government purchases of goods and services, and net exports.

Table A-1   Allocation of the Gross Expenditures for the Health Goal to the National Income Accounts (in millions of 1969 dollars)

Item	Estimated for 1980	Disposition
1. Gross expenditures	$148,370	
2. Overlaps with other goals	82,925	Subtracted from health goal and added to other goals that include health expenditures.
(a) Personal consumption expenditures for health	74,125	$58,555 already included in consumer expenditures growth projection. Remaining $15,570 added to total for household consumption goal.
(b) Health research and development	4,600	Already included in estimates for research and development goal.
(c) Private outlays for the construction of health facilities	4,200	$3,270 already included in growth projection for gross private domestic investment. $930 added to total for plant and equipment goal.
3. Net expenditures	65,445	The expenditures remaining after deducting for overlaps are made up of government purchases of goods and services for health that are added to the government sector of the national income accounts.

In assessing the output requirements for attaining the goals, it is important to recognize that the growth GNP projected for 1980 on the basis of recent trends also specifies or implies substantial expenditures in the individual goal areas. So, the projected growth GNP of $1.4 trillion in 1980 assumes personal consumption expenditures for health care amounting to $58.5 billion. This estimate implies that the proportion of consumer outlays represented by health care will increase from 7.4 percent in 1969 to 7.9 percent in 1980. Similarly, the growth projection contains an estimated $3270 million in private (mainly nonprofit) outlays for the construction of health facilities. This is more than three-fourths of the corresponding $4.2 billion projection for these facilities in the health goal. The procedures used in eliminating the double counting and taking into account the goals expenditures already included in the growth projection are summarized for the health goal in Table A–1.

After the expenditures for the individual goals have been translated into national income accounting categories, three other items must be taken into account to complete the GNP-for-Goals estimate. For one, changes in business inventories must be allowed for. As in NPA's long-term growth forecast, inventory investment is reckoned at approximately 7 percent of private outlays for plant and equipment or the equivalent of slightly more than 1 percent of the GNP. The second addition is for general government, that is, for the costs of a variety of government operations such as law enforcement, fire protection, or legislative functions that are not included in the estimates for individual goals. On the basis of past experience and NPA forecasts, general government outlays are reckoned at 15 percent of government purchases other than for general government. Account must also be taken of the foreign transactions sector of the national income accounts. The net exports derived from NPA's growth projection for 1980 are estimated at $10.2 billion.[3] Allowing for the feedback effects of the outlays for attaining the international aid goal in increasing exports on the assumption that 75 percent of the economic aid supplied to the developing nations returns to the United States in the form of purchases of American goods and services, the net export balance is projected to increase to $12.6 billion by 1980. After making these adjustments, the distribution of the hypothetical GNP corresponding to achievement of the goals is summarized in Table A–2. The individual goal expenditures represent the net cost of the goals after the double counting and transfers have been elimianted, with the costs allocated to the appropriate economic sector of the national income accounts. (See Table A–1 for an example of how the goal costs are allocated.)

[3] Derived from *U.S. Economic and Demographic Projections: 1972–81, op. cit.,* p. 52. Estimates have been adjusted from 1958 to 1969 dollars.

Table A-2 Estimated Hypothetical GNP for Goals in 1980 and its Distribution by Economic Sector (in millions of 1969 dollars)

Goal Area	GNP =	Con- sumption +	Invest- ment +	Govern- ment	Net + Exports
Household consumption	$ 931,270	$930,370	$	$ 900	$
Private plant and equipment	207,807		207,807		
Housing	74,200		69,800	4,400	
Urban development	18,450			18,450	
Social welfare	8,550			8,550	
Manpower training	5,811			5,811	
Health	65,445			65,445	
Education	93,500			93,500	
Transportation	25,000			25,000	
National defense	64,500			64,500	
International aid	1,280			1,280	
Research and development	28,300			28,300	
Environmental quality	27,050			27,050	
Agricultural support	4,500			4,500	
Total attributable to individual goals	1,555,663	930,370	277,607	347,686	
Additional items	78,980				
Inventory change			14,300		
General government				52,060	
Net exports					12,620
Hypothetical GNP for Goals	$1,634,643	$930,370	$291,907	$399,746	$12,620

Attainment of the entire system of goals would require both a larger GNP and one distributed differently by economic sector than is the case in NPA's GNP projection for 1980 based on past trends or the actual Gross National Product in 1969. Consumption, for example, would account for a smaller share of the nation's output while gross private investment and government purchases would make up a larger share. These differentials are described in Table A–3.

Table A-3   Estimated Distribution of GNP by Economic Sector, 1969, NPA 1980 Growth Projection, and Hypothetical GNP for Goals in 1980

Item	1969	1980 Growth Projection	1980 Hypothetical GNP for Goals
GNP (in billions of 1969 dollars)	$930.3	$1398.9	$1634.6
Distribution by sector			
Consumption	62.0%	62.0%	56.9%
Investment	14.9	16.0	17.9
Government	22.6	21.3	24.4
Net exports	0.2	0.7	0.8
Total	100.0%	100.0%	100.0%

The distribution of the 1980 GNP corresponding to attainment of the system of goals is primarily an extrapolation of the present distribution of sectoral outlays in each of the goal areas. Accordingly, the projected distribution reflects the current distribution between public and private outlays in each goal area, and the increase in outlays required to attain specific goals, rather than judgments concerning the most efficient or the most desirable distribution of activities between the public and private sectors. If the household consumption goal were attained, the dollar outlays for personal consumption would be $64 billion greater than the comparable expenditures in the growth projection. However, outlays in the consumption sector in the goals estimate are a smaller proportion of the GNP because the rapid growth in expenditures is projected for the human welfare service goals, areas in which government spending predominates, or in goal areas such as urban development whose attainment would involve massive increases in private outlays for plant and equipment. Significantly, the increase in the weight of the government sector in the national income accounts in the goals estimate takes place in the absence of an increase listed for expenditures for the national defense goal.

Since attainment of the goals would concentrate the growth in expenditures more heavily in some sectors than others, the projected "gap" in resources for achieving all 14 goals would also be more heavily concentrated in these sectors. The sectoral distribution of the deficit is described in Table A–4.

Table A-4   Estimated Distribution of Deficit in Resources for Attaining Goals in 1980 by Economic Sector (in billions of 1969 dollars)

Item	GNP	Con-sumption	Invest-ment	Govern-ment	Net Ex-ports
Growth projection for 1980	$1398.9	$866.6	$223.8	$298.3	$10.2
Estimated requirements for goals	1634.2	930.4	291.9	399.7	12.6
Defiicit for goals	235.7	63.8	68.1	101.4	2.4
Deficit as percent of growth projection	17%	7%	30%	34%	24%

Although three-fourths of the outlays for the goals represent expenditures in the private sector, well over two-fifths of the deficit—43 percent—is concentrated in the government sector. Requirements for government purchases to attain the system of goals would be about a third greater than the estimates of government purchases in 1980 in the growth projection. Within the private sector, the deficit would be considerably greater in the investment than in the consumption sector, three-tenths as compared with less than one-tenth of the projected output in their respective sectors in NPA's growth forecast. The distribution of GNP by sector suggests, therefore, that attaining a series of goals similar to the ones considered would involve a higher savings rate than at present or than otherwise anticipated in 1980, and an increase in Federal, state, and local tax schedules to make possible a reallocation of resources from consumption to private investment and the government sector.

Since the anticipated resources are unlikely to be sufficient for attaining all goals, the relevant questions for policy in the 1970's will concern questions of standards, available resources and, consequently, of priorities. The resource requirements for attaining alternative combinations of priorities that are feasible within the constraints set by the available resources can be assessed in greater or lesser detail in terms of the national income and product accounts. The input-output matrix offers a more detailed classification of the nation's use of resources in terms of interindustry classifications. These systems of economic accounts can provide a framework for converting the study of the resource requirements for national goals into an operational tool of priority analysis.

APPENDIX B

ABSTRACT OF STANDARDS
FOR INDIVIDUAL GOALS

Goal Area

Abstract of Standards

Agricultural Support

Illustrates implications of income parity objective and objective of assuring an adequate food supply in terms of three policy options for raising disposable income per person in the farm economy by 1980 to 90 percent of the anticipated nonfarm income level. Options considered include direct control of farm output on a scale sufficient to raise farm prices to attain income objective. A second option entails continuing the crop subsidies and land diversion programs of the 1960's. The third is unconstrained production through elimination of supply control measures with farmers receiving income supplements if farm prices yield incomes below target level. Cost estimates present both program costs to government (the goal costs) and indirect costs to consumers in the form of anticipated higher prices and foregone consumption. In addition to costs listed for income parity objective, outlays for goal standard also include expenditures for job training and mobility assistance programs to encourage the movement of low-income members of the farm labor force into nonfarm employment.

Education

Objectives for elementary and secondary education reflect recommendations in recent studies such as reports of National Education Finance Project for major expansion in early childhood education for 3- and 4-year-olds, kindergarten programs for all five-year-olds, and implementation of schools' responsibility to provide adequate special and remedial education programs for physically, mentally, and emotionally handicapped children.[a] Objectives also include expanded support for innovations in education such as computer-assisted instruction, and emphasis on movement toward equalization of expenditures per pupil within each state and between states. Enrollment in higher education projected to increase by 50 percent in 1970's as compared with approximately 100 percent in the 1960's with most rapid increase in two-year community colleges, and in representation of nonwhites, low-income groups, and adults beyond school leaving age in college population. Objectives also entail experimentation with three-year undergraduate programs and extended reliance on deferred tuition plans for financing higher education.

Environmental Quality

Scenario for environmental quality goal stresses role of pollution abatement as primary objective in measures intended to protect quality of natural environment. Standards for air and water pollution abatement reflect objectives in 1972 Clean Water Act to attain pollution reduction efficiencies of 90 percent or greater in next decade by utilizing the "best available" technologies by the early 1980's. Ob-

[a] National Education Finance Project, *Alternative Programs for Financing Education*, 1971.

jectives also include elimination of open dumping as means for solid waste disposal and substantial expansion of programs to reduce acid mine drainage, aircraft noise, radiation hazards, and damages to land from surface mining. Concern with natural resources aspects of environmental quality centers on development of new energy sources, especially sources of "clean energy," and on expanding areas for parks and open spaces to meet needs of an urbanized society.

Health

Objectives include emphasis on improvement in delivery of health services through increased role for health maintenance organizations and community health centers, greater use of paraprofessionals and physicians' assistants, and similar innovations. To enlarge access to modern medical technologies, by 1980 nonpoor and nonaged families are expected to receive level of health insurance coverage equivalent to that currently enjoyed by families with "high coverage" plans with provision for expansion of dental and psychiatric benefits. Expansion of access for lower-income and rural populations includes measures to enable persons in these groups to obtain same number of annual physicians' and dentists' visits as are available generally to the population.

Household Consumption

Scenario for household consumption goal based on priority decisions reflected in behavior of consumers who have been spending over nine-tenths of the additions to their disposable personal income for consumer goods and services. Projections take into account changes in consumer spending patterns stemming from changes in average household income, and from shifts toward spending larger share of disposable income for durables and services and smaller share for nondurable items. Projections also build in increases stemming from larger personal consumption expenditures that would be generated by attainment of other goals, especially the social welfare and health goals. Finally, goal standard includes allowance equivalent to one-tenth of 1 percent of personal consumption expenditures for consumer information and protective services.

Housing

Standards derived from target in 1968 Housing and Urban Development Act calling for construction or rehabilitation of 26 million housing units in the 1969 to 1978 period. This total includes six million subsidized units for low– and moderate-income families, elimination or rehabilitation of housing units lacking major plumbing facilities or with an average of more than one person per room. Projections of housing expenditures in 1980 allow for new household formation in 1970's, for replacement demand for housing, for demands for better housing and vacation homes as income levels rise, and for housing demands for persons with special housing needs such as the aged and the physically handicapped.

International Aid

Scenario for goals standard assumes outlay of 1 percent of Gross Domestic Product from public and private sources for capital supply and technical assistance to eliminate "savings gap" for raising per capita incomes in the less developed nations. Scenario anticipates shift in character of public aid from predominantly bilateral assistance to equal division by 1980 between bilateral and multilateral aid. Food for Peace and military assistance programs projected to continue at $1 billion a year or less.

Manpower Training

Scenario for manpower training goal stresses that "work and welfare go together" so that attainment of manpower training goal implies replacement of present public welfare assistance program by nationwide income maintenance measures offering greater incentives to work or seek training. Consistent with this emphasis, standard provides for retraining 2 percent of labor force a year in the 1970's, with 80 percent of training slots set aside for poor persons. To provide women who are heads of low-income families with greater options to participate in work or training, projections include estimated costs in 1980 for operating day-care facilities for preschool and school age children from 700,000 low-income families headed by a woman.

National Defense

Outlays for national defense goal in 1980 are derived from three scenarios based on different assumptions about relations between the U.S.A. and the U.S.S.R. and the People's Republic of China in the next decade. "The alternatives reflect differences in the levels of threat faced by the United States rather than differences in the level of national security each would buy."[b] These alternatives include an optimistic "arms reduction" scenario stressing partial disarmament, a "limited arms stabilization" scenario assuming continuation of the existing state of international relations, and an "arms buildup" alterna-

[b] T. Lieser, *National Defense Goal Area: Alternative Projections to 1980,* National Planning Association (unpublished), 1970.

tive predicated on a return to the Cold War tensions of the 1950's and early 1960's. Each scenario has its particular constellation of armed forces size, number and types of nuclear deterrents, military procurement requirements, and defense-related research and development effort. These constellations provide the basis for the cost estimates for the national defense goal.

Private Plant and Equipment

Projections based on estimates of growth in capital stock by industrial sector required to produce output to sustain projected rate of growth in the GNP, plus the additional plant and equipment expenditures specified by individual goals, utilities in the urban development goal, and pollution abatement equipment in the environmental quality goal, for example. The aggregate volume of investment is derived from historical capital-output ratios by industry and from replacement rates based on the age distribution of the plant and equipment in use. Estimates also take into account derived investment in plant and equipment implied when the attainment of goals would substantially increase personal consumption expenditures (e.g., the social welfare goal).

Research and Development

Scenario for research and development goal anticipates a future in which defense-related R & D grows at a rate similar to GNP while large percentage increases in public R & D outlays are concentrated on "civilian society" areas such as health, transportation, pollution abatement, or basic research. Accordingly, Federal expenditures for the conduct of R & D in 1980 in areas other than defense, space, and atomic energy are projected to reach

40 percent of the total Federal expenditure as compared with 14 percent in 1969. Resources for R & D originating in the private sector (including industry, universities, and nonprofit organizations) are projected to increase at the same rate as the Federal Government's outlays.

Social Welfare

Emphasis on expansion of income support derived from recent legislation, Administration and congressional proposals, and special studies. Standard includes as largest component retirement benefits from public and private sources sufficient to provide income to a retired couple in 1980 equivalent to the Bureau of Labor Statistics' "modest" budget for an aged couple in urban areas—$4200 in 1969. Other objectives include introduction of national family allowance system supplying Federal income supports to provide minimum income of $4200 to a four-person family by 1980. Also included are benefits for wage loss because of disability amounting to two-thirds of wage loss for a fully disabled person up to a maximum of $7950 a year, an amount consistent with the Bureau of Labor Statistics' intermediate budget for a family of four taking into account that disabled individuals need not pay work-related expenses. Standard for unemployment compensation benefits envisages uniform national benefit levels at 65 percent of a state's weekly wage together with inclusion in system of government and farm workers now excluded. Income-in-kind measures such as school lunch or Food Stamp programs projected to continue but to increase more slowly than money income transfers to poor.

Transportation

Outlays projected for goal in 1980 include costs of transportation equipment and facilities and of R & D to provide more efficient, safe, and economical movement of people and goods with minimum negative side effects such as greater pollution. Scenario for goal anticipates shifts in "mix" of transportation modes involving stabilization of proportion of freight moved by rail at 40 percent of intercity freight. Lesser rate of increase is projected in automobile passenger miles than in passenger miles traveled by public carriers with ratio of automobile to public carrier passenger miles estimated to decline from 6.5 to 1 in 1969 to 3.5 to 1 by 1980. Also included are capital outlays for a high-speed intercity ground transportation system concentrated in high density urban corridors ranging up to 500 miles. Transportation-oriented R & D is listed as doubling by 1980, with emphasis on safer, more economical, and less-polluting motor vehicles.

Urban Development

Includes projections of expenditures for physical facilities, generally derived from other goals, to provide metropolitan areas with adequate housing, public utilities, mass transportation, schools, hospitals, cultural and recreational facilities, and industrial, commercial and government buildings in the next decade. Facility needs based on anticipated population growth in metropolitan areas, demographic changes and shifts in the location of economic activity within metropolitan areas, replacement needs, and past distribution of facilities. Projected capital outlays include expenditures to provide all metropolitan areas with a million or more population with a rapid rail mass transit system by the end of the next decade.

APPENDIX C

STATISTICAL TABLES

Table C-1 **Selected Economic Framework Indicators,**
1962, 1969, and Projected 1980[a]

| | 1962 | 1969 | 1980 | Average Annual Rates of Growth | |
				1962-1969	1969-1980
Population (in millions)[b]	186.5	202.7	227.8	1.2%	1.1%
Civilian labor force (in millions)	70.6	80.7	99.6	1.9	1.9
Employment (in millions)	66.7	77.9	95.1	2.2	1.8
Unemployment (in millions)	3.9	2.8	4.4	−4.6	4.2
Unemployment rate	5.5	3.5	4.4	N.A.[c]	N.A.[c]
Gross National Product (in billions of 1969 dollars)	$ 679.1	$ 930.3	$1398.9	4.6	3.8
GNP per capita	$3642.0	$4590.0	$6141.0	3.4	2.7

[a] Taken from *U.S. Economic and Demographic Projections: 1972-81,* National Planning Association, Report No. 72-N-2, 1973, and unpublished NPA data.

[b] Population estimate is based on the Census Bureau Series E intermediate fertility assumption that the average number of children per thousand women at the end of the child-bearing period will converge from the 1970 level of 2398 to 2110 by the year 2000. See U.S. Department of Commerce, Bureau of the Census, "Population Estimates and Projections," *Current Population Reports,* Series P-25, No. 476, February 1972.

[c] Not applicable.

Table C-2   Selected Productivity and Output Indicators in the Private
Economy, 1962-1969, and Projected 1969-1980[a]

	Average Annual Rates of Growth	
	1962-1969	1969-1980
Gross private product[b]	4.7%	3.8%
Private employment	1.8	1.3
Private man-hours	1.3	1.0
Capital stock[c]	4.2	4.6
Gross private product per private employee	2.8	2.5
Gross private product per private man-hour	3.3	2.8
Capital stock per private employee	2.3	3.3
Private man-hours per worker (per year)	− .5	− .5

[a] U.S. Economic and Demographic Projections: 1972-81, op. cit., pp. 4, 44, 58 and unpublished NPA data.
[b] Refers to gross product originating in the private sector.
[c] Refers to the stock of producers' durable equipment and private nonresidential structures.

Table C-3   U. S. Population by Age, 1962, 1969, and Projected 1980[a]
(in thousands)

	Number			Percent Distribution		
	1962	1969	1980	1962	1969	1980
Under 16 years	61,600	62,100	60,800	33.0%	30.6%	26.7%
16–24 years	23,200	31,300	37,400	12.5	15.4	16.4
25–34 years	22,500	24,700	36,900	12.1	12.2	16.2
35–64 years	42,800	64,800	69,100	30.0	32.0	30.3
65 years and over	17,500	19,800	23,700	9.4	9.8	10.4
Total population	186,500	202,700	227,800	100.0%	100.0%	100.0%

[a] U.S. Economic and Demographic Projections: 1972-81, op. cit.

Table C-4   Poverty Population, 1969 and Projected 1980
Under Alternative Poverty Income Criteria[a]
(dollar totals in 1969 dollars)

	1969	1980	
		Static Poverty Income Criteria[b]	Dynamic Poverty Income Criteria[b]
Families (in thousands)	4,950	3,255	3,525
Unrelated individuals (in thousands)	4,851	4,665	4,870
Total consumer units (in thousands)	9,801	7,920	8,395
Total persons (in thousands)	24,289	17,030	18,270
Poverty income deficit (in millions of dollars)[c]	$10,120	$ 7,800	$ 8,400
Deficit per person for poverty population	$ 417	$ 460	$ 460
Poverty income criteria			
Family of four	$ 3,721	$ 3,721	$ 4,220
Unrelated individual	$ 1,834	$ 1,834	$ 2,080

[a] U.S. Department of Commerce, Bureau of the Census, *24 Million Americans, Poverty in the United States: 1969,* Series P. 60, No. 76, December 1970, pp. 79-82. 1980 figures are NPA estimates based on NPA projections of income distribution.

[b] The constant poverty income criteria assumes no change in the income cutoff designations set by the Government in 1969 (other than those reflecting price changes), while the dynamic criteria assumes that the cutoff point would rise by one-half the projected rise in real average family income, projected to be 2.3 percent annually (see Table C-5).

[c] The "poverty income deficit" is the difference between the income received by the poor and the income required to put them just beyond the poverty income level.

Table C-5 Selected Indicators of Personal Income and Its Disposition, 1962, 1969, and Projected 1980[a]
(dollar totals in 1969 dollars)

				Average Annual Rates of Growth	
	1962	1969	1980	1962–1969	1969–1980
Personal income (in billions)	$ 521.1	$ 750.3	$1159.9	5.3%	4.0%
Disposable personal income (in billions)	453.6	634.2	945.7	4.9	3.7
Personal taxes[b] (in billions)	67.5	116.2	214.2	8.1	5.7
Personal consumption expenditures (in billions)	418.1	579.6	866.6	4.8	3.7
Personal savings (in billions)	25.4	37.9	53.0	5.9	3.1
Personal tax, consumption and savings rates					
Taxes as a percent of personal income	13.0%	15.5%	18.5%		
Consumption as a percent of disposable income	92.2	91.4	91.6		
Savings as a percent of disposable income	5.6	6.0	5.6		
Total consumer units (in thousands)	58,011	65,689	79,296	1.8	1.7
Personal income per consumer unit	$ 8,983	$11,439	$14,627	3.5	2.3
Disposable income per consumer unit	7,819	9,667	11,926	3.6	1.9
Taxes per consumer unit	1,164	1,772	2,701	6.2	3.9
Personal consumption per consumer unit	7,207	8,837	10,929	3.0	2.0
Savings per consumer unit	438	578	668	4.0	1.3

[a] Taken from *U.S. Economic and Demographic Projections: 1972–81, op. cit.,* and unpublished NPA data. All income data was deflated by the personal consumption expenditures deflator of the U.S. Department of Commerce, Bureau of Economic Analysis.

[b] Includes personal tax and nontax payments, excludes contributions to social insurance trust funds.

Table C-6   Distribution of Personal Consumption Expenditures by Type,
                   1969 and Projected 1980[a]

	1969	1980
Total outlays (in billions of 1969 dollars)	$579.6	$866.6
Percent distribution by type		
Food	22.6%	19.6%
Clothing	10.3	11.3
Personal care	1.7	1.7
Housing	14.5	13.4
Household operation	14.2	14.0
Medical care	7.4	7.9
Personal business	5.7	6.3
Transportation	13.4	14.6
Recreation	6.4	7.3
Private education and research	1.7	1.8
Religious and welfare activities	1.4	1.5
Foreign travel and other net	.7	.6
Total	100.0	100.0

[a] *U.S. Economic and Demographic Projections: 1972–81, op. cit.* Data
in this table refer to the outlays and distribution of expenditures under the
"growth" projection which assumes an average annual growth in GNP of 3.8
percent.

Table C-7 Estimated Effect of Attainment of Individual Goals on the Distribution of Consumer Expenditures by Type in Household Consumption Goal in 1980

	Growth Projection	Increments From Attaining Social Welfare Goal	Increments From Other Goals	Total Household Consumption Goal
		Dollar Outlays (in billions of 1969 dollars)		
Food	$169.9	$ 9.4	$ .3	$179.6
Clothing and personal care	112.7	4.6	.1	117.4
Housing and household operation	237.4	11.7	3.2	252.3
Medical care	68.5	3.1	15.7	87.3
Transportation	126.5	4.3	2.3	133.1
Other items	151.6	3.3	5.8	160.7
Total	$866.6	$36.4	$27.4	$930.4
		Percent Distribution		
Food	19.6%	25.8%	1.1%	19.3%
Clothing and personal care	13.0	12.5	.3	12.6
Housing and household operation	27.4	32.2	11.7	27.1
Medical care	7.9	8.6	57.3	9.4
Transportation	14.6	11.8	8.4	14.3
Other items	17.5	9.1	21.2	17.3
Total	100.0%	100.0%	100.0%	100.0%

Table C-8 Distribution of Expenditures for Individual Goals by Source of Funds, 1962, 1969, and Projected 1980
(in millions of 1969 dollars)

Goal Area	1962			1969			1980		
	Total Expenditure	Percent Public	Percent Private	Total Expenditure	Percent Public	Percent Private	Total Expenditure	Percent Public	Percent Private
Household consumption	$420,000	—%	100.0%	$ 579,600	—%	100.0%	$ 931,300	.1%	99.9%
Private plant and equipment	58,680	—	100.0	99,300	—	100.0	207,800	—	100.0
Housing[a]	37,500	4.0	96.0	35,420	3.3	96.7	85,400	5.9	94.1
Urban development[a]	72,750	32.1	67.9	89,925	31.1	68.9	196,000	26.3	73.7
Social welfare	46,400	84.3	15.7	72,964	82.8	17.2	188,800	88.6	11.4
Manpower training	100	100.0	—	1,756	100.0	—	6,000	100.0	—
Health	43,500	25.3	74.7	63,827	37.3	62.7	148,400	44.1	55.9
Education	41,800	76.1	23.9	64,350	75.3	24.7	123,800	75.5	24.5
Transportation	39,300	33.8	66.2	61,400	24.4	75.6	104,300	24.0	76.0
National defense	66,500	100.0	—	81,025	100.0	—	80,900	100.0	—
International aid	6,100	90.2	9.8	5,375	75.5	24.5	15,500	55.2	44.8
Research and development	21,100	67.8	32.2	27,279	58.7	41.3	48,800	58.1	41.9
Agriculture	8,200	100.0	—	7,750	100.0	—	11,000	100.0	—
Environmental quality	10,900	57.3	42.7	15,785	50.1	49.9	55,400	48.1	51.9
Total	$872,830	25.3%	74.7%	$1,205,756	24.5%	75.5%	$2,023,100	28.2%	80.8%

[a] Housing outlays are by ownership of structure rather than source of funds.

Table C-9 Changes in Expenditures for Individual Goals by Source of Funds, 1962-1969, and Projected Change 1969-1980
(in million of 1969 dollars)

	1962-1969				1969-1980			
Goal	Total Change in Expenditures	Percent Public	Percent Private		Total Change in Expenditures	Percent Public	Percent Private	
Consumption	$159,600	%	100.0%		$351,670	.3%	99.7%	
Private plant and equipment	40,620		100.0		108,500		100.0	
Housing[a]	− 2,080	− 15.9	− 84.1		49,980	7.8	92.2	
Urban development[a]	17,175	26.7	73.3		106,085	22.3	77.7	
Social welfare	26,564	80.3	19.7		115,786	92.2	7.8	
Manpower training	1,656	100.0			4,213	100.0		
Health	20,327	63.0	37.0		84,543	49.3	50.7	
Education	22,550	73.8	26.2		59,450	75.8	24.2	
Transportation	22,100	7.7	92.3		42,900	23.4	76.6	
National defense	14,525	100.0			− 125	−100.0		
International aid	− 725	−199.3	99.3		10,075	44.4	55.6	
Research and development	6,179	27.6	72.4		21,471	57.2	42.3	
Agriculture	− 450	− 5.5			3,250	100.0		
Environmental quality	4,885	34.0	66.0		39,565	47.4	52.6	
Total	$332,926	22.3%	77.7%		$997,353	27.5%	72.5%	

[a] Housing outlays are by ownership of structure rather than source of funds.

284

Table C-10 Comparison of Goal Classification Contained in the Initial Goals 1966 Report[a] and the Current Goals Report

Classification in the Initial 1966 Goals Report	Classification in the Current 1974 Goals Report	Comments
Consumer expenditures and saving	Household consumption	Change in title only
Private plant and equipment	Private plant and equipment	No change
Housing	Housing	No change
Urban development	Urban development	No change
Social welfare	Social welfare	No change
Manpower retraining	Manpower training	The original goal—"manpower retraining,"—was primarily related to the problems of workers displaced from their jobs as the nature and location of economic activity shifted (e.g., blue-collar workers displaced by automation, declining employment in the coal mining industry, the movement of textile plants from the north to the south) while the present goal focuses primarily on the training of disadvantaged individuals with frequently only marginal prior labor force attachment for entry level positions.
Health	Health	No change
Education	Education	No change
Transportation	Transportation	No change
National defense	National defense	No change
International aid	International aid	No change
Research and development	Research and development	No change
Space	Research and development	Outlays for space represent an overlap with the R & D goal because the entire NASA budget is considered R & D. Outlays

Table C-10 (Continued)

Classification in the Initial 1966 Goals Report	Classification in the Current 1974 Goals Report	Comments
		for Space peaked in 1966 at $5.9 billion (current dollars) and have since declined to $3.1 billion in 1974 (current dollars). This fact, coupled with the reluctance of Congress to set specific objectives for future manned flights (e.g., to land astronauts on Mars by 1980), indicates that space exploration is no longer assigned the same priority.
Area redevelopment		Area redevelopment through infusion of "seed money" into depressed areas appeared to have been an emerging goal during the early 1960's; however, outlays of the magnitude envisioned by the initial study never materialized. Expenditures by the Area Redevelopment Administration were $215 million in 1962, and outlays for its successor organization, the Economic Development Administration, were only slightly higher in 1969 at $282 million (in current dollars). Some area redevelopment has taken place through the funding of regional commissions such as the Appalachian and Ozark Regional Commissions. However, the objectives of these groups are less specific than the comprehensive and concentrated development projects discussed in area redevelopment goal (i.e., most of the commission funds are allocated to highway construction rather than developing industrial parks and other community infrastructure). Additionally, some aspects of area redevelopment

	are incorporated in the agriculture goal such as the work of the Soil Conservation Service, Rural Electrification Administration, and Farmers Home Administration, as well as the mobility and training allowances provided in the goal.
Natural resources	
Environmental quality	The earlier natural resources goal focused on the need for a clean and adequate water supply, recreational facilities, national and state parks, and mineral research. The current environmental quality goal contains all of these elements but adds consideration of air pollution, solid waste disposal, noise pollution, "clean" energy needs, acid mine drainage, and radiation exposure, as well as more stringent regulations regarding water pollution. Pollution abatement considerations stem from a body of legislation such as the Clean Air and Water Acts and their amendments, with set standards for emission levels in both the public and private economies.
Agriculture	No change
Agriculture	

[a] Leonard A. Lecht, *Goals, Priorities and Dollars*, New York, The Free Press, 1966.

INDEX